ACBL Bridge Series

Play
of the
Hand

in the
21st Century

ISBN-13:978-0-939460-94-6
ISBN-10: 0-939460-94-7

Updated ACBL Bridge Series

Play of the Hand in the 21st Century is the second in a series of texts developed by the American Contract Bridge League.

These materials were written in 1986 by Audrey Grant. In 2006, the ACBL enlisted Betty Starzec, a Senior TAP Teacher-Trainer, to update the series to more accurately convey the latest duplicate bridge ideas and philosophy. The update complements the *Learn to Play Bridge* computer programs written for the ACBL by world champion Fred Gitelman.

There are five textbooks and teacher manuals with coordinating E-Z Deal decks of cards:

Volume One —
Bidding in the 21st Century – The Club Series

Volume Two —
Play of the Hand in the 21st Century – The Diamond Series

Volume Three —
Defense in the 21st Century – The Heart Series

Volume Four —
Commonly Used Conventions in the 21st Century – The Spade Series

Volume Five —
More Commonly Used Conventions in the 21st Century – The Notrump Series

Trained teachers across North America offer bridge courses using these materials. Information on teachers in your area is available on the ACBL web site **www.acbl.org** through the Find a Teacher link.

Coordinated decks of E-Z Deal Cards, which allow the reader to deal out the exercise hands at the end of each chapter, are available for each bridge text.

These materials can be purchased through Baron Barclay Bridge Supply 1-800-274-2221.

The American Contract Bridge League

The American Contract Bridge League (ACBL) is dedicated to the playing, teaching and promotion of contract bridge.

The membership of 160,000+ includes a wide range of players — from the thousands who are just learning the joy of bridge to the most proficient players in North America.

ACBL offers a variety of services, including:

- *Tournament play.* Thousands of tournaments: North American Bridge Championships (three a year), as well as tournaments at the regional, sectional, local and club levels — are sanctioned annually.

- *A magazine.* The Bridge Bulletin, a monthly publication, offers articles for all levels of players on tournaments, card play, the Laws, personalities, special activities and much more.

- *A ranking plan.* Each time a member does well in any ACBL event, whether at the club level or at a North American Bridge Championship, that member receives a masterpoint award. Players achieve rankings and prestige as a result of their cumulative masterpoint holdings.

- *A teaching program.* ACBL has trained more than 5,000 people through the Teacher Accreditation Program (TAP) to teach beginning bridge lessons. You can find a teacher in your area at ACBL's web site — **www.acbl.org**, Find a Teacher or with the ACBL mobile app.

- *A newcomer program.* ACBL offers special games and programs for players new to bridge and new to duplicate. The Intermediate-Newcomer (IN) Programs at the three North American Bridge Championships are very popular and are offered as examples of what ACBL hopes regionals and sectionals will offer to their local newcomers.

- *Access to 3,200 bridge clubs.* ACBL offers sanctioned bridge play at clubs across the United States, Canada, Mexico, Bermuda, on cruise ships and even at a few foreign-based bridge clubs. You can locate a club in your area at ACBL's web site — **www.acbl.org**, Find a Club or the ACBL mobile app.

- **A charity program.** Since 1964, the ACBL Charity Foundation has made substantial contributions to a wide range of charitable organizations, now with $100,000 in annual allocations.

- **A cooperative advertising program.** ACBL assists teachers, clubs, units and districts by subsidizing costs incurred for advertising programs designed to recruit students and promote bridge lessons and games.

- **A Junior program for players age 25 and under.** ACBL offers a funded teaching program, a funded school bridge lesson series program, student membership, a youth web site — Youth4bridge.org — and special events.

- **Membership benefits.** Special hotel rates at tournaments, airline discounts, an 800 line for member services, discounted entry fees at most tournament play, recognition for levels of achievement, discounted Hertz car rental, FedEx Office and Office Max discounts for printing services are offered.

ACBL has been the center of North American bridge activity since it was founded in 1937. You can enjoy the fun, friendship and competition of bridge with an ACBL membership available online at www.acbl.org. You can now follow the latest bridge news on Facebook and Twitter.

TABLE OF CONTENTS

CHAPTER 8 — PUTTING IT ALL TOGETHER

CHAPTER 9 — JACOBY TRANSFERS

APPENDIX

INTRODUCTION

The American Contract Bridge League's (ACBL) *Play of the Hand in the 21st Century* student text is the second in a series of bridge books for beginning and advancing players. It is preceded by the *Bidding in the 21st Century* and followed by three others: *Defense in the 21st Century*, *Commonly Used Conventions in the 21st Century* and *More Commonly Used Conventions in the 21st Century.*

The sanctioning body for bridge in North America, the ACBL, developed these books to address the needs of students and teachers. They are a comprehensive set of materials that reflect current bridge bidding and playing standards. The original series of books, written by Audrey Grant, has been used successfully by bridge teachers and students for more than 20 years.

In the late 1900s, the ACBL produced a computer program, *Learn to Play Bridge I* and subsequently *Learn to Play Bridge II,* written by bridge champion Fred Gitelman. The response to these programs has been tremendous with more than 150,000 copies now in circulation. (LTPB can be downloaded for free by visiting the ACBL's web site, **www.acbl.org**, or Fred Gitelman's web site at **www.bridgebase.com**).

Betty Starzec, a senior TAP Teacher-Trainer, updated the material, not only to convey more accurately the latest bridge ideas and philosophy but also to be used as a tool in conjunction with the *Learn to Play Bridge* programs. *The ACBL Bridge Series* texts encompass these changes:

- 25 total points required for games of 3NT, 4♠ and 4♥.
- Opening bids still require 13 total points or more. Therefore, the opener's bidding ranges as well as responder's ranges were adjusted slightly in order to conform to the 25 total points required for game. For example, responder's ranges are 6–9 total points for the minimum range, 10–11 total points for the medium range and 12+ total points for the maximum range.
- 1NT opening bids are 15–17 and are based on high-card points (HCP).
- 2NT opening bids are 20–21 HCP.
- Overcalls will be allowed with as few as 10 total points with an upper limit of 17 total points.
- Each text book contains a bonus chapter. The bonus chapter for the *Play of the Hand Series* is *Jacoby Transfers.*
- Strong 2♣ bids are used along with weak two-bids.

The goal of this update is to enable the reader to learn basic bridge or to review and improve bridge techniques in a logical and progressive fashion. More importantly, the reader will have fun while learning the fundamental concepts of modern bridge bidding, play and defense which will be beneficial for a lifetime.

CHAPTER 1
Making a Plan

THE PLAN

For most players, the play of the hand is the most exciting part of the game. You and your partner have exchanged information through the bidding and have decided on what you both think is the best contract. Now one member of the partnership, the declarer, must try to take the required number of tricks. When you are declarer, often you will have to depend on lady luck to help *bring home the contract*. The more you learn about the play of the hand, the more frequently she will be on your side.

As declarer, it's tempting to start to play without making a plan. Usually you can see a couple of tricks that can be taken right away, and you may feel that everyone's eyes are on you — waiting for you to do something. If you do start with no plan in mind, however, halfway through the play you will often find yourself looking longingly at winners in one hand with no way to reach them. Or you may realize after the deal is finished how you could have made your contract. Learn to take a few moments at the beginning of each deal to make a plan; it is well worth the effort.

The Planning Steps

There are four basic steps when making a plan, whether your goal is to put someone on the moon or play a bridge hand:

1. **Determine your objective.** Start by deciding exactly what you want to do. To put someone on the moon, your objective is to land the astronaut and return that person safely to earth. When playing a bridge hand, your objective is to fulfill your contract.

2. **Determine how close you are to your objective**. By assessing your current situation, see how far you must go to reach your goal. If you're standing on earth, you must travel 240,000 miles to reach the moon. If you're playing a contract that requires nine tricks and you have only seven, you'll need to find two more tricks to make the contract.

3. **Determine the resources you have available**. Once you know what you must do to meet your objective, look at the various resources at your disposal that may help you meet it. Several alternatives may be available. You may have a manned satellite already in orbit, the materials to build a spaceship or the technology to build a transporter ("Beam me up, Scottie"). At the bridge table, you may be able to promote an extra

trick, take a finesse or ruff a loser in dummy.

4. **Decide how to put it all together**. Select the best option from among the various choices. Plan to do things in the right order and prepare for any contingency. Should you build the spaceship first or train the astronaut first? When playing a hand, the best play in an individual suit may not be best when you take the whole deal into consideration.

The PLAN for Playing a Bridge Hand

To help remember the four steps, use the following PLAN:

1. **P**ause to consider your objective
2. **L**ook at your winners and losers
3. **A**nalyze your alternatives
4. **N**ow put it all together

Let's take a closer look at each of the steps in the PLAN.

STEP ONE — THE OBJECTIVE

The first step in the PLAN is to *Pause to consider your objective*. Whether you are playing your first hand of bridge or are a world champion, consider your goal. A seasoned player does this automatically but nevertheless does it. Considering your objective is as simple as reminding yourself of how many tricks you need to make the contract. However, there is a different focus depending on whether you, as declarer, are playing in a suit contract or in notrump.

The Objective in a Notrump Contract

In notrump, consider your objective from the point of view of how many tricks, or winners, you need. In 1NT, you need seven winners: the book of six tricks plus one. In 7NT, you need all 13 tricks: six plus seven.

The Objective in a Suit Contract

In a suit contract, consider your objective from the point of view of losers, the number of tricks you can afford to lose. In a contract of 4♠, you can afford three losers. If the opponents take three of the 13 tricks available, you will still end up with 10. In a 6♥ contract, you can afford only one loser. If you lose one trick, you still may take the remaining 12 to make your contract.

Winners or Losers?

It may seem simpler to count either winners or losers and not worry about whether the contract is in notrump or a suit. In a notrump contract, however, you can predict winners more easily because the opponents can't ruff them. It's not as easy to determine your losers since you have no trump suit to stop the opponents, and the number of tricks they take may depend on how long a suit they have.

In a suit contract, the effect of the trump suit generally makes it easier to focus on losers. The trump suit allows you to avoid losing tricks that you might have to lose at notrump. You can eliminate losers by ruffing them in dummy or discarding them on extra winners.

Remember, counting winners or losers is only a matter of perspective. There are times when you need to consider your potential losers in a notrump contract if you must give up the lead to the opponents. In a suit contract, you may need to look at the source of your winners. When you are starting to use the PLAN, though, count winners in notrump and losers in a suit contract.

STEP TWO — COUNTING WINNERS

The second step in the PLAN is to *Look at your winners and losers.* By doing this and comparing the result to the objective determined in the first step, you can see how much work you must do to reach your goal.

In a notrump contract, start by counting winners or sure tricks — those you can take without giving up the lead. If your objective is to take nine tricks and you can count seven winners, you need to find two additional tricks to make your contract.

Counting Winners in a Suit

How do you count winners? Start by looking at your combined (declarer's hand and dummy's hand) holding in each suit to decide how many winners, or sure tricks, you have. Then add up the total for all four suits. Consider these examples:

DUMMY: A K Q J
DECLARER: 5 4 3 2

Four sure tricks: the ace, the king, the queen and the jack can be taken without giving up the lead.

DUMMY: K Q J 10
DECLARER: 5 4 3

This suit has a lot of potential. Before you can take any tricks, however, the opponents will get the lead with the ace. Therefore, count no sure tricks.

Winners don't have to be all in the same hand. Compare this holding with the first example:

DUMMY: A K 5 4
DECLARER: Q J 3 2

You have four winners. Since both hands have the same number of cards, taking four tricks in any order won't be difficult.

The maximum number of winners you can count is the number of cards in the longer hand (*i.e.,* the hand that has more cards in the suit than the other hand):

DUMMY: A K
DECLARER: Q J

Although there are four high cards, only two tricks are available because that's the number of cards in the longer hand.

DUMMY: A K 3
DECLARER: Q J

Now there are three winners because the longer side is three cards in length. Only one high card will be wasted.

DUMMY: A K Q 3 2
DECLARER: J 10

You have five top cards: the ace, the king, the queen, the jack and the 10. The longer side has five cards, so five winners are available in this suit.

You don't need all of the high cards if the opponents will have no cards left in the suit after you play your high cards:

DUMMY: A K Q J 2   Since you have nine cards in the combined
DECLARER: 6 5 4 3   hands, the opponents can hold only four. After
                         you play the ace, the king, the queen and the
jack, the opponents will have no cards left in the suit, and your 2 will be
a winner. Count five winners in the suit.

DUMMY: A K 3 2   Similarly, this suit combination will produce
DECLARER: Q 8 7 6 5 4   six winners.

DUMMY: A K 3   This suit probably will produce six tricks, but
DECLARER: Q 8 7 6 5 4   one of the opponents may hold all four of the
                         missing cards: J–10–9–2. Count three winners
even though this suit will be one of the first places you look for extra
tricks if you need them.

Counting Winners in a Deal

Let's count the number of sure tricks in an entire deal. The contract
is 3NT. Your objective is to take nine tricks. How many winners do you
have?

DUMMY
♠ 9 8 7
♥ A K Q
♦ Q J 6 4 2
♣ 9 8

DECLARER
♠ K Q J 10
♥ 7 6 3
♦ A K 5 3
♣ A 7

There are no sure tricks in spades although
there is potential for extra tricks after the ace
is played. You can't count sure tricks yet, since
you can't take them without giving the lead to
the opponents. There are three heart winners:
the ♥A, the ♥K and the ♥Q; five diamond
winners: the ♦A, the ♦K, the ♦Q, the ♦J,
and either the ♦2, the ♦4 or the ♦6 (the
opponents have only four diamonds, so the
♦2, the ♦4 or the ♦6 will be a winner); and
one club winner: the ♣A. The total is nine
tricks. You have what you need to make your
contract.

STEP TWO — COUNTING LOSERS

In a trump contract, start by counting your losers — the tricks you may have to lose to the opponents. If your objective is to make 4♠ and you can count four losers, you must find a way to eliminate one of your losers in order to make your contract.

Counting Losers in a Suit

How do you count losers? Counting losers is usually more challenging than counting winners. Start by looking at each suit in turn. Focus on your (declarer's) holding in the suit, but look across at dummy to see if any high cards can help out. Then add up the losers in all four suits.

Consider the following examples, remembering to focus on declarer's holding:

DUMMY: Q 4

DECLARER: A K 3

There is one loser, the 3 in declarer's hand. Does dummy have any high-card help? Yes, the queen will take care of the 3, so count no losers in this suit.

DUMMY: 7 5 4

DECLARER: J 6 3

There are no winners in declarer's hand, and dummy can provide no help. Count three losers in this suit. The opponents can take only three tricks in the suit because you will use your trump suit to win the trick if they lead this suit a fourth time.

The number of losers in a side suit (a suit other than the trump suit) is never counted as more than the number of cards in declarer's hand. This is because it's assumed that declarer will play a trump if the suit is led again. Declarer eventually may run out of trumps, but this isn't usually a concern when initially planning the play. This problem will be discussed further in Chapter 7.

The situation is different if declarer has more cards than dummy. Compare these examples:

DUMMY: 8 7 5 4

DECLARER: 3 2

Declarer has only two cards in the suit — with no high cards to help in dummy. Declarer counts two losers in the suit.

DUMMY: 3 2
DECLARER: 8 7 5 4

There are four losers. Even though dummy has only two cards, the focus is on declarer's hand.

Sequences

When you have a sequence of cards in the combined hands and are missing one or more higher-ranking cards, count your losers as the number of missing high cards. For example:

DUMMY: K Q J
DECLARER: 9 4 2

Missing the ace, count only one loser.

DUMMY: Q 10 4
DECLARER: J 6 3

The ace and the king of the suit are missing. Count two losers.

DUMMY: J 8 4 3
DECLARER: 10 9 7 2

The ace, the king and the queen are missing. Count three losers.

It's interesting to note the difference between counting winners and losers when you have a sequence of cards in a suit. You count only one loser when you have the king, the queen and the jack, and yet you count no winners for the suit. A winner, by definition, is a sure trick — one you can take without giving up the lead. Keep in mind that the actual cards in the suit are the same in both cases. The change in perspective helps to simplify problem solving. It's easier to view the sequence of king, queen and jack as having only one loser in a trump contract, even though, until the ace is played, they are technically all losers.

Unsupported High Cards

If you have only one high card by itself and the opponents have one or more higher cards, count it as a loser. Your high card may win a trick, but count it as a loser when making your initial plan. For example:

DUMMY: K 3
DECLARER: 8 6

There are two losers in declarer's hand. Dummy has the king, which may be a trick, depending on which opponent has the ace. For now, count this suit as two losers.

DUMMY: 8 7 3
DECLARER: Q 6 2

Count this suit as three losers. True, the queen might win a trick, but that depends on where the king and the ace are. It's best to be cautious.

Broken Sequences

Sometimes the high cards are in broken sequences — you are missing one or more high cards. Look carefully at these suits to determine the number of losers. Consider these examples:

DUMMY: 9 7 2
DECLARER: A Q J

You have one loser, the king. You may be able to eliminate this loser by trapping it, as you will see later. For now, count one loser.

DUMMY: K J 10
DECLARER: 8 7 5

You are missing two of the top five cards — the ace and the queen. Count two losers.

DUMMY: K J 4
DECLARER: 6 3 2

You are missing three of the top five cards — the ace, the queen and the 10. It's possible to lose all three tricks, so count three losers.

DUMMY: A Q 10
DECLARER: 7 4 2

The ace will take a trick, but you are missing the king and the jack. Count two losers.

Other Combinations

Sometimes you need to consider both the high cards and the length of the suit. Look at this example:

DUMMY: K Q 7 6
DECLARER: 5 4 3 2

You are missing the ace, the jack, the 10, the 9 and the 8. How many losers you actually have depends on which opponent has the ace and how the missing cards are divided. If they are divided 3–2 (three in one opponent's hand, two in the other), you will lose at most two tricks and may lose only one. If they are divided 4–1, you lose two or three tricks. A conservative view would be two losers, and you plan in later steps to eliminate one of them.

Such combinations may be difficult to estimate when you are just starting to play bridge. As you become more familiar with the various techniques for handling such card combinations, you'll find it easier to estimate your losers.

Counting Losers in a Deal

Let's count the losers in an entire deal. The contract is 4 ♠ so you can afford only three losers. How may losers do you have?

DUMMY
♠ K 4 3
♥ A Q 2
♦ 6 4 3 2
♣ J 10 7

DECLARER
♠ Q J 10 8 7 6
♥ 6 3
♦ A K
♣ Q 4 3

There is one loser in spades, the ♠A. There are two low hearts in declarer's hand, but dummy has the ♥A to take care of one of them. Dummy also has the ♥Q, but that may not prevent the loss of a trick to the ♥K. Count one loser in this suit. There are no losers in diamonds since declarer has only two cards in the suit, the ♦A and the ♦K. After they have been played, declarer will be able to ruff diamonds if they are led. There are two losers in clubs since the ♣A and the ♣K are missing. The total is four losers — one more than you can afford.

Quick and Slow Losers

As you develop your PLAN, it will become important to distinguish between two types of losers — quick and slow. A quick loser is one that the opponents can take as soon as they get the lead. A slow loser is one that they could take eventually, but not immediately, since you have one or more winners still left in the suit.

In the above hand, for example, the spade and club losers are quick losers. The opponents get to make the opening lead and are in a position to take the ♠A, the ♣A and the ♣ K right away. The heart loser is slow. Since you have the ♥A, the opponents can't take the ♥K right away.

If you have too many quick losers, you don't want to give up the lead, since the opponents will be in a position to defeat your contract. If the losers are slow, you can afford to give up the lead if necessary since you will regain it before the opponents take too many tricks. As you will see in later chapters, differentiating between quick and slow losers often will affect how you plan to play the hand. Here are more examples:

DUMMY: K Q J DECLARER: 4 3 2	This suit has only one loser but it's a quick loser. As soon as the opponents get the lead, they can take the ace.
DUMMY: A 4 3 DECLARER: 8 7 2	The two losers in this suit are both slow, because if the opponents lead the suit, you can win the first trick with the ace. In Chapter 4,

we'll look at how you might eliminate such losers before the opponents have a chance to take them.

STEP THREE — THE ALTERNATIVES

After completing the first two steps of your PLAN, you'll know what your objective is and how far you are from it. Sometimes, you'll have the winners you need or no more losers than you can afford. In that case, you can skip over the third step and go right to *Putting it all together.* More frequently, you'll need to develop some extra winners or eliminate some losers to make your contract. The third step of the PLAN tells you to *Analyze your alternatives.*

The Alternatives in a Notrump Contract

You can use a variety of techniques to develop the extra winners you need when playing in a notrump contract:

> • Promoting high cards
> • Developing long suits
> • Finessing (leading toward the high card)

When analyzing your alternatives, look at the combined holding in each suit to see which technique may produce one or more of the extra tricks you need. In future chapters, you'll see how each method can be used to develop extra winners.

The Alternatives in a Suit Contract

The techniques used in notrump can also be applied to suit contracts to help eliminate extra losers. Because of the effect of the trump suit, two additional methods are commonly used to eliminate losers:

> • Ruffing losers in dummy
> • Discarding losers

In later chapters, we'll see how to use these alternatives.

STEP FOUR – THE OVERALL STRATEGY

The last step of the PLAN reminds you to *Now put it all together.* You may have more than one alternative for developing the extra tricks you need or eliminating extra losers. Select the best alternative or combine your chances whenever possible. Even if you have the tricks you need, there are some pitfalls to watch out for. In later chapters, you will learn to be careful with entries between the two hands and to keep an eye on what the opponents are doing.

Even if you have all of the tricks you need, you should keep some things in mind when putting it all together.

Avoiding Temptation

Sometimes, you may find yourself trying to get more tricks than you need to make your contract. Look at this example. The contract is 3NT, and the opening lead is the ♣5.

DUMMY
♠ K Q 4
♥ 7 5 2
♦ K J 10
♣ A Q 7 6

DECLARER
♠ A 3 2
♥ K 8 6
♦ A Q 7 5 3
♣ 3 2

You may be tempted to try to win the first trick with dummy's ♣Q. It seems like a good opportunity to get an extra trick. How are you to know whether this play is a good idea?

Before deciding on the play in a particular suit, make your PLAN. The first step tells you to *Pause to consider your objective.* You need nine tricks to make the contract of 3NT. The second step reminds you to *Look at your winners and losers.* Count your sure tricks: three spades, five diamonds and one club —a total of nine winners. On this deal, the third step, *Analyze your alternatives,* is unnecessary since you already have enough tricks to meet your objective. Move to the fourth step, *Now put it all together,* and concentrate your energy on taking your nine winners.

Your PLAN shows that you can make the contract without playing the ♣Q on the first trick. What could go wrong if you forgot to PLAN and yielded to the temptation to play the ♣Q? If the ♣Q were taken by your right-hand opponent's ♣K, RHO might lead a heart. Your ♥K could be trapped. You might lose four (or more) heart tricks along with the club trick and be defeated in a contract you could have made.

Always make your PLAN. If you have all of the tricks you need, take them before something goes wrong.

Avoid Stranding a Suit

Sometimes you have to be careful of the order in which you take your tricks. Take a look at the following suit combination:

DUMMY: A Q J 2   Counting winners, you, as declarer, have four
DECLARER: K 3   sure tricks: the ace, the king, the queen and the jack. When a suit is unevenly divided between your hand and dummy, you need to plan the order in which you will play your winners. Suppose you start by winning a trick with dummy's ace, playing the 3 from your hand. Next you lead dummy's 2 to your king. You have taken two tricks but now you have a problem. The queen and the jack are left in dummy. You must lead from your hand, but you have no cards left in the suit. Sometimes dummy will have a winner in another suit that will let you get to dummy, but you won't always be so fortunate. The secret is to start by winning the first trick with the high card from the short side. Win the first trick with the king in your hand, and then play the 3 to dummy's ace. Now, you are in the correct hand at the right time and can take the queen and the jack.

Examples:

DUMMY:	J 10 2	To take five winners, start by winning the
DECLARER:	A K Q 4 3	first two tricks with dummy's jack and 10.

Then play dummy's 2 to your ace, king and queen.

DUMMY:	A K 3	Win the first trick with the high card in the
DECLARER:	Q 2	short hand, the queen. Then play the 2 to

dummy's ace and king.

Avoid Letting the Opponents Ruff Your Winners

If you are declaring a trump contract, you may lose an extra trick if an opponent plays a trump on one of your side suit winners. You can prevent this by playing the trump suit before taking your winners in the side suit. Draw the opponents' trumps until they have none left.

When to draw trumps will be discussed further in later chapters. For now, start by drawing the opponents' trumps if you have no more losers than you can afford.

GUIDELINES FOR DEFENSE

While this book concentrates on the play of the hand, more frequently you will find yourself defending. One of the most important aspects of defense is the opening lead, since you must decide what to lead before you get to look at dummy. Here are a few guidelines to help you get started when leading against notrump contracts.

Choosing the Suit to Lead against a Notrump Contract

Because there is no trump suit in a notrump contract, once you get the lead as a defender and have established winners in a suit, you can take them. Declarer is powerless to stop you. A defender's objective, therefore, is to establish enough tricks to defeat the contract, get the lead and take them. While high cards are a potential source of tricks, an equally important source is the small cards in long suits. You generally won't have enough high cards to defeat the contract right away, so you must work at establishing low cards as winners, using high cards to help you get the lead back.

With the advantage of the opening lead, you normally want to start the defense by establishing tricks in the longest suit in the combined defenders' hands — the longer the suit, the greater the potential for establishing low cards as winners. Unfortunately, you can't see your partner's hand when making the opening lead, so you must try to determine which is your side's longest suit.

If your partner has bid a suit, you have some information about the deal. With nothing clearly better to do, lead your partner's suit. If the opponents have bid a suit, showing some length in the suit, avoid leading that suit. With no other clues, choose the longest suit in your hand. If you have a choice of long suits, pick the stronger suit.

Suppose you are leading against a contract of 3NT with the following hand:

♠ J 10 9 8 7	Left to your own devices, you would choose your
♥ A K	longest suit and lead a spade. Your hope is to establish
♦ J 10 9	some of your spades as winners while keeping your
♣ 8 4 2	high cards in the other suits to help you regain the
	lead. If your partner has bid diamonds, you would

lead a diamond instead.

Always keep your objective in mind. If the contract were 6NT, rather than 3NT, you would need only two tricks to defeat it. You would start by taking the ♥ A and the ♥ K.

Choosing the Card to Lead against a Notrump Contract

Once you have selected the suit, decide which card in the suit to lead. If you have three or more high cards (A, K, Q, J or 10) that are touching (*e.g.*, K–Q–J–7–4, Q–J–10–7), lead the top card. Leading the top card of an honor sequence tells your partner that you have the next-lower card but don't have the next-higher card.

If, as is common, you don't have a sequence of touching high cards, lead a low card. For reasons we won't go into here, you lead your fourth-highest card if you have a suit of four or more cards (*e.g.,* K–J–7–5, Q–10–8–6–3). Since you usually lead your longest suit against a notrump contract (picking the stronger suit if you have a choice), you might hear bridge players use the adage, *"Lead the fourth highest from your longest and strongest suit against notrump."* This is good advice if you have nothing better to guide you.

Here are some examples of choosing the opening lead against a 3NT contract with nothing to guide you.

♠ A 3
♥ Q J 10 6 3
♦ 9 5 3
♣ J 6 3

Pick your longest suit, hearts. With three touching high cards, lead the top card, the ♥Q.

♠ K J 6 3
♥ 7 3
♦ J 9 4 2
♣ Q 6 5

With a choice of long suits, pick the stronger, spades. With no honor sequence, lead low, the ♠3.

♠ 2
♥ Q 4
♦ K 10 8 7 4 2
♣ A J 6 3

Pick your long suit, diamonds. Traditionally, you would select the fourth-highest card, the ♦7. At this stage in your bridge career, it wouldn't make much difference if you chose the ♦4 or the ♦2 instead.

BIDDING REVIEW

To refresh your memory, here is a review of some of the bidding concepts covered in the first book in this series, *Bidding*, which may prove useful when bidding the practice deals.

HAND VALUATION

High-card Points		*Distribution Points*	
Ace	4 points	Five-card suit	1 point
King	3 points	Six-card suit	2 points
Queen	2 points	Seven-card suit	3 points
Jack	1 point	Eight-card suit	4 points

Opening the Bidding 1NT or One of a Suit

With fewer than 13 total points, pass.

With 15 to 17 HCP and a balanced hand, bid 1NT.

With 13 to 21 points:

    With a five-card or longer suit:

- Bid your longest suit.
- Bid the higher ranking of two five-card or two six-card suits.

    With no five-card or longer suit:

- Bid your longer minor suit.
- Bid the higher ranking of two four-card minor suits or the lower ranking of two three-card minor suits.

Responses to Opening of 1NT

0 to 7
- Bid 2 ♦, 2 ♥, or 2 ♠ with a five-card or longer suit (2 ♣ is reserved for the Stayman convention*).
- Otherwise, pass.

8 or 9
- Bid 2NT (the Stayman convention* can be used to uncover an eight-card major suit fit).

10 to 15
- Bid 4 ♥ or 4 ♠ with a six-card or longer suit.
- Bid 3 ♥ or 3 ♠ with a five-card suit.
- Otherwise, bid 3NT (the Stayman convention* can be used to uncover an eight-card major suit fit).

The Stayman convention will be discussed in Chapter 5.

Responses to Opening Bids of One of a Suit

0 to 5   • Pass

6 to 9   **Responding to a major suit**
- Raise to the two level with three-card support.
- Bid a new suit at the one level.
- Bid 1NT.

           Responding to a minor suit
- Bid a new suit at the one level.
- Bid 1NT.
- Raise to the two level with five-card support.

10 or 11   **Responding to a major suit**
- Raise to the three level with three-card or longer support.
- Bid a new suit.

           Responding to a minor suit
- Bid a new suit.
- Raise to the three level with five-card or longer support.

12 or more   **Responding to a major suit**
- Jump to 2NT with a balanced hand and 13 to 15 HCP.*
- Jump to 3NT with a balanced hand and 16 to 18 HCP.**
- Bid a new suit.

           Responding to a minor suit
- Bid a new suit.
- Jump to 2NT with a balanced hand and 13 to 15 HCP.
- Jump to 3NT with a balanced hand and 16 to 18 HCP.

---

* If you have a game-going hand with three-card support for partner's major suit opening bid, you know the Golden Game should be in partner's major suit. Therefore, you should bid a new suit before jumping to game in partner's major suit.

** If you have 16 to 18 HCP with three-card support for partner's major suit opening bid, some players (especially duplicate players) prefer to bid 3NT with an absolutely balanced hand (4-3-3-3). However, bidding a new suit and jumping to game in opener's major is still a standard treatment.

SUMMARY

When you are declarer, take the time to make a PLAN before you start to play:

1. **P**ause to consider your objective
2. **L**ook at your winners and losers
3. **A**nalyze your alternatives
4. **N**ow put it all together

Consider your objective in terms of the number of winners you must take or losers you can afford to make your contract. **In notrump contracts, count your winners. In trump contracts, count your losers.** If you need to develop extra winners or eliminate extra losers, look at each suit to see what alternatives are available. When putting it all together, take your tricks if you have enough to make the contract. Remember to **play the high card from the short hand first** and to **draw trumps if playing in a suit contract**.

When defending against a notrump contract, use the adage **fourth highest from your longest and strongest** to guide you when selecting an opening lead.

Exercise One — The Objective

In a contract of 3NT, the objective is to take nine tricks. In a contract of 2♣, the objective is to lose no more than five tricks. Look at the following contracts and decide the objective, counting winners in notrump and losers in a trump contract.

1) 3♣　　　2) 6NT　　　3) 4♠　　　4) 1NT　　　5) 2♦

_____　　_____　　_____　　_____　　_____

Exercise Two — Counting Winners

Count the number of sure winners in each suit — the tricks that can be taken without giving up the lead.

DUMMY:　　1) A K Q　2) A J　　3) Q J 7 5　4) A 8 3 2　5) K Q
DECLARER:　4 2　　　　K Q　　A K 4 3 2　K 9 5　　4 2

_____　　_____　　_____　　_____　　_____

Exercise Three — Counting Losers

Count the number of losers that declarer has in each suit — the tricks that could be lost to the opponents. Are the losers quick or slow?

DUMMY :　　1) K Q J 4　2) J 10 9 8　3) 9 8 6 2　4) A 5　　5) K 6 4
DECLARER:　9 8　　　　5 4 3 2　　A 5　　　9 8 6 2　8 5

Losers:　　_____　　_____　　_____　　_____　　_____

Quick/Slow:　_____　　_____　　_____　　_____　　_____

DUMMY:　　6) Q 4 2　7) K 7 6　8) 7 4 3 2　9) K Q 5　10) A J 10
DECLARER:　9 8 3　　J 10 9 3　A K J　　7 4 2　　8 4 2

Losers:　　_____　　_____　　_____　　_____　　_____

Quick/Slow:　_____　　_____　　_____　　_____　　_____

Exercise One *Answers* — The Objective

1) To lose no more than four tricks.
2) To take 12 tricks.
3) To lose no more than three tricks.
4) To take seven tricks.
5) To lose no more than five tricks.

Exercise Two *Answers* — Counting Winners

1) Three sure tricks.
2) Two sure tricks since there are only two cards on each side of the table.
3) Five sure tricks. The opponents have only four cards in the suit and even if one opponent has all four cards, the 2 will still be a winner.
4) Two sure tricks.
5) No sure tricks. Promote a winner by giving up the lead.

Exercise Three *Answers* — Counting Losers

1) One loser; quick.
2) Three losers; quick.
3) One loser; slow.
4) Three losers; slow.
5) Two losers; quick.
6) Three losers; quick.
7) Two losers; one quick and one slow.
8) One loser; slow.
9) Two losers; one quick and one slow.
10) Two losers; slow.

Exercise Four — High Card from the Short Side

With which card would declarer win the first trick in each of the following suits?

DUMMY: 1) A Q J 10 3   2) A 4   3) A J 4   4) Q 5   5) K Q 6
DECLARER: K 2   K Q 5   K Q 7 3   A K J 7   A J 9

_____   _____   _____   _____   _____

Exercise Five — Leading against a Notrump Contract

Which card would the opening leader select from each of the following hands against a contract of 3NT?

1) ♠ J 6 3
   ♥ Q 7
   ♦ K Q J 8 5
   ♣ 10 8 4

2) ♠ 9 4
   ♥ J 10 8 6
   ♦ Q J 10 8
   ♣ A 7 3

3) ♠ 10 8 6 5 2
   ♥ A J 7
   ♦ K 5
   ♣ Q 5 2

_____   _____   _____

Exercise Six — Review of Opening Bids

As dealer, what would be the opening bid with each of the following hands?

1) ♠ K 9 7
   ♥ J 4
   ♦ Q J 9 8 4
   ♣ K 7 3

2) ♠ A Q
   ♥ K 10 5
   ♦ K J 4
   ♣ Q J 10 8 4

3) ♠ A K J 5
   ♥ 3
   ♦ Q 10 7 5 3
   ♣ Q 9 4

4) ♠ Q 10 8 7 4
   ♥ A K
   ♦ A K 10 7 3
   ♣ 6

5) ♠ A J 5 3
   ♥ Q J 6
   ♦ A 4
   ♣ Q 9 6 2

6) ♠ K 8 4 2
   ♥ 7
   ♦ A Q J 5
   ♣ A K Q 4

_____   _____   _____

Exercise Four *Answers* — High Card from the Short Side

    1) The king   2) The ace   3) The ace or jack

    4) The queen   5) It doesn't matter

Exercise Five *Answers* — Leading against a Notrump Contract

    1) ♦K   2) ♦Q   3) ♠5

Exercise Six *Answers* — Review of Opening Bids

    1) Pass   2) 1NT   3) 1♦

    4) 1♠   5) 1♣   6) 1♦

Exercise Seven — Review of Responses to 1NT Opening Bids

Partner opens the bidding 1NT. What response should be made with each of the following hands?

1) ♠ J 8 4
   ♥ Q 6 2
   ♦ 10 8 5 3
   ♣ J 9 3

2) ♠ 10 8 6 4 3 2
   ♥ J 5
   ♦ 9 6
   ♣ J 10 9

3) ♠ K 9
   ♥ Q J 8
   ♦ J 10 8 3
   ♣ Q 8 6 3

4) ♠ A 5
   ♥ J 10 8 6 4 3
   ♦ K Q 6
   ♣ 5 2

5) ♠ K J 9 8 3
   ♥ A 4 2
   ♦ 7 2
   ♣ Q 10 3

6) ♠ 7 2
   ♥ K 5
   ♦ Q 10 9 7 5 2
   ♣ A 4 2

Exercise Eight — Review of Responses to Opening Bids in a Suit

Partner opens the bidding 1 ♥. What response should be made with each of the following hands?

1) ♠ J 7 3
   ♥ 9 4
   ♦ Q 4 3
   ♣ 10 8 7 6 2

2) ♠ 8 2
   ♥ Q J 5
   ♦ J 9 6 4 2
   ♣ K 8 3

3) ♠ Q 9 6 4
   ♥ A 2
   ♦ 7 4 3
   ♣ Q 9 5 2

4) ♠ Q J 10
   ♥ 6 2
   ♦ K 9 7 6 3
   ♣ J 10 5

5) ♠ 8 4
   ♥ Q 6
   ♦ A 8 3 2
   ♣ K Q 10 6 2

6) ♠ A K 4
   ♥ K 10 6 5
   ♦ 10 9 6 3
   ♣ 8 7

Exercise Seven *Answers* — Review of Responses to 1NT Opening Bids

    1) Pass   2) 2♠   3) 2NT

    4) 4♥   5) 3♠   6) 3NT

Exercise Eight *Answers* — Review of Responses to Opening Bids in a Suit

    1) Pass   2) 2♥   3) 1♠

    4) 1NT   5) 2♣   6) 3♥

Exercise Nine — Counting Winners

(E–Z Deal Cards: #1, Deal 1 — Dealer, North)

Turn up all of the cards on the first pre-dealt deal. Put each hand dummy-style at the edge of the table in front of each player.

The Bidding

Neither North nor East has enough to open the bidding. With a balanced hand and 16 HCP, what opening bid best describes South's hand?

West passes. North is the captain and decides the level and strain of the contract. With 11 total points and no interest in the major suits, what should North's decision be?

Dealer:	♠ 7 5
North	♥ 7 3 2
	♦ A Q 10 6 3
	♣ A 9 2

♠ K Q J 10 6
♥ A 10 6
♦ 9 7
♣ 10 6 5

N W E S

♠ 9 4 3
♥ Q J 9 8 4
♦ 2
♣ J 8 7 4

♠ A 8 2
♥ K 5
♦ K J 8 5 4
♣ K Q 3

How will the auction proceed from there?

What will the contract be? Who will be the declarer?

The Play

Which player makes the opening lead? What will the opening lead be?

Declarer starts by making a PLAN:
1. **P**ause to consider your objective
2. **L**ook at your winners and losers
3. **A**nalyze your alternatives
4. **N**ow put it all together

After going through the four steps, how will declarer play the hand?

Exercise Nine *Answers* — Counting Winners

The Bidding

- South opens 1NT.
- North responds 3NT.
- Pass, pass, pass.
- The contract is 3NT. South is the declarer.

The Play

- West makes the opening lead of the ♠K.
- South needs nine tricks and has nine winners. South takes nine tricks and runs.

Exercise Ten — Taking Winners

(E–Z Deal Cards: #1, Deal 2 — Dealer, East)

Turn up all of the cards on the second pre-dealt deal and arrange them as in the previous deal.

The Bidding

East has a balanced hand. Why can't it be opened 1NT? What would East open?

South passes. Does West have a suit that can be bid at the one level? Why can't West bid a new suit at the two level? What will West respond?

How will the auction proceed from there?

What will the contract be? Who will the declarer be?

```
Dealer:        ♠ Q 6
  East         ♥ K J 6 3 2
               ♦ K 10 4
               ♣ 9 4 2
♠ 10 5 2              ♠ A 8 4 3
♥ 9 7 4        N     ♥ A 10 5
♦ 7 5 3      W   E   ♦ A 9 8 6
♣ A K J 3        S   ♣ Q 5
               ♠ K J 9 7
               ♥ Q 8
               ♦ Q J 2
               ♣ 10 8 7 6
```

The Play

Which player makes the opening lead? What will the opening lead be?

Declarer starts by making a PLAN. After going through the four steps, how will declarer play the hand? In putting it all together, why must declarer be careful about how the club suit is played?

Exercise Ten *Answers* — Taking Winners

The Bidding

- East opens 1♦; there aren't enough points to open 1NT.
- West doesn't have a suit to bid at the one level; West can't bid a new suit, clubs, at the two level with only 8 points.
- West responds 1NT.
- Pass, pass, pass.
- The contract is 1NT. West is the declarer.

The Play

- North leads the ♥3.
- Declarer has seven winners, enough to make the contract, so declarer will take seven tricks.
- The ♣Q must take the first club trick so the club winners in declarer's hand are not stranded.

Exercise Eleven — Counting Losers

(E–Z Deal Cards: #1, Deal 3 — Dealer, South)

Turn up all of the cards on the third pre-dealt deal and arrange them as in the previous deal.

The Bidding

South doesn't have enough to open the bidding. With 17 HCP and a balanced hand, what will West open?

North passes. East is the captain. At what level does the partnership belong? What should the strain of the contract be? What will East respond?

How will the auction proceed from there?

```
Dealer:      ♠ K 9 7 4 3
South        ♥ 7 5 4 2
             ♦ 10 6
             ♣ K 8
♠ J 5 2              ♠ 10 6
♥ A Q 9       N      ♥ K J 10 8 6 3
♦ A Q 8     W   E    ♦ K J 5
♣ A 9 7 3     S      ♣ 6 2
             ♠ A Q 8
             ♥ —
             ♦ 9 7 4 3 2
             ♣ Q J 10 5 4
```

What will the contract be? Who will be the declarer?

The Play

Which player makes the opening lead? What will the opening lead be?

Declarer starts by making a PLAN. After going through the four steps, how will declarer play the hand? In putting it all together, what precaution must declarer take?

Exercise Eleven *Answers* — Counting Losers

The Bidding

- West opens 1NT.
- The level the partnership belongs in is game; the strain is hearts. East responds 4♥.
- Pass, pass, pass.
- The contract is 4♥. East is the declarer.

The Play

- The opening lead is the ♣Q from South.
- Declarer can afford three losers and has only three losers.
- Declarer must be careful to draw trumps so unexpected losers aren't created.

Exercise Twelve — Drawing Trumps

(E–Z Deal Cards: #1, Deal 4 — Dealer, West)

Turn up all of the cards on the fourth pre-dealt deal and arrange them as in the previous deal.

The Bidding

West doesn't have enough to open the bidding. What will North's opening bid be?

East passes. Does South have support for partner's major suit? What will South respond?

How will the auction proceed from there?

What will the contract be? Who will be the declarer?

Dealer:	♠ K Q J 10 3
West	♥ A Q 5
	♦ 9 4
	♣ 8 6 3

♠ A 7   ♠ 9 5 2
♥ 9 7 6 4 3 2   ♥ J 8
♦ A J 6   ♦ K Q 10 2
♣ 9 4   ♣ K Q J 10

```
        N
      W   E
        S
```

♠ 8 6 4
♥ K 10
♦ 8 7 5 3
♣ A 7 5 2

The Play

Which player makes the opening lead? What will the opening lead be?

Declarer starts by making a PLAN. Why can declarer skip to the fourth question in the plan after answering the first two questions? Why may declarer be tempted to delay drawing trumps and play another suit? Why isn't this a good idea?

Exercise Twelve *Answers* — Drawing Trumps

The Bidding

- North opens 1♠.
- South can support partner's major and bids 2♠.
- Pass, pass, pass.
- The contract is 2♠. North is the declarer.

The Play

- East leads the ♣K.
- Declarer has five losers and can afford five losers. Declarer doesn't need to look for ways to eliminate the losers.
- Declarer may not want to give up the lead.
- If declarer doesn't draw trumps, the opponents may ruff one of the winners.

CHAPTER 2

Developing Tricks –
Promotion and Length

Promoting High Cards

Developing Long Suits

Promotion and Length
Combined

Guidelines for Defense

Bidding Review

Summary

Exercises

Sample Deals

The first step of the PLAN tells you to *Pause to consider your objective.* Once you have determined your goal, the second step of the PLAN reminds you to *Look at your winners and losers.* After you have completed these two steps, you'll find yourself in one of two situations: either you have enough winners (or few enough losers) to make your contract or you don't. As you saw in the first chapter, if you have enough tricks, you can skip over the third step and concentrate on putting it all together. This may require some care — taking your tricks in the right order or driving out the opponents' trumps first. You don't have to worry about developing additional tricks or eliminating extra losers.

Usually, however, when you compare the number of tricks you need to make your contract with the number of tricks you have, you'll find that you have too few winners or too many losers. This is where the third step in the PLAN, *Analyze your alternatives,* comes into use. In this chapter, we'll look at two ways to develop the extra tricks you need — through promotion and length. These methods are useful in both notrump and suit contracts.

PROMOTING HIGH CARDS

The most common and certain method of developing tricks is through the force of your own high cards to drive out the opponents' higher cards. Let's see how this works.

The Value of High Cards

The more high cards you have in a suit, the greater the potential the suit has for taking tricks. This is true even when the opponents have one or more higher cards. Here is an example:

DUMMY: K Q J 10   There are no sure winners in this suit. You
DECLARER: 5 4 3 2   can, however, use the king to drive out the opponents' ace and promote your queen, jack and 10 into three winners.

With a suit such as this, it doesn't matter whether you lead the king, the queen, the jack or the 10. They all have equal power. To keep discussions simple, we will assume that you lead your highest card in such situations. Note that the opponents are not forced to win the first trick with their ace. Whether they do or don't win the first trick will make no difference in the result if the contract is notrump. You can continue by leading the queen or the jack to make them take the ace and still end up with three winners.

In a suit contract, you would view the above holding a little differently. Count it as one loser. You still have to promote three winners by driving out the opponents' ace.

The idea of promotion is straightforward. You are making a trade-off. You are willing to give the opponents one or more tricks in return for developing one or more tricks of your own.

Consider this combination:

DUMMY: 4 3 2

DECLARER: Q J 10

You are missing the ace and the king but you have the next three highest cards in the suit. Use the queen to drive out the opponents' king and the jack to drive out the ace. This will promote your 10 into a winner.

Sometimes a lot of patience is required to develop tricks through the promotion of high cards.

DUMMY: J 10 9 8

DECLARER: 5 4 3 2

A trick is available in this suit after the opponents' ace, king and queen have been played. This may seem like a lot of work to take one trick since you have to give up the lead three times. Remember that a trick won by a low card is as worthwhile as a trick won by an ace. You're taking a little time to turn a low card into an ace.

When the Suit Is Unevenly Divided

Cards that have been promoted into winners become tricks only if you can reach them. If both dummy and declarer have the same number of cards in a suit, there is no problem. You will always have a low card left on one side of the table to get to the winners on the other side. If the cards are unevenly divided with more on one side of the table than the other, you must be more careful. Look at this layout of the diamond and club suits in a deal.

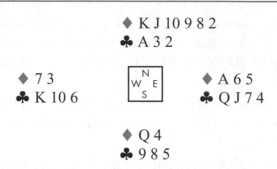

♦ K J 10 9 8 2
♣ A 3 2

♦ 7 3   ♦ A 6 5
♣ K 10 6   ♣ Q J 7 4

♦ Q 4
♣ 9 8 5

The diamond suit has no sure tricks. With all of the high cards except the ace, you plan to promote five diamond winners by driving out the opponents' ♦ A. Even though the diamond suit is divided unevenly between two hands, there doesn't appear to be a problem — you can use the ♣ A in the dummy to reach your winners once they are established. You still must be careful, however, of the order in which you play your cards.

Suppose you start by playing the ♦ 4 from your hand to dummy's ♦ K. East can make things difficult in one of two ways. If East wins this trick and leads back a club, your ♣ A will be driven out. If you lead dummy's ♦ 2 back to your established ♦ Q, you'll be in your hand with no way back to dummy! You don't have any more small diamonds and the ♣ A is gone. Another possibility is that East refuses to win the first trick. Now, you would lead the ♦ 2 back to your ♦ Q. East may refuse again to take the ace. You've won two tricks but you're in your hand and again you don't have any diamonds left. You can play a club to dummy's ♣ A, lead another diamond and force East to take the ♦ A. Now you're in the same position as before. Dummy's remaining diamonds are established but you can't get to them.

The solution is to use the same principle we came across in Chapter 1 when taking winners: Play the high card from the short side first. Look at the difference this makes. Start by playing the ♦ Q from your hand. If East wins the ace, you won't have a problem taking your remaining winners. If East doesn't win the ace, continue by leading your ♦ 4 to dummy's ♦ K. If East wins the ace, you have the ♣ A in dummy to get to your established winners. If East refuses to take the ace, you're in dummy and can continue leading diamonds. Play the ♦ J and force East to take the ace. Once again, the ♣ A remains in dummy as a way to get to the established winners.

A small change in the order of play makes a big difference! Here are some more examples:

DUMMY: J 3

DECLARER: K Q 10 4

To establish three winners, start by playing the high card from the short side first. If you are in the dummy, lead the jack. If you are in your hand, lead the 4 to dummy's jack.

DUMMY: Q 10 8 3 2

DECLARER: K J 5

Start by leading the king from your hand. If the opponents do not take their ace, continue by leading your remaining high card from the short side, the jack.

Losing Tricks to the Opponents

When you have all of the tricks you need, you generally take your winners and get on with the next deal. The situation is different when you have to develop extra tricks. As you have seen with the idea of promotion, the development of tricks may involve giving up the lead to the opponents.

At first glance, this may appear dangerous. Every time you give up the lead, the opponents have a chance to take their tricks — they may be able to defeat your contract. Losing tricks is a normal part of the game. If you are in a contract of 3NT, you don't need to take 12 or 13 tricks, only nine. You can afford to lose four tricks. You also don't need to take the first nine tricks. The idea is to lose tricks when you gain the most by doing so.

Most of the time, it is best to take your losses early. If you need to promote tricks in a suit, go to work on that suit. Give up tricks as necessary while you still have winners left in the other suits. Your other winners will prevent the opponents from taking tricks. They also will help you regain the lead and take your newly-established winners.

The concept of taking your losses early is easier to understand by look-ing at a full deal. The contract is 3NT and the opening lead is the ♥Q.

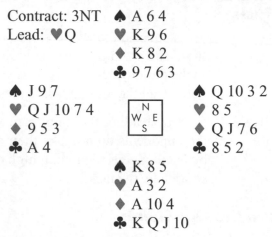

Contract: 3NT   ♠ A 6 4
Lead: ♥Q   ♥ K 9 6
                 ♦ K 8 2
                 ♣ 9 7 6 3

♠ J 9 7   ♠ Q 10 3 2
♥ Q J 10 7 4   ♥ 8 5
♦ 9 5 3   ♦ Q J 7 6
♣ A 4   ♣ 8 5 2

                 ♠ K 8 5
                 ♥ A 3 2
                 ♦ A 10 4
                 ♣ K Q J 10

Since the contract is 3NT, you need nine tricks to fulfill the contract. You have two sure tricks in spades, two in hearts and two in diamonds. That's a total of six. Three more tricks need to be developed. It's time to *Analyze your alternatives* and look at each suit to consider the potential for developing extra tricks. The club suit jumps out at you. By driving out the opponents' ace, you can promote the remaining three clubs into the winners you need.

When putting it all together, remember to take your losses early. Lead clubs immediately after you win the first trick. After the opponents win their ace, you still have high cards left in all of the other suits. You can win a trick in whichever suit they play and regain the lead. Now that you have your nine winners, you can take your tricks and run.

Look at what would happen if you did not lose the club trick early. Suppose you start by taking your winners: the ♥A, the ♥K, the ♠A, the ♠K, the ♦A and the ♦K. You have six tricks in the bag. When you belatedly lead the ♣K to get your extra winners, the opponents are in control. By taking your ♥A and ♥K, you have promoted all of West's remaining hearts into winners. Similarly, you have set up winning spade and club tricks in the opponents' hands. When they get in with the ♣A, they will take enough of their winners to defeat your contract.

Think about the defenders' point of view. When West leads the ♥Q,

West is hoping to promote the lower-ranking hearts into winners — just as you intend to promote your clubs into winners. If you take the ♥ A and the ♥ K right away, you are helping West's team, not your own!

DEVELOPING LONG SUITS

Tricks can also be developed through length. A long suit contains a lot of trick-taking potential. The more cards your side holds in a suit, the fewer the opponents hold. After the suit has been played a few times, the opponents won't have any cards left in the suit. All of your remaining cards will be winners, whether they are high cards or low cards.

The Division of a Suit

When you first start playing bridge, keeping track of the cards you hold in a suit is enough to keep you busy. What the opponents hold remains a mystery. As your experience and confidence grow, it becomes increasingly important to consider the opponents' holding in each suit. The key is to recognize that each suit has only 13 cards. If you and your partner have eight of them, the opponents have five; if you and your partner have nine cards, the opponents have only four.

When you are declarer, you know the exact number of cards the opponents hold in each suit but not how they are divided between the opponents' hands. For example, if you have seven cards in a suit, their six cards could be divided 3–3 (three in one opponent's hand and three in the other) or 4–2 or even 5–1 or 6–0.

Sometimes the opponents' bidding will suggest how the missing cards are divided. More often, you will have to guess (and find out for sure as the deal is played out). Since it is important to know what to expect, here are some useful guidelines:

- **An even number of missing cards will divide slightly unevenly most of the time.** For example, if the opponents have four cards, they are likely to be divided 3–1 rather than 2–2; if the opponents have six cards, they are likely to be divided 4–2 rather than 3–3; if the opponents have eight cards, they are likely to be divided 5–3 rather than 4–4.

- **An odd number of missing cards will divide as evenly as possible most of the time.** For example, if the opponents have three cards, they are likely to be divided 2–1; if the opponents have five cards, they are likely to be divided 3–2; if the opponents have seven cards, they are likely to be divided 4–3.

Here is the same information on the likely division of the opponents' cards shown in tabular form:

NUMBER OF MISSING CARDS	LIKELY DISTRIBUTION
3	2–1
4	3–1
5	3–2
6	4–2
7	4–3
8	5–3

Let's see how to make use of this information when looking for extra winners or trying to eliminate losers.

Developing Long Suits

Some suits will develop extra tricks through length no matter how the missing cards are divided.

For example:

DUMMY: A K Q J 3 2 You have nine cards; the opponents have four.
DECLARER: 6 5 4 Even if one opponent has all four of the missing cards, that opponent won't have any left by the time you have played the ace, the king, the queen and the jack. Your 3 and 2 will be winners.

In some cases, you will have to hope for a favorable division of the opponents' cards:

DUMMY: A K Q 2   You have eight cards; the opponents have five.
DECLARER: 6 5 4 3   If one opponent has all five of the missing cards or four of the five, that opponent will have a high card left after you have played your ace, king and queen.

The missing cards will most likely be distributed 3–2. If this is the case, you will take four tricks from the suit instead of three.

A typical layout of the missing cards might be:

A K Q 2

J 9 7   [N W E S]   10 8

6 5 4 3

In the following example, you'd have to be lucky to get an extra trick:

DUMMY: K Q 3 2   You have seven cards; the opponents have six.
DECLARER: A 5 4   You'll get an extra trick if the missing cards are divided 3–3. After you have played the ace, the king and the queen, neither opponent will have any left. Your remaining low card will be a winner. However, it is more likely that the missing cards will divide 4–2, and they could be divided 5–1 or 6–0.

Frequently, you must let the opponents win one or more tricks to establish a long suit.

DUMMY: A K 3 2   You have eight cards; the opponents have five. You hope the missing cards are divided 3–2. Even if that is the case, you can't win all of the tricks. To develop an extra trick you must give up a trick.

The complete layout of the suit could be:

A K 3 2

J 9   [N W E S]   Q 10 8

7 6 5 4

After you play your ace and king, East still has the queen left. Play the suit again, letting East win a trick. When you regain the lead, you will have the only cards left in the suit and will take a trick with them. You get three of the four tricks by giving up one trick to the opponents.

Here are more examples where you must give up tricks in order to establish long suits:

DUMMY: A 4 3 2
DECLARER: 8 7 6 5

You have eight cards; the opponents have five. If the missing cards are divided 3–2, you can develop a second trick by giving up two tricks.

DUMMY: A 9 7 6 5
DECLARER: 8 4 3 2

You have nine cards; the opponents have four. If the opponents' cards are divided 2–2, you can take four tricks in the suit by taking your ace and then giving up a trick. If the opponents' cards are divided 3–1, you can still take three tricks, but you'll have to give up two tricks first. If one opponent has all four of the missing cards, you can eventually establish one extra trick but you'll have to give up three tricks to do so.

DUMMY: K 6 5 4 3
DECLARER: A 2

You have seven cards; the opponent have six. You can try playing the ace and the king and then leading the suit again from dummy. If the missing cards are divided 3–3, you'll establish two extra winners in dummy. If the suit is divided 4–2, you'll have to get back to dummy and give up another trick to finally set one up for yourself. If the suit breaks 5–1 or 6–0, you take only the two tricks you started with — the ace and the king.

DUMMY: A K Q 3 2
DECLARER: 6 5 4

You won't have to lose any tricks if the opponents' cards divide 3–2, as is likely. If they divide 4–1, you'll have to give up a trick to set up your remaining low card as a winner.

DUMMY: 10 8 7 4 3
DECLARER: 9 6 5 2

The more cards you have in a suit, the more potential for developing tricks. Lead the suit, giving up a trick. When you regain the lead, play the suit again, giving up another trick. If the missing cards are divided 2–2, your remaining cards are winners. If not, lead the suit again at your next opportunity and you can still establish two tricks.

A Complete Deal

Let's take a look at the development of a long suit in a complete deal. You're in 3NT and the opening lead is the ♠3.

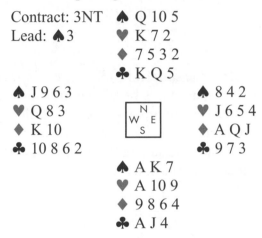

Contract: 3NT ♠ Q 10 5
Lead: ♠3   ♥ K 7 2
              ♦ 7 5 3 2
              ♣ K Q 5

♠ J 9 6 3   ♠ 8 4 2
♥ Q 8 3   ♥ J 6 5 4
♦ K 10   ♦ A Q J
♣ 10 8 6 2   ♣ 9 7 3

              ♠ A K 7
              ♥ A 10 9
              ♦ 9 8 6 4
              ♣ A J 4

Your objective is to take nine tricks, and you start with eight winners: three sure tricks in spades, two in hearts and three in clubs. You need to find one more trick. When you *Analyze your alternatives,* the only suit that presents some potential is diamonds. Even though you have no high cards in the suit, you do have eight cards in the combined hands. The opponents have only five, and you hope they are divided 3–2.

Now put it all together and remember the earlier advice to take your losses early. After winning the first spade trick, play a diamond immediately, giving up a trick. Whatever the opponents lead back, you can win and lead another diamond, giving up a second trick in the suit. Since you still have winners left in all of the other suits, you can win whatever the opponents lead and play a diamond once again. Although you lose this trick also, you have finally established the extra trick you need. You can take your remaining winners when you regain the lead.

This may seem like a lot of work, but making your PLAN and knowing how to develop long suits really pays off when you make a contract like this one.

When the Suit Is Unevenly Divided

When a suit is unevenly divided between your hand and dummy, be careful not to strand the winners in the long hand after you establish them. Look at this layout of a suit:

```
            A K 4 3 2
                 ┌───┐
                 │ N │
        Q J 9    │W  E│    10 8
                 │ S │
                 └───┘
            7 6 5
```

You have eight cards in the suit. If the missing cards are divided 3–2, you plan to develop two more tricks by giving up one trick. If dummy had no high cards in other suits to provide an entry, deciding which trick to give up to the opponents is crucial. Suppose you try taking the ace and the king and then leading the suit again, giving West a trick with the queen. The remaining cards in the suit are:

```
              4 3
            ┌───┐
            │ N │
            │W  E│
            │ S │
            └───┘
```

You have two winners in dummy but no way to reach them! Instead, remember the advice to *take your losses early* and give up the first trick by playing a low card from both hands.

Now the suit looks like this:

```
            A K 4 3
                 ┌───┐
                 │ N │
        Q J      │W  E│    10
                 │ S │
                 └───┘
            7 6
```

You have lost one trick. When you regain the lead, take the ace and the king. You will be in the dummy to take your remaining two winners. In fact, you could achieve the same result by winning the first trick and giving up the second trick.

Here is a similar case:

A 9 7 6 3

K J [N W E S] Q 10 5

8 4 2

To establish extra winners in this suit, you must give up two tricks. If dummy has no high cards in other suits to provide an entry, keep the ace until the suit is established. Give up a trick by playing a low card from both hands. This is called *ducking a trick.* When you regain the lead, duck another trick by playing low from both hands. The remaining cards are:

A 9 7

[N W E S] Q

8

Now you are in business. When you regain the lead, play your 8 to dummy's ace and take your two established winners.

PROMOTION AND LENGTH COMBINED

It is often possible to combine the idea of promotion with that of length when developing tricks in a suit.

Promotion and Long Suits Working Together

Take a look at this suit layout:

K Q J 3

10 5 [N W E S] A 9 2

8 7 6 4

There are no sure tricks. Your plan is to promote the queen and the jack into winners by playing the king to drive out the opponents' ace. Since you have eight cards in the combined hands, you will take another trick if the suit divides 3–2. After the king, the queen and the jack have been played, the opponents won't have any cards left in the suit.

DUMMY: 7 5 3

DECLARER: Q J 10 4 2

You can lead the queen to drive out the king and the jack to drive out the ace, promoting your 10 into a winner. If the opponents' cards are divided 3–2, your 4 and 2 also will be winners.

DUMMY: 6 5 3 2

DECLARER: K Q J

You plan to promote two tricks by using your king to drive out the opponents' ace. You may end up with a third trick if the missing cards are divided exactly 3–3. You will have to be lucky, since the missing cards are more likely to be divided 4–2. Even if they are 3–3, you will need a high card in another suit in the dummy in order to reach your winner.

Another Look at Winners and Losers

Knowing about promotion and the development of long suits helps you decide whether you need to develop extra winners or eliminate losers. Take a look at your holding in this suit:

A 6 4 3

? W N E S ?

9 7 5 2

When counting winners, you would count one sure trick. When counting losers, you would count three losers. When analyzing your alternatives, you would see that you are missing only five cards which are probably divided 3–2. You hope the actual layout is something like this:

A 6 4 3

K J 10   W N E S   Q 8

9 7 5 2

In a notrump contract, you could plan to develop an extra winner by giving up two tricks. In a suit contract, you could plan to eliminate one of your losers by giving up two tricks. Two sides of the same coin.

Of course, there is no guarantee that you can develop an extra winner or eliminate a loser. The actual layout could be:

A 6 4 3

K J 10 8
$$\boxed{\begin{array}{c} N \\ W \quad E \\ S \end{array}}$$
Q

9 7 5 2

You can't get more than your one sure trick, and you still have three losers in the suit. This is why you count one sure trick or three losers in the second step of your PLAN. Hoping that the missing cards are divided 3–2 is one of your alternatives in the third step. You may have better prospects elsewhere.

Choosing the Suit to Develop

Sometimes you will have a choice of suits to develop. In general, pick the suit that will give you the most tricks. This is usually the suit in which you have the most cards. Compare these two suits:

1)   DUMMY: A K 6 5 2   2)   DUMMY: A K 6 5 2

DECLARER: 4 3   DECLARER: 7 4 3

If you need to develop two more tricks to make your contract, the second suit has much more potential than the first. In the first case, you have only seven cards; the opponents have six. You hope that the missing cards are divided 3–3 and plan to give up one trick while developing two more. It's more likely, however, that the missing cards are divided 4–2. They could be 5–1 or 6–0.

In the second case, you have eight cards and are missing five. It is quite likely that the missing cards are divided 3–2. By giving up a trick in the suit, you can develop the two extra winners you need.

If you have the same number of cards in both suits, the suit that is more unevenly divided has more potential for extra tricks. Compare these two suits:

1)   DUMMY: A K 6 5   2)   DUMMY: A K 6 5 2

DECLARER: 7 4 3 2   DECLARER: 7 4 3

In both cases, you have eight cards and the opponents have five. If the missing cards are divided 3–2, you can develop one extra trick in the first example by giving up a trick. In the second example, however, you will get two extra tricks if the suit divides 3–2.

GUIDELINES FOR DEFENSE

In the previous chapter, you saw that you generally lead from your longest suit against a notrump contract in the hope of establishing enough winners to defeat declarer. When you lead against a suit contract, there are other considerations.

Choosing the Suit to Lead against a Trump Contract

When defending against a notrump contract, often you are willing to give up one or two tricks to establish your long suit. If you can regain the lead, you can take all of your winners. When defending against a suit contract, it may not do you much good to develop your long suit. By the time you get to lead your winners, declarer usually will be able to ruff them. If you must give up a trick while establishing your winners, you may never get it back.

Instead of automatically leading your longest suit, you often look for a safe suit to lead — one that is unlikely to present declarer with a trick that declarer could not get without help. A suit with an honor sequence is usually safe (*e.g.,* K–Q–J or Q–J–10) or a suit with no high cards (*e.g.,* 8–7–4–2). A suit with only one high card is usually more dangerous (*e.g.,* K–7–5–2). If you have two touching high cards, it is somewhere in between (*e.g.,* Q–J–4–2). Leading the king from K–Q–3–2 is likely to set up at least one trick for the defense and maybe more if your partner has the ace or the jack.

A different approach is for the defenders to use declarer's trump suit. Try leading a short suit of one or two cards. Your plan is to try to win a trick by ruffing when the suit is led again.

Most of the time, it isn't a good idea to lead a trump because you'll be helping declarer draw trumps. If you think that declarer may be planning to ruff some losers with dummy's trumps, however, leading a trump might work out well.

If partner has bid a suit, you should lead partner's suit unless you have an alternative that is clearly better. If partner hasn't bid and you don't have a clear-cut choice, you still must pick a suit. If possible, choose one that the opponents did not bid.

Let's see how you would choose a lead against a contract of 4♠ with the following hand:

♠ 7 4 3   The safest suit to lead is clubs since you have an
♥ K 8 6 2   honor sequence. Even if declarer has the ace and
♦ 3 2   the king, you will start to drive them out. Eventu-
♣ Q J 10 2   ally you may establish a club trick for your side. If
         partner has the ace or the king, you may get two or
         three tricks. If one of the opponents has bid clubs,
you can try leading your short suit, diamonds. You may get to use one of your trumps to ruff one of declarer's winning diamond tricks.

Leading a heart from your king is dangerous. It would be fine if partner had bid hearts or if the opponents had bid all of the other suits. If the opponents' bidding has suggested that dummy may have only one or two hearts, you could lead a trump. You hope that the trump lead will stop declarer from ruffing heart losers in dummy. Perhaps dummy has bid spades, diamonds and clubs, indicating that there are very few — if any — hearts in the hand.

Choosing the Card to Lead against a Suit Contract

Once you have selected the suit, decide which card in the suit to lead. If you have two or more high cards that are touching, lead the top card (*e.g.,* K–Q–3 or Q–J–8–7). As when leading the top card of an honor sequence against a notrump contract, you are telling partner that you have the next-lower card but not the next-higher card.

If you are leading a short suit, lead the top card (*e.g.,* 7–2 or 5–4). Otherwise, lead a low card (*e.g.,* Q–7–4 or K–J–6–3). Against notrump contracts, you traditionally lead your *fourth-highest* card if you have a suit of four or more cards (*e.g.,* Q–9–5–4–2).

Here are some examples of choosing the right opening lead against a contract of 4♥ with nothing else to guide you.

♠ K Q J   Leading a spade is safe and offers a good opportunity
♥ J 5   to develop two tricks in the suit. With touching high
♦ J 8 4 2   cards, lead the top card, the ♠K.
♣ A 6 5 3

♠ Q 7 5 2   This time you can try leading your short suit, the ♦ 5.
♥ 8 4 3   Perhaps partner can win the trick with the ace and
♦ 5   lead another diamond to let you ruff one of declarer's
♣ 10 9 7 3 2   winners. If partner has another ace, partner may be
               able to win another trick and lead another diamond
for you to ruff — four tricks from only two aces!

♠ K 10 7   No lead is really attractive. Anything could be right.
♥ 6 4 2   You could try the ♣J since you also have the ♣10.
♦ Q 9 6 2   You could also lead a trump if you think declarer
♣ J 10 3   may be planning to use dummy's trumps to ruff some
               losers. Even a low diamond or spade could prove to
be the best lead.

BIDDING REVIEW

Rebids by Opener

Opener's bid of one in a suit describes a hand with 13 to 21 points. That is too wide a range for responder to determine the level at which the partnership belongs. When opener makes a rebid, opener tries to narrow the description of the strength of the hand into one of three categories:

Minimum Hand	13 to 15 points
Medium Hand	16 to 18 points
Maximum Hand	19 to 21 points

At the same time, opener tries to further describe the distribution of the hand so that responder can determine the appropriate strain. The rebid opener chooses depends on partner's initial response as shown in the following summaries:

Rebids by Opener after a 1NT Opening Bid

After responder's sign-off:

- Pass.

After responder's invitational bid of 2NT:

- Pass with 15 HCP.
- Bid 3NT with 16 or 17 HCP.

After responder's forcing bid of 3 ♥ or 3 ♠:

- Bid four of the major with three or more cards in the major.
- Bid 3NT with two cards in the major.

Opener's Rebid after Responder Raises a Major Suit

With 13 to 15 points (minimum hand):

- Pass.

With 16 to 18 points (medium hand):

- Raise to the three level.

With 19 to 21 points (maximum hand):

- Jump raise to the four level (game).

Opener's Rebid after Responder Raises a Minor Suit

With 13 to 15 points (minimum hand):

- Pass.

With 16 to 18 points (medium hand):

- Raise to the three level.

With 19 to 21 points (maximum hand):

- Jump to 3NT (game).

Opener's Rebid after Responder Bids 1NT

With 13 to 15 points (minimum hand):

- Pass with a balanced hand.
- Bid a second suit of four cards or longer if it is lower-ranking than the original suit.
- Rebid the original suit at the two level.

With 16 to 18 points (medium hand):

- Bid a second suit of four cards or longer, even if it is higher-ranking than the original suit.
- Rebid the original suit at the three level.

With 19 to 21 points (maximum hand):

- Bid 3NT with a balanced hand.
- Bid a second suit of four cards or longer, jumping a level (jump shift), if it is lower-ranking than the original suit.
- Rebid the original suit, jumping to game.

Opener's Rebid after Responder Bids a New Suit

With 13 to 15 points (minimum hand):

- Raise partner's major to the cheapest available level with four-card support. Count dummy points.
- Bid a second suit of four cards or longer if it can be bid at the one level. A suit that ranks below the original one can be bid at the two level.
- Rebid the original suit at the cheapest available level.
- Bid notrump with a balanced hand at the cheapest available level.

With 16 to 18 points (medium hand):

- Raise partner's major, jumping one level, with four-card support. Count dummy points.
- Make a jump rebid in notrump, showing a balanced 18 or 19 HCP hand.
- Rebid the original suit, jumping one level.
- Bid a second suit of four cards or longer even if it is higher-ranking than the original and must be bid at the two level.

With 19 to 21 points (maximum hand):

- Raise partner's major, jumping two levels, with four-card support. Count dummy points.
- Bid a second suit of four cards or longer, jumping one level (jump shift).
- Bid 3NT — a double jump suggesting a hand with a long solid suit and stoppers in all unbid suits.
- Rebid the original suit, jumping to game.

Opener's Rebid after Responder Jump Raises Opener's Suit

With 13 to 15 points (minimum hand):

- With 13, pass.
- With 14 or 15, raise to game.

With 16 to 18 points (medium hand):

- Raise to game.

With 19 to 21 points (maximum hand):

- Bid the appropriate game.

Opener's Rebid after Responder Bids 2NT

With 13 to 15 points (minimum hand):
- With a balanced hand, raise to 3NT.
- With an unbalanced hand, bid a second suit of four cards or longer or rebid the original suit.

With 16 to 18 points (medium hand):
- With a balanced hand, raise to 4NT, inviting opener to bid a slam with a maximum.
- With an unbalanced hand, bid a second suit of four cards or longer or rebid the original suit.

With 19 to 21 points (maximum hand):
- With a balanced hand, raise to 6NT.
- With an unbalanced hand, bid a second suit of four cards or longer or rebid the original suit.

Rebids by Responder

When you make your rebid as responder, you put your hand into one of the following categories according to the point count. Use dummy points if planning to support opener's major suit.

Minimum Hand	6 to 9 points
Medium Hand	10 or 11 points
Maximum Hand	12 or more points

By combining this information with the strength and distribution shown by opener's rebid, you try to decide the level and strain of the contract. When you have enough information, sign off in the appropriate contract. If you need more information, make an invitational or forcing bid. The bid you choose depends on whether opener has shown a minimum, medium, or maximum hand.

RESPONDER'S REBID

Opener's Range	Responder's Range	Final Level	Responder's Option
13 to 15 (Minimum)	6 to 9	Partscore	• Pass • 1NT • Two-level bid of a suit already mentioned by the partnership
	10 or 11	Partscore or Game	• 2NT • Three-level bid of a suit already mentioned by the partnership
	12 or more	Game	• Bid a Golden Game • Bid a new suit at the three level
16 to 18 (Medium)	6 or 7	Partscore	• Pass • Cheapest bid of a suit already mentioned by the partnership
	8 or 9	Game	• Bid a Golden Game • Bid a new suit
	10 or 11	Game	• Bid a Golden Game
	12 or more	Game	• Bid a Golden Game or Slam • Bid a Slam, if appropriate
19 to 21 (Maximum)	6 to 9	Game	• Pass • Bid a Golden Game • Bid a new suit
	10 or 11	Game	• Bid a Golden Game • Pass in game • Bid a new suit
	12 or more	Game or Slam	• Bid a Golden Game or slam, if appropriate

SUMMARY

When you come to the third step in your PLAN, *Analyze your alternatives,* there are a number of ways to develop extra winners or eliminate losers. Extra tricks can be developed by **promotion,** driving out the opponents' higher cards so your high cards can take tricks. Tricks can also be developed by playing a long suit so the small cards are good after the opponents run out of the suit.

You can expect the missing cards to divide in the following manner:

> • An even number of missing cards will divide slightly unevenly most of the time.
>
> • An odd number of missing cards will divide as evenly as possible most of the time.

Don't be afraid to give up tricks to the opponents in order to develop tricks for yourself. If you do need to give up tricks, remember the advice: **Take your losses early.** Make sure you can reach your winners once they are established. You want to retain a high card in the hand that contains the winners you are establishing.

When you have a choice of suits to develop, pick the longer suit. With equal-length suits, pick the suit that is more unevenly divided between declarer's hand and dummy.

Exercise One — Promotion

How many tricks do you expect to take from each of the following suits? How many times would you have to give up the lead before you could enjoy your winners?

DUMMY:	1) K Q J 10	2) J 10 9 8	3) Q 10 3	4) K 3	5) J 8 7
DECLARER:	7 6 4 2	5 4 3 2	J 7 4	Q 7	10 9 4

_____   _____   _____   _____   _____

Exercise Two — High Card from the Short Side

Assume that an ace in another suit is in dummy. How many tricks do you expect to get from the following suits? How would you play these suit combinations? What could happen if you weren't careful?

DUMMY:	1) K J 10 9 4	2) Q J 3	3) K Q 10 3	4) J 10 5	5) Q 10 9 8 3
DECLARER:	Q 7	K 4	J 4	Q 7	K J

_____   _____   _____   _____   _____

Exercise Three — The Division of the Opponents' Cards

If the opponents hold the following number of cards in a suit, how would you expect them to be divided between the two hands?
1) 3   2) 4   3) 5   4) 6   5) 7   6) 8   7) 9

_____   _____   _____   _____   _____   _____   _____

Exercise One *Answers* — Promotion

1) Three, after giving up the lead once.
2) One, after giving up the lead three times.
3) One, after giving up the lead twice.
4) One, after giving up the lead once.
5) No tricks.

Exercise Two *Answers* — High Card from the Short Side

1) Four, by playing the queen first.
2) Two, by playing the king first.
3) Three, by playing the jack first.
4) One, by playing the queen first.
5) Four, by playing the king first.

In all of the examples, try to win the first trick with the high card from the short side; otherwise, your winners may be stranded even though you have one entry to dummy to go with your long suit.

Exercise Three *Answers* — The Division of the Opponents' Cards

1) 2–1	2) 3–1	3) 3–2
4) 4–2	5) 4–3	6) 5–3
7) 5–4		

Exercise Four — Developing Tricks through Length

If the opponents' cards are divided as you would expect, how many tricks are you most likely to get from each of the following suits? How many tricks would you get if the suits are divided as favorably as possible?

DUMMY:	1) A K 6 3	2) A 5 4 2	3) A 8 7 4 2	4) K 8 7 5 3 2	5) A K 8 6 2
DECLARER:	7 5 4 2	K Q 3	K 6 3	A 4	7 5 4 3

_____ _____ _____ _____ _____

Exercise Five — Stranding a Suit

Assuming that dummy has no high cards other than those in this suit, how would you play the suit to avoid stranding your established winners in dummy? How many tricks would you expect to take? How would you expect the opponents' cards to be divided?

DUMMY:	1) A K 7 6 3	2) A 8 6 4 2	3) A K 8 7 4 2	4) A 8 6 3 2	5) A 7 6 2
DECLARER:	8 5 2	K 9 3	6 3	7 5 4	K 4 3

_____ _____ _____ _____ _____

Exercise Six — Leading against a Suit Contract

Which card would you lead from each of the following hands against a contract of 4♠?

1) ♠ J 6 3	2) ♠ 10 9 4	3) ♠ J 5 2
♥ A 6 3	♥ Q 10 6 5 3	♥ K 8 7
♦ K Q J	♦ 10 9 7 3	♦ Q 5 2
♣ J 9 5 4	♣ 3	♣ K Q 10 9

_____   _____   _____

Exercise Four *Answers* — Developing Tricks through Length

1) Three. Three, if the opponents' cards divide 3–2.
2) Three. Four, if the opponents' cards divide 3–3.
3) Four. Four, if the opponents' cards divide 3–2.
4) Five. Five, if the opponents' cards divide 3–2.
5) Four. Five, if the opponents' cards divide 2–2.

Exercise Five *Answers* — Stranding a Suit

1) Lose the first (or second) trick. Expect four winners when the opponents' cards divide 3–2.
2) Lose the first trick and then play the king (or vice versa). Expect four tricks when the opponents' cards divide 3–2.
3) Lose the first trick. Expect five tricks when the opponents' cards divide 3–2.
4) Lose the first two tricks. Expect three tricks when the opponents' cards divide 3–2.
5) Lose the first trick, then play the king (or vice versa). Expect only two tricks, since the most likely division of the opponents' cards is 4–2. You can take three tricks if they divide 3–3.

Exercise Six *Answers* — Leading against a Suit Contract

1) ♦ K   2) ♣ 3   3) ♣ K

Exercise Seven — Review of Rebids by Opener

You open the bidding 1♥ and your partner responds 1♠. What do you rebid with each of the following hands?

1) ♠ 7 6 4 2
   ♥ A Q J 4 3
   ♦ A 2
   ♣ Q 3

2) ♠ Q 5
   ♥ K 10 5 3 2
   ♦ K J 4
   ♣ A J 10

3) ♠ 5
   ♥ K Q 10 7 3
   ♦ A J 2
   ♣ Q J 9 4

4) ♠ 7 4
   ♥ A K J 7 6 2
   ♦ K 7 3
   ♣ J 4

5) ♠ A J
   ♥ Q J 7 6 2
   ♦ A Q 4
   ♣ K Q 9

6) ♠ K 8 4 2
   ♥ A Q J 6 2
   ♦ 5
   ♣ K Q 4

7) ♠ 7 4
   ♥ A K Q 7 6 2
   ♦ A K 3
   ♣ 10 3

8) ♠ A K 7 4
   ♥ K Q J 6 2
   ♦ 4 2
   ♣ A J

9) ♠ A 8
   ♥ A K Q 6 2
   ♦ 5 3
   ♣ K Q J 4

Answers to Exercise

Exercise Seven *Answers* — Review of Rebids by Opener

1) 2♠	2) 1NT	3) 2♣
4) 2♥	5) 2NT	6) 3♠
7) 3♥	8) 4♠	9) 3♣

Exercise Eight — Review of Rebids by Responder

Your partner opens the bidding 1 ♦, you respond 1 ♥ and your partner rebids 1NT. What do you rebid with each of the following hands?

1) ♠ 7 6 4 2
   ♥ K Q 4 2
   ♦ A 4
   ♣ 8 6 2

2) ♠ 3
   ♥ K 10 5 3
   ♦ K J 5 4
   ♣ 8 6 4 2

3) ♠ A 5
   ♥ J 9 8 7 4 3
   ♦ J 8 2
   ♣ 9 4

4) ♠ K 6 3
   ♥ A Q J 6
   ♦ 10 7 3
   ♣ J 5 4

5) ♠ 10 8
   ♥ K Q J 7 6 2
   ♦ K 9 2
   ♣ 10 5

6) ♠ 6 2
   ♥ K J 6 2
   ♦ A 6 5 3 2
   ♣ Q 4

7) ♠ A 8 7 4
   ♥ K Q 6 3
   ♦ K 3
   ♣ J 10 4

8) ♠ 4
   ♥ Q J 9 8 6 2
   ♦ A J 2
   ♣ K 10 3

9) ♠ Q 8
   ♥ A J 5 4
   ♦ K Q 7 5 3
   ♣ Q 3

Answers to Exercise

Exercise Eight *Answers* — Review of Rebids by Responder

1) Pass	2) 2 ♦	3) 2 ♥
4) 2NT	5) 3 ♥	6) 3 ♦
7) 3NT	8) 4 ♥	9) 3NT

Exercise Nine — Promotion in a Notrump Contract

(E–Z Deal Cards, #2, Deal 1 — Dealer, North)

Turn up all of the cards on the first pre-dealt deal. Put each hand dummy-style at the edge of the table in front of each player.

The Bidding

Does North have enough to open the bidding? With a choice of suits, which suit does North choose?

East passes. Can South bid a suit at the one level? What does South respond?

West passes. Can North support partner's suit? Can North bid a new suit at the one level? Which rebid describes North's hand?

Dealer:	♠ A 6 5
North	♥ J 4
	♦ A 7 6 4
	♣ A 9 8 3

♠ 9 4   ♠ Q J 10 7 3
♥ A 7 6   ♥ 9 8 5 2
♦ Q J 9 8   ♦ K 3
♣ K J 10 5   ♣ Q 7

             ♠ K 8 2
             ♥ K Q 10 3
             ♦ 10 5 2
             ♣ 6 4 2

East passes. South asks what level and what strain is best for the partnership. What will South's rebid be?

What will the contract be? Who will be the declarer?

The Play

Which player makes the opening lead? What will the opening lead be?

```
  Declarer starts by making a PLAN:
  1. Pause to consider your objective
  2. Look at your winners and losers
  3. Analyze your alternatives
  4. Now put it all together
```

How many extra winners does declarer need? Which suit can provide them? How does declarer plan to play the suit? Should declarer win the first trick in dummy or in declarer's hand? Why?

Exercise Nine *Answers* — Promotion in a Notrump Contract

The Bidding

- North opens with 1 ♦.
- South responds 1 ♥.
- North can't support hearts or bid a new suit at the one level and responds with 1NT.
- South passes.
- The contract is 1NT. North is the declarer.

The Play

- East leads the ♠Q.
- Declarer needs three more tricks to make the contract. The heart suit can provide them.
- Declarer plans to try to win the first heart trick with the ♥J, the high card from the short side.
- Declarer should win the first trick in hand because the ♠K is needed as an entry to dummy's hearts.

Exercise Ten — Promotion in a Suit Contract

(E–Z Deal Cards, #2, Deal 2 — Dealer, East)

Turn up all of the cards on the second pre-dealt deal and arrange them as in the previous deal.

The Bidding

East has a balanced hand. Why can't East open 1NT? Why can't East open with the longest suit? What will East open?

South passes. What does West respond?

North passes. What does East rebid?

South passes. West decides on the level and strain

```
Dealer:      ♠ 9 2
East         ♥ K Q 6 5 2
             ♦ 10 6
             ♣ 10 8 4 3
♠ A K J 4 3           ♠ Q 10 6 5
♥ 10 3        N       ♥ J 8 4
♦ Q 9 7    W   E      ♦ K J 3
♣ K 7 2       S       ♣ A Q 6
             ♠ 8 7
             ♥ A 9 7
             ♦ A 8 5 4 2
             ♣ J 9 5
```

for the partnership. What rebid does West make? What will the contract be? Who will be the declarer?

The Play

Which player makes the opening lead? What will the opening lead be?

How many losers can declarer afford in a 4♠ contract? How many losers are there?

Declarer starts by making a PLAN. After going through the four steps, how will declarer play the hand? What could interfere with declarer making the contract? When should West draw trumps? What cards can be promoted into winners?

Exercise Ten *Answers* — Promotion in a Suit Contract

The Bidding

- There aren't enough points to open 1NT. East can't open spades, the longest suit, because East is playing five-card majors. East opens 1♣.

- West reponds 1♠, a forcing bid. West knows there is enough strength for game but doesn't yet know the strain.

- East rebids 2♠.

- West places the contract in 4♠. West is the declarer.

The Play

- North leads the ♥K.

- West has three losers. West can afford three losers. If West doesn't draw trumps right away, an unexpected loser could appear. After drawing trumps, West plays the diamond suit to promote two extra tricks.

Exercise Eleven — Using Length in a Notrump Contract

(E–Z Deal Cards, #2, Deal 3 — Dealer, South)

Turn up all of the cards on the third pre-dealt deal and arrange them as in the previous deal.

The Bidding

What is South's opening bid?

West passes. Does North have a suit to bid at the one level? What does North respond?

East passes. Can South support partner's suit? Does South have another suit to bid at the one level? Does South have a balanced hand? What does South rebid to finish describing the hand?

```
Dealer:        ♠ J 8 2
South          ♥ A 6 3 2
               ♦ K 4 2
               ♣ A 8 4
♠ Q 10 4              ♠ K 7 6 3
♥ Q 10 8       N      ♥ J 9 7 5
♦ J 8        W   E    ♦ Q 10 9
♣ Q 10 7 5 2   S      ♣ J 9
               ♠ A 9 5
               ♥ K 4
               ♦ A 7 6 5 3
               ♣ K 6 3
```

West passes. At what level does the partnership belong: partscore, game or maybe game? In what strain should the partnership play? What rebid should North make?

What will the contract be ? Who will be the declarer?

The Play

Which player makes the opening lead? What will the opening lead be?

Declarer starts by making a PLAN. How many additional tricks does declarer need? Which suit offers the potential for developing the extra winners? How does declarer plan to make the contract?

Exercise Eleven *Answers* — Using Length in a Notrump Contract

The Bidding

- South opens 1 ♦.
- North responds 1 ♥, a suit that can be bid at the one level.
- South can't support partner's suit or bid a new suit at the one level. South has a balanced hand and rebids 1NT.
- North, with 12 points, knows the partnership belongs in game. North bids game by bidding 3NT.
- The contract is 3NT. South is the declarer.

The Play

- West leads the ♣5.
- Declarer needs two extra tricks to make the contract. Diamonds provide the opportunity.
- Declarer wins the opening lead and then plays diamonds, even though the defenders get one trick in the suit. After declarer has lost this one trick, two extra winners are established.

Exercise Twelve — Using Length in a Suit Contract

(E–Z Deal Cards, #2, Deal 4 — Dealer, West)

Turn up all of the cards on the fourth pre-dealt deal and arrange them as in the previous deal.

The Bidding

Neither West nor North has enough to open the bidding. What will East's opening bid be?

South passes. Does West have support for partner's major suit? What will West respond?

North passes. Does East have a minimum, medium or maximum hand? How will East show the strength of East's hand?

```
Dealer:        ♠ 10 5
West           ♥ Q 9 8 5
               ♦ Q 10
               ♣ Q 9 6 5 3
♠ K J 7                    ♠ A Q 8 4 2
♥ J 7 2          N         ♥ 4
♦ A 7 6 2      W   E       ♦ K 9 4 3
♣ 10 8 2         S         ♣ A K 7
               ♠ 9 6 3
               ♥ A K 10 6 3
               ♦ J 8 5
               ♣ J 4
```

South passes. What does West do now? What will the contract be? Who will be the declarer?

The Play

Which player makes the opening lead? What will the opening lead be?

Declarer starts by making a PLAN. How many losers does declarer have? How can one of the losers be eliminated? What must declarer hope for? What is declarer's first play?

Exercise Twelve *Answers* — Using Length in a Suit Contract

The Bidding

- East opens 1♠.
- With support for partner's suit, West responds 2♠.
- With a medium hand, East bids 3♠.
- With 9 points, West accepts the invitation and bids 4♠.
- The contract is 4♠. East is the declarer.

The Play

- South leads the ♥A.
- There are four losers. Declarer has to eliminate a loser in the diamond suit if the missing diamonds are divided 3–2.
- Declarer draws trumps first.

CHAPTER 3
Developing Tricks – The Finesse

In the last chapter, extra tricks were developed by promoting high cards that were in sequence or by developing low cards that were in long suits. Another popular way of getting tricks is by finessing. This is an attempt to win a trick with a high card when the opponents have a higher card to play. Although this may seem like an impossible task, it's only a matter of where the cards are positioned.

LEADING TOWARD A HIGH CARD

Finessing against the Ace

Look at this layout of a suit:

```
              K 4
               ┌─────┐
               │  N  │
          ?    │W   E│    ?
               │  S  │
               └─────┘
              3 2
```

You don't have a sure trick in this suit since the opponents have the ace. You do hold the second-highest card, the king. Is there any way to get a trick with the king? If you had the queen, it would be easy to get a trick in this suit, as you saw in the last chapter. You could lead the king and promote your queen into a winner. In this case, you have nothing to promote. If you lead the king, the opponents will win with the ace, and you'll have nothing but low cards left.

Suppose you lead the 4 instead of the king. The opponents can win the trick with one of their high cards and then take your king with their ace. Again, no trick.

Since leading the king or the 4 from dummy doesn't work, consider leading a low card from your hand toward the high card in the dummy. This gives you a chance to win a trick with your king. Why? West must play before you choose the card to play from dummy. If West has the ace, you're sure to get a trick.

Suppose this is the layout:

K 4

A J 10 8 6 |N W E S| Q 9 7 5

3 2

If West plays the ace, you play the 4 from dummy. Later you can win a trick with the king. If West doesn't play the ace, you play the king. Either way, you get a trick with your king because East doesn't hold the ace.

What if East has the ace? The layout would be like this:

K 4

Q 9 7 5 |N W E S| A J 10 8 6

3 2

You lead a low card from your hand, and West also plays a low card. If you play your king, East wins with the ace; if you don't play your king, East wins with a lower card. East can then play the ace to take your king. Notice, however, that you can't get a trick in any other fashion if this is the layout when *you* have to play the suit.

By leading toward your king, you give yourself a chance. If West has the ace, you get a trick with your king. If East has it, you don't get a trick. This is the concept of a *finesse*. You hope that one or more of the missing high cards lies in a particular opponent's hand.

How often will West have the ace rather than East? Unless you are unluckier than the average bridge player, half the time. It's a 50–50 proposition.

A finesse is similar to the idea of developing long suits presented in the previous chapter. There, you hoped the opponents' cards were divided in a friendly fashion. Here, you hope some of the opponents' cards are located in a friendly fashion. By leading *toward* your king in the last example, you give yourself a chance to profit if the ace lies where you want it to be.

Finessing against the King

In the previous example, you finessed against the ace, the higher card held by the opponents. You can also finesse against a missing king.

```
        A Q 4
          N
  ?    W     E    ?
          S
        5 3 2
```

You have one sure trick, the ace. You'd like to get a second trick with your queen. Leading the queen won't do any good because the opponents will win with their king. Since the opponents also hold the jack, you haven't even promoted another winner. How do you go about getting a trick with your queen? You have to follow the same principle of leading toward the card you hope will win a trick. You hope West has the king and the complete layout is something like this:

```
             A Q 4
               N
  K J 8 6   W     E    10 9 7
               S
             5 3 2
```

If you lead a low card from your hand toward dummy, West must play before you choose dummy's card. If West plays the king, win with your ace and your queen will become a second trick. If West plays a low card, finesse with the queen. It will win the trick when East has no higher card to play. Of course your finesse will lose if East has the king, and you'll be back to the one sure trick you already had.

Here is a different layout in which you are missing the king:

```
        A 5 4
          N
  ?    W     E    ?
          S
        Q 3 2
```

The principle is the same. Try to win a trick with your queen by leading a low card from dummy toward the queen. This time you are hoping

East has the king, and the complete layout is like this:

```
            A 5 4
                N
987        W       E     K J 10 6
                S
            Q 3 2
```

Whether or not East plays the king, you'll get a trick with your queen. But suppose the layout is:

```
            A 5 4
                N
K J 10 6   W       E     9 8 7
                S
            Q 3 2
```

When you lead a low card from dummy toward your queen, West wins with the king. You're back to one trick in the suit. Could you do better by leading the queen instead of leading toward it? No, West would play the king, making you use dummy's ace to win the trick. Since you don't have the jack or the 10, none of the remaining cards would be promoted into a winner. Instead, the opponents' jack and 10 would be promoted. Leading the queen gains you nothing. It doesn't matter whether West or East holds the king, you won't get an extra trick either way.

Finessing against the Queen

When you hope to take a trick with the jack and the opponents have the queen, you are finessing against the queen. Consider this layout:

```
            A K J
                N
?          W       E     ?
                S
            5 3 2
```

You have two sure tricks, the ace and the king. Since the jack could be a winner, lead toward the jack from your hand. If West plays a low card, play (finesse with) the jack. If West has the queen, your jack will win the trick, and you'll end up with three tricks. If East has the queen, you won't win a trick with the jack, but you'll be left with the two sure tricks you already had.

The ace and the king don't have to be in the same hand. In the following example, you are still looking for the queen:

A J 4

?   [N W E S]   ?

K 6 2

The king is played first, and then a low card is led toward dummy's ace and jack. If West has the queen, you can finesse the jack and take three tricks.

In the previous examples, you did not have to lose a trick if the queen was favorably located. When the jack is in the hand opposite the ace and king, you may have to lose a trick to get a trick with your jack.

J 4

?   [N W E S]   ?

A K 6 2

The ace and king are two sure tricks. If you need a third trick, you must use the idea of leading toward the card you hope will win a trick. Lead a low card from your hand toward dummy's jack as your first play. You are hoping West has the queen, and that the complete layout looks something like this:

J 4

Q 10 8 3   [N W E S]   9 7 5

A K 6 2

If West plays the queen, you play the 4 from dummy. Later you will get a trick with your jack as well as your ace and king. If West doesn't play the queen, play dummy's jack. It will win the trick while you still have the ace and the king left.

Finessing for Lower Cards

Sometimes you have to finesse for cards lower than the queen. Consider this layout:

<pre>
              A K Q 10 2
                    ┌─────┐
    J 9 8 5   │ N │   7
                    │W   E│
                    │ S │
                    └─────┘
                 6 4 3
</pre>

With eight cards in the suit, you would normally play the ace, the king and the queen, hoping the missing cards were divided 3–2. In this situation, however, when you play the ace and the king, East shows out (discards) on the second round. It becomes apparent that West started with four cards including the jack.

To avoid losing a trick, return to your hand with a high card in another suit, and then lead your remaining low card toward dummy. If West plays a low card, finesse with dummy's 10. You'll end up taking all of the tricks in the suit.

Using the Finesse

Now that you have an understanding of the principle of the finesse, let's see how you would use it in a complete deal. The contract is 3NT and the opening lead is the ♦ Q.

<pre>
Contract: 3NT   ♠ 7 4
Lead: ♦ Q   ♥ A 6 5
                   ♦ 8 7 3 2
                   ♣ A K 6 3
     ♠ J 9 2   ┌─────┐   ♠ K 10 8 3
     ♥ J 7 2   │ N │   ♥ Q 10 9 4
     ♦ Q J 10 9   │W   E│   ♦ K 6 5
     ♣ 10 5 4   │ S │   ♣ 9 7
                    └─────┘
                   ♠ A Q 6 5
                   ♥ K 8 3
                   ♦ A 4
                   ♣ Q J 8 2
</pre>

The objective in 3NT is nine tricks. You have one sure trick in spades, two in hearts, one in diamonds and four in clubs, for a total of eight. When analyzing your alternatives, you can see the opportunity for a finesse in spades. You hold the ace and the queen, but you're missing the king. None of the other suits offer any hope for an extra trick.

When you put your PLAN together, take into consideration the fact that you need to be in the dummy to lead toward the spades in your hand. Therefore, after winning the ♦ A, plan to use one of your high cards in another suit to get to dummy. Then, lead a low spade toward your hand and finesse with the ♠ Q if East plays a low spade. Since East has the ♠ K, you'll make the contract.

Here is another opportunity for a finesse. This time, you are playing in a trump contract of 3 ♦. West leads the ♠ J.

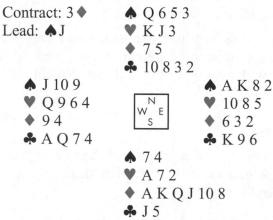

```
Contract: 3 ♦        ♠ Q 6 5 3
Lead: ♠ J            ♥ K J 3
                     ♦ 7 5
                     ♣ 10 8 3 2

♠ J 10 9                         ♠ A K 8 2
♥ Q 9 6 4         N              ♥ 10 8 5
♦ 9 4          W     E           ♦ 6 3 2
♣ A Q 7 4         S              ♣ K 9 6

                     ♠ 7 4
                     ♥ A 7 2
                     ♦ A K Q J 10 8
                     ♣ J 5
```

You can afford four losers, and you have two spades, one heart and two club losers. You can't do much about the spade and club losers, but the ♥ J offers you an opportunity in the heart suit. When you get the lead, draw trumps, then play the ♥ A and lead a low heart toward dummy's ♥ K and ♥ J. When West plays a low heart, finesse with the ♥ J, making the contract when East does not have the ♥ Q.

REPEATING A FINESSE

Sometimes, you can finesse more than once in the same suit. This is called a *repeating finesse*.

Repeating a Finesse against the Ace

Look at the following combination of cards:

K Q 5

?   [N W E S]   ?

7 4 3

As we saw in the previous chapter, you can get one trick from this combination of cards using promotion. Lead the king to drive out the opponents' ace and establish your queen as a trick. However, by using the principle of the finesse, you can get two tricks if West has the ace. You hope the complete layout is something like this:

K Q 5

A J 9 2   [N W E S]   10 8 6

7 4 3

Following the idea of leading toward the high card, lead a low card from your hand toward dummy. If West plays the ace, play the 5 from dummy — later you will get two tricks with your king and the queen. If West plays a low card, play the queen (or the king) from dummy. Since East does not have the ace, the queen will win the trick. The situation is now similar to one we have seen before:

K 5

A J 9   [N W E S]   10 8

7 4

You want to lead toward the high card again in order to try to take a trick with the king. To do this, you must return to your hand in another suit. Then you can *repeat the finesse* by leading toward the king. Whether or not West takes the ace, you'll end up with two tricks in the suit.

If East started with the ace, East will take your king or queen — you'll win only one trick. The repeated finesse is not a sure thing. It lets you take two tricks when the ace is favorably placed.

Repeating a Finesse against the King

Here is another example of a repeated finesse. This time, you are missing the king.

A Q J

? [W N E S] ?

6 5 3

Start by leading a low card from your hand toward dummy. If West plays a low card, play the jack (or the queen). If East doesn't have the king, your finesse will work and the jack will win the trick. Now, get back to your hand in another suit and repeat the finesse by leading another low card toward dummy. When West plays a low card, finesse with the queen. You'll end up with three tricks whenever West's holding includes the king.

The Repeated Finesse in Action

Let's take a look at the use of the repeated finesse in a critical situation. You are in a 4♠ contract with a rather precarious holding in the trump suit. West leads the ♣K.

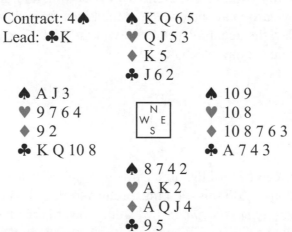

Contract: 4♠   ♠ K Q 6 5
Lead: ♣K   ♥ Q J 5 3
                     ♦ K 5
                     ♣ J 6 2

♠ A J 3   ♠ 10 9
♥ 9 7 6 4   ♥ 10 8
♦ 9 2   [W N E S]   ♦ 10 8 7 6 3
♣ K Q 10 8   ♣ A 7 4 3

                     ♠ 8 7 4 2
                     ♥ A K 2
                     ♦ A Q J 4
                     ♣ 9 5

You can afford to lose three tricks in your contract of 4♠. There are no losers in hearts or diamonds but you will lose the first two tricks in clubs. Therefore, you can afford to lose only one spade trick. You're missing the ace, as well as the jack, the 10 and the 9. You could lead the king to drive out the ace and promote your queen, but even if the missing cards divided 3–2, you'd lose a second spade trick.

Instead, use the art of the finesse. Suppose the opponents take the ♣K and the ♣Q and lead another club. You ruff with the ♠2 and lead the ♠4 toward dummy. If West takes the ♠A, life is a bit easier. Whatever West leads back, you can win and continue by playing the ♠K and the ♠Q. When the suit divides 3–2, you'll end up with only three losers.

If West plays a low spade, play dummy's ♠Q (or the ♠K), which will win the trick. Now come back to your hand by leading the ♥3 to your ♥K (for example). Lead another low spade toward dummy. No matter when West takes the ♠A, you'll end up losing only one spade trick and you'll make the contract.

FINESSING AGAINST TWO CARDS

Sometimes, you must finesse against more than one missing card. The general guideline is to lead toward the *lower* of your high cards first. Let's see how this works:

Missing the King and the Jack

Suppose you have these cards:

A Q 10

?   W N E S   ?

7 4 2

If dummy did not have the 10, this would be the situation for a simple finesse against West's king. However, the 10 provides an additional possibility since you can consider finessing against the jack as well as the king. Following the general principle of leading toward the high card, start by leading a low card from your hand toward dummy. What if West plays low? Should you play the queen or the 10?

Playing the 10, the lower card, gives you an opportunity to make the maximum number of tricks. Suppose this is the complete layout:

```
              A Q 10
                 ┌───┐
                 │ N │
   K J 8 5       │W  E│      9 6 3
                 │ S │
                 └───┘
               7 4 2
```

If you play the 10, it will win the trick because West has the king and the jack. Now you can come back to your hand and lead another low card toward dummy's remaining ace and queen. This time, you finesse the queen and end up winning all three tricks.

Suppose you played dummy's queen the first time. It would win the trick but the remaining cards would be:

```
               A 10
                 ┌───┐
                 │ N │
    K J 8        │W  E│      9 6
                 │ S │
                 └───┘
                7 4
```

If you led another low card toward dummy, West would play the jack to force dummy's ace. West would win the next trick with the king, and you'd take only two tricks.

If West doesn't have the king and the jack, your play of the 10 will not lose anything. Suppose the complete layout is:

```
              A Q 10
                 ┌───┐
                 │ N │
    J 8 5        │W  E│      K 9 6 3
                 │ S │
                 └───┘
               7 4 2
```

You play the 2, West plays the 5 and you play dummy's 10. East wins the king. Now your ace and queen are established as two sure tricks.

What would happen if this were the layout?

```
              A Q 10
                 ┌───┐
                 │ N │
    K 8 5        │W  E│      J 9 6 3
                 │ S │
                 └───┘
               7 4 2
```

You play the 2, West plays the 5 and you play dummy's 10. East wins the jack. Later, you can repeat the finesse by playing a low card to dummy's queen. This time, your finesse will work, and you'll end up with two tricks.

Of course, the complete layout may be:

A Q 10

8 5 3   N W E S   K J 9 6

7 4 2

Your first finesse of the 10 will lose to East's jack, and your second finesse of the queen will lose to East's king. You'll end up with only one trick, but there was nothing else you could have done. The two missing cards were both unfavorably located.

Missing the King and the Queen

Take a look at this layout:

A J 10

?   N W E S   ?

8 5 3

This time, the king and the queen are missing. You have a sure trick with the ace. It would be nice to get a second trick since you also have the jack and the 10.

Start by leading a low card from your hand. If West plays low, follow the principle of playing the lower of your high cards first, and play dummy's 10.

This will win the trick if the complete layout is:

A J 10

K Q 9 6   N W E S   7 4 2

8 5 3

Since East has neither the king nor the queen with which to win the trick, you'll end up winning two tricks.

When you lead a low card toward dummy, West may play the queen (or the king) rather than a low card. You can win this trick with the ace, and you can use the jack to drive out West's remaining high card. This play will establish the 10 as a second trick.

Most of the time, West won't have both of the missing high cards. Leading low to the 10, however, will work out even if East has either the king or the queen. Suppose the complete layout is:

A J 10

Q 9 6   K 7 4 2

8 5 3

You play the 3, West the 6 and dummy the 10. East can win with the king. The remaining cards will be:

A J

Q 9   7 4 2

8 5

When you regain the lead, you can play another low card toward dummy. If West contributes the 9, you play dummy's jack. This time your finesse is successful, and you once again end up winning two tricks.

You would also win two tricks if East had the queen and West had the king. Only if East held the king and the queen would both of your finesses lose, and you'd end up with one trick. When that happens, you will have at least given it your best try.

Missing the Ace and the Queen

Look at this combination of cards:

K J 10

?   [N W E S]   ?

6 4 3

Missing the ace and the queen, start by leading a low card toward dummy, playing the 10 if West plays low. If West started with the ace and the queen, the 10 will win the trick:

K J 10

A Q 7 5   [N W E S]   9 8 2

6 4 3

Come back to your hand and repeat the finesse. You'll end up with two tricks.

Even if East has the ace, playing the 10 may be successful:

K J 10

Q 7 5   [N W E S]   A 9 8 2

6 4 3

East must play the ace to win the trick. Later, you can take another finesse against West's queen to end up with two tricks.

If East has the queen, you'll win only one trick:

K J 10

A 7 5   [N W E S]   Q 9 8 2

6 4 3

When you lead low toward the 10, East will win the queen. Later you can use the king to drive out West's ace, establishing your jack. It wouldn't have helped to lead low to the king the first time. You'd win the trick but the opponents would win the next two tricks with their queen and ace.

Playing the lower card first, the 10, gains when West has the queen. It costs nothing if East has the queen.

Example of Finessing against Two Cards

Suppose you are playing in a contract of 3NT on the following deal. West leads the ♥Q.

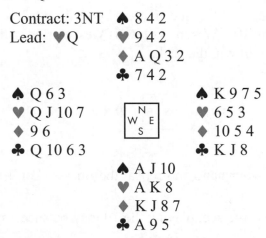

```
               Contract: 3NT    ♠ 8 4 2
               Lead: ♥Q         ♥ 9 4 2
                                ♦ A Q 3 2
                                ♣ 7 4 2
        ♠ Q 6 3                              ♠ K 9 7 5
        ♥ Q J 10 7         N                 ♥ 6 5 3
        ♦ 9 6           W       E            ♦ 10 5 4
        ♣ Q 10 6 3         S                 ♣ K J 8
                                ♠ A J 10
                                ♥ A K 8
                                ♦ K J 8 7
                                ♣ A 9 5
```

You need nine tricks. You have one sure spade trick, two heart tricks, four diamond tricks and one club trick, for a total of eight. When you *Analyze your alternatives,* the spade suit offers the only chance to develop the extra trick you need.

When you come to the fourth step of the PLAN, *Now put it all together,* you must be careful of the order in which you play the cards. Since you lack the ♠K and the ♠Q, you'll have to lead twice from dummy toward your hand. The ♦A and the ♦Q are the only high cards in dummy so you must use them appropriately.

After winning the first heart trick, lead a diamond to dummy's ace (or queen) so you can lead a spade toward your hand. When East plays a low spade, play the ♠10, the lower of your high cards. West will win the ♠Q and probably lead another heart. Win the heart and lead a diamond to dummy's queen. Now lead another spade toward your hand. When East plays a low spade, play your ♠J. This finesse is successful, and you have the ninth trick you need to make the contract.

LEADING A HIGH CARD

When You Can Afford to Lead a High Card

Earlier, we looked at this holding in a suit:

```
            A 5 4
          ┌───────┐
          │   N   │
  ?       │ W   E │   ?
          │   S   │
          └───────┘
            Q 3 2
```

Starting with one sure trick, the ace, you can try to get a second trick by leading toward the queen, hoping that East has the king. But if West has the king, leading toward your queen won't work.

If West has the king, it might seem reasonable to lead the queen from your hand since the ace is in dummy. However, this won't do you any good.

Suppose the complete layout is:

```
              A 5 4
            ┌───────┐
            │   N   │
  K J 9 6   │ W   E │   10 8 7
            │   S   │
            └───────┘
              Q 3 2
```

When you lead the queen, West will cover (play a higher card) with the king to make you use the ace to win the trick. The opponents will win the next two tricks since they have the jack and the 10.

The situation is different if you have the jack and the 10:

```
              A 5 4
            ┌───────┐
            │   N   │
  K 9 6 3   │ W   E │   8 7 2
            │   S   │
            └───────┘
              Q J 10
```

Here, you can afford to lead the queen. If West covers with the king, you can win the ace and your jack and 10 are promoted into winners. If West doesn't cover with the king, play low from dummy — your queen will win the trick since East doesn't have the king. Then you can repeat the finesse by leading the jack (or 10) from your hand.

If East has the king instead of West, you'll lose the finesse but you'll still win two tricks since you have the ace and the jack left.

How can you tell when to lead a high card and when to lead toward a high card? The secret is to look at the other cards you hold in the suit. You can lead a high card if you can afford to have an opponent cover it with a higher card. Otherwise, you should lead toward the high card.

In the above example, you can afford to lead the queen — if West covers with the king, your jack and 10 will be promoted into winners. In the earlier example, you could not afford to lead the queen — if West covers with the king, the opponents' jack and 10 will be promoted into winners.

Take a look at this layout:

                        A K 3
                       ┌───┐
                       │ N │
            Q 8 7 5   │W E│   9 4 2
                       │ S │
                       └───┘
                       J 10 6

You have two sure tricks with the ace and the king. If you lead the ace and the king, however, you'll take only two tricks in the suit unless one of the opponents holds a singleton or doubleton queen. Holding the jack and the 10 gives you an opportunity to trap the queen if West has it. Can you afford to lead the jack? Yes. If West covers with the queen, you can win the trick, and your 10 is promoted into a winner.

Contrast that layout with the following:

                       A K 3 2
                       ┌───┐
                       │ N │
              ?   │W E│   ?
                       │ S │
                       └───┘
                       J 6 5 4

Again, you are missing the queen. Can you afford to lead the jack to trap the queen in West's hand? This time you don't have the 10. If you lead the jack, West can cover with the queen and the opponents' 10 will be promoted into a trick. Leading the ace and the king is better — you hope that one of the opponents started with a singleton or doubleton queen.

For example, the complete layout may be:

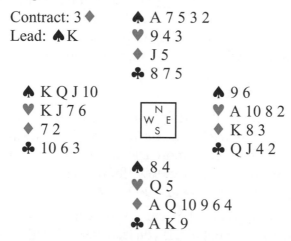

A K 3 2

Q 9   10 8 7

J 6 5 4

By playing the ace and the king, you can take all four tricks in the suit. If you lead the jack and West covers with the queen, East eventually will win a trick with the 10.

Leading a High Card

Leading a high card often allows you to repeat a finesse. Take a look at the following deal.

Contract: 3 ◆   ♠ A 7 5 3 2
Lead: ♠K   ♥ 9 4 3
                      ◆ J 5
                      ♣ 8 7 5

♠ K Q J 10   ♠ 9 6
♥ K J 7 6   ♥ A 10 8 2
◆ 7 2   ◆ K 8 3
♣ 10 6 3   ♣ Q J 4 2

                      ♠ 8 4
                      ♥ Q 5
                      ◆ A Q 10 9 6 4
                      ♣ A K 9

You can afford four losers in a contract of 3 ◆ . You have one spade loser, two heart losers, one club loser and one possible diamond loser. You're missing the ◆ K, but you plan to eliminate your diamond loser by taking a finesse against East's (hoped-for) king.

After winning with dummy's ♠A, you lead the ♦J. If East covers with the ♦K, you win the ♦A and take the rest of the diamond tricks. If East does not cover with the ♦K, you play a low diamond from your hand — dummy's jack will win the trick. Now you lead dummy's ♦5 and repeat the finesse, trapping East's king.

Suppose you had led dummy's ♦5 first, rather than the ♦J. When East played a low diamond, you would win with the 9 (or the 10 or the queen), but now you would be in your hand with no way to return to dummy to repeat the finesse. East eventually would win a trick with the ♦K. Knowing that you can afford to lead the ♦J is the key to making the contract.

GUIDELINES FOR DEFENSE

When you are to make the opening lead and your partner has bid a suit, it's a good idea to *lead partner's suit unless you clearly have a better alternative.* You and your partner must cooperate on defense. If your partner has opened the bidding or overcalled in a suit, you have a strong indication of which suit is most likely to produce tricks for the defense. You can begin immediately to help partner develop tricks in that suit.

Leading Partner's Suit

If you have a singleton in partner's suit, you have no choice of cards to lead. If you have a doubleton, lead the top card, *e.g.,* the king from K–3 or the 7 from 7–5. With three or more cards, lead the top of two or more touching high cards, otherwise lead low (fourth best if you have four or more). For example, **Q**–J–5, K–8–**2**, Q–9–8–**4**–3.

In general, avoid leading a low card when you have the ace and are defending against a trump contract. If you lead the suit, lead the ace. This is an exception to leading low when you don't have touching high cards.

Here are some examples of choosing the opening lead against a 3NT contract when your partner has opened the bidding 1 ♥ :

♠ Q 9 4 2	You have no good reason to lead anything other than
♥ J 5	partner's suit. With a doubleton, lead the top card,
♦ J 7 6 2	the ♥ J.
♣ 10 8 3	

♠ 6 4	You have no good reason to lead anything other than
♥ Q 6 2	partner's suit. With three cards but without touching
♦ 10 8 6 3	high cards, lead a low card, the ♥ 2.
♣ Q 9 6 4	

♠ K 7 2	With touching high cards, lead the top card, the ♥ Q,
♥ Q J 8 3	rather than fourth best. Leading the ♥ Q tells partner
♦ 9 6 2	that you have the next-lower card, the ♥ J, but not
♣ J 10 3	the next-higher card, the ♥ K. Of course, you would
	also lead the ♥ Q if you had a doubleton. Partner will

often be able to tell when you hold two cards in the suit from the auction, the number of cards in dummy and partner's own holding.

Returning Partner's Suit

In addition to leading your partner's suit, it's also a good idea to return partner's suit unless you have something clearly better to do. This means that when you first gain the lead, you should play a card in the suit that partner originally led. Again, remember that you are working as a partnership — since partner chose a suit to lead, in most cases you should work together to develop tricks in that suit.

The card you lead back in partner's suit is the same card you normally would lead from your remaining holding. For example, suppose you originally had K–7–3 in a suit. Partner leads the 4, and you play the king on the first trick. If you get a chance to lead the suit back, lead the 7, the top of your remaining doubleton. If you started with K–7–3–2, you would lead back the 2 — low from your remaining three cards.

BIDDING REVIEW

Making an Overcall

When the opponents open the bidding, you can consider whether to overcall using the following guidelines:

Requirements for an Overcall in a Suit

- A five-card or longer suit (for both majors or minors). Try to have a six-card suit to overcall at the two level.
- 8 to 16 HCP (10-17 total points) – Overcall at the two level suggests a hand that is strong enough to have opened the bidding.

Requirements for a 1NT Overcall*

- 15 to 18 HCP
- Balanced hand
- Some strength in the opponent's suit

Advancing After an Overcall

If partner overcalls 1NT, you can use the same responses as when partner opens the bidding 1NT. If partner overcalls in a suit, use the following guidelines:

With a minimum hand (8 or 9 points):

- Pass if already at the two level.
- Raise partner's suit to the two level with three-card or longer support.
- Bid a new suit at the one level with no support and a good five-card suit of your own.

---

* Notrump overcalls of 15 to 18 HCPs are very common in the bridge world. This range allows you to overcall 1NT after a 1 ♣ opening bid with a hand like this:

♠	A J 10
♥	K J 10
♦	Q J 9
♣	A Q x x

This hand is not good enough to rebid notrump after making a takeout double (showing a good 18-19 HCPs). It does not have a source of tricks (long suit), and it requires that the advancer have entries in order to take any finesses against the opening bidder. A 1NT overcall with this hand is more than adequate.

With a limit raise or better hand (10 or 11+ points):

- Make a cuebid to describe a limit raise hand with support for partner's overcall and then –
  - Stop below game in the appropriate partscore if partner shows less than an opening hand with the rebid.
  - Bid game if partner shows more than the minimum overcall by bidding another suit.
- Bid a new suit (even if it's at the two level).
- Bid game if you have enough total points opposite a minimum overcall.

  Notrump advances show no fit for partner (most likely two card support) and no suit of your own, but it does show strength in the opponent's suit:
  - Advance to 1NT with 8 to 11 HCP.
  - Advance to 2NT with 12 to 15 HCP.
  - Advance to 3NT with 16+ HCP.

SUMMARY

When you come to the third step in your PLAN, *Analyze your alternatives,* one of the methods that can help you establish extra winners or eliminate losers is the **finesse.** The principle of the finesse is to **lead toward the high card** that you are hoping will win a trick.

If you are finessing for more than one missing card, lead toward the lower of your high cards first.

Sometimes, you can afford to lead a high card to trap a missing card in an opponent's hand. You should lead a high card only if you can afford to have an opponent cover it with a higher card.

When partner has bid a suit and you are defending, you should **lead partner's suit** unless you have a clearly better alternative. Also, if your partner has led a suit, you should **return partner's suit when you get an opportunity,** unless you have something clearly better to do.

Exercise One — The Finesse

In the following examples, how many sure tricks are there? How could you get an extra trick?

DUMMY:	1) A Q 3	2) 4 3	3) A K J	4) Q 4 2	5) K J 3
DECLARER:	7 6 5	K 5	7 5 3	A 7 3	A 5

_____   _____ _____   _____   _____

Exercise Two — The Repeated Finesse

How would you play each of the following suits to get the maximum number of tricks? For you to succeed, where would the missing high card have to be?

DUMMY:	1) 7 4 3	2) A Q J	3) 8 7
DECLARER:	K Q 5	5 3 2	A K J 10

_____   _____   _____

Exercise Three — Suit Development

Combining the ideas of the finesse and the development of long suits, determine how many tricks you could take with each of the following combinations. Assume the location and division of the missing cards is as favorable as possible.

DUMMY:	1) Q 4 3	2) K Q 3 2	3) K 9 7 5 2	4) A Q J 3 2	5) 9 7 4
DECLARER:	A 8 7 6 5	7 6 5 4	8 6 3	7 6 5	A K J 3

_____ _____   _____   _____   _____

Exercise One *Answers* — The Finesse

1) One sure trick; one potential trick with the queen.
2) No sure tricks; one potential trick with the king.
3) Two sure tricks; one potential trick with the jack.
4) One sure trick; one potential trick with the queen.
5) Two sure tricks; one potential trick with the jack.

Exercise Two *Answers* — The Repeated Finesse

1) Lead toward declarer's hand twice. If the opponent on your right holds the ace, you'll take two tricks.
2) Lead toward dummy twice, taking the finesse. If the opponent on your left holds the king, you'll take three tricks.
3) Lead toward declarer's hand twice, taking the finesse. If the opponent on your right holds the queen, you'll take four tricks.

Exercise Three *Answers* — Suit Development

1) Lead toward the queen. If the opponent on your left has the king and the missing cards divide 3–2, you'll take four tricks.
2) Lead twice toward the king and the queen. If the opponent on your left has the ace and the missing cards divide 3–2, you'll take three tricks.
3) Lead toward the king. If the opponent on your left has the ace and the missing cards divide 3–2, you'll take three tricks.
4) Lead toward dummy twice, taking the finesse. If the opponent on your left has the king and the missing cards divide 3–2, you'll take all five tricks.
5) Lead toward the jack. If the opponent on your right has the queen and the missing cards divide 3–3, you'll take four tricks.

Exercise Four — Leading the High Card

How would you play each of the following suits to get the maximum number of tricks?

DUMMY:	1) A 7 3	2) J 10 9	3) Q 7	4) Q J 5 2	5) J 4
DECLARER:	Q J 10	A K 3 2	A 9 3	A 6 3	A Q 10 9

_____　_____　_____　_____　_____

Exercise Five — Leading toward the Lower High Card First

How can you take the maximum number of tricks with each of the following combinations? How must the missing cards be located?

DUMMY:	1) A Q 10	2) 5 4 3	3) A J 10
DECLARER:	7 5 3	K J 10	8 6 4

_____　　_____　　_____

Exercise Six — Leading Partner's Suit

Which card would you lead from the following combinations if your partner has bid the suit?

1) Q J 3　　2) J 3　　3) K 7 4　　4) 10 8 6 2　　5) A J 3

_____　_____　_____　_____　_____

Exercise Four *Answers* — Leading the High Card

1) Lead the queen. If it's not covered with the king, play low from dummy.

2) Lead the jack from dummy. If it's not covered, play low from your hand, taking the finesse.

3) Lead low from your hand toward the queen in dummy.

4) Lead toward dummy, hoping the opponent on your left has the king.

5) Lead the jack. If it's not covered, play low, taking the finesse.

Exercise Five *Answers* — Leading toward the Lower High Card First

1) Lead low toward dummy and finesse the 10, hoping the opponent on your left has both the king and the jack.

2) Lead low toward the K–J–10 and finesse the 10 (or the jack), hoping the opponent on your right has the queen.

3) Lead low toward the dummy, finessing the 10. You hope either the king or the queen is on your left.

Exercise Six *Answers* — Leading Partner's Suit

1) Queen

2) Jack

3) 4

4) 2

5) Ace against a suit; 3 against notrump

Exercise Seven — Review of Overcalls

What would you bid with each of the following hands if the opponent on your right opened the bidding 1 ♦ ?

1) ♠ A Q J 10 7
   ♥ K 3
   ♦ 6 4 2
   ♣ A 6 3

2) ♠ K Q J
   ♥ A Q J
   ♦ K J 10
   ♣ 10 9 6 3

3) ♠ J 8 5 3
   ♥ A Q
   ♦ Q J 6 2
   ♣ Q J 7

4) ♠ K J 10 6 3
   ♥ A Q 8 6 5
   ♦ 6
   ♣ Q 4

5) ♠ J 5 3
   ♥ 4 2
   ♦ A K J 8 4
   ♣ A 7 5

6) ♠ J 10
   ♥ A 8 4
   ♦ Q 9 2
   ♣ Q 10 8 6 3

Exercise Eight — Review of Advances after Overcalls

How would you advance the bidding with each of the following hands? The opponent on your left opens the bidding 1 ♦ , your partner overcalls 1 ♥ and your right-hand opponent passes?

1) ♠ A J 10 7
   ♥ Q 8 3
   ♦ 6 2
   ♣ J 10 6 3

2) ♠ J 9 8 6 2
   ♥ 3
   ♦ Q 5 3
   ♣ 10 9 6 2

3) ♠ J 8 5
   ♥ 5 4
   ♦ A Q 10 3
   ♣ Q 9 7 4

4) ♠ A K 10 6 3
   ♥ 8 5
   ♦ J 7 4
   ♣ K 7 3

5) ♠ A 5 3
   ♥ Q J 4 2
   ♦ 6
   ♣ K Q 8 7 5

6) ♠ K J 10
   ♥ Q 4
   ♦ Q J 9 2
   ♣ A K 3 2

Exercise Seven *Answers* — Review of Overcalls

    1) 1♠   2) 1NT   3) Pass

    4) 1♠   5) Pass   6) Pass

Exercise Eight *Answers* — Review of Advances after Overcalls

    1) 2♥   2) Pass   3) 1NT

    4) 1♠   5) 4♥   6) 3NT

Exercise Nine — Taking a Finesse

(E–Z Deal Cards: #3, Deal 1 — Dealer, North)

Turn up all of the cards on the first pre-dealt deal. Put each hand dummy-style at the edge of the table in front of each player.

The Bidding

What opening bid best describes North's hand?

East has an opening bid and a good five-card suit. What bid can East make to compete?

South passes. With support for partner's suit, West can use dummy points to evaluate the hand. At what level does the partnership belong? How can West find out the level? In what strain? What will West bid?

```
Dealer:      ♠ A K Q 10 6
North        ♥ 8 3
             ♦ K J 4
             ♣ 9 5 2
♠ 9 8 7 2              ♠ J 4 3
♥ K 9 6 5     N        ♥ A Q J 10 2
♦ 9 7      W   E       ♦ A Q
♣ A K Q       S        ♣ 10 4 3
             ♠ 5
             ♥ 7 4
             ♦ 10 8 6 5 3 2
             ♣ J 8 7 6
```

How will the auction proceed from there? What will the contract be? Who'll be the declarer?

The Play

Which player makes the opening lead? What will the opening lead be? Why?

> ## Declarer starts by making a PLAN:
> 1. **P**ause to consider your objective
> 2. **L**ook at your winners and losers
> 3. **A**nalyze your alternatives
> 4. **N**ow put it all together

After going through the four steps, how does declarer plan to eliminate the extra loser? What precaution must declarer take after the opening lead if North continues to lead spades?

Exercise Nine *Answers* — Taking a Finesse
The Bidding

- North opens 1 ♠.
- East overcalls 2 ♥.
- Possibly game in hearts. West makes a cuebid of 2 ♠.
- Pass, 4 ♥, pass, pass, pass. The contract is 4 ♥. East is the declarer.

The Play

- South leads the ♠ 5, partner's suit.
- Declarer loses the first three spade tricks but can ruff the next spade with a high heart to avoid an overruff. Declarer must draw trumps ending up in dummy in order to finesse for the ♦ K.

Exercise Ten — A Repeated Finesse

(E–Z Deal Cards: #3, Deal 2 — Dealer, East)

Turn up all of the cards on the second pre-dealt deal and arrange them as in the previous deal.

The Bidding

East has 13 points. What is East's opening bid?

South has a balanced hand with 16 HCP. What bid best describes South's hand?

West passes. North is the captain. At what level does the partnership belong? In what strain should the partnership play? How does North advance the bidding?

```
Dealer:        ♠ 10 8 4
East           ♥ A J 3
               ♦ 9 4 2
               ♣ K Q 9 2
♠ 7 6 3 2                    ♠ K 9 5
♥ Q 7 6         N            ♥ K 10 8 4
♦ 8 6        W     E         ♦ K Q J 10 5
♣ 10 8 5 3      S            ♣ 7
               ♠ A Q J
               ♥ 9 5 2
               ♦ A 7 3
               ♣ A J 6 4
```

How will the auction proceed from there? What will the contract be? Who'll be the declarer?

The Play

Which player makes the opening lead? What will the opening lead be? Why?

Declarer starts by making a PLAN. After going through the four steps, how will declarer play the hand? In *Putting it all together,* what precaution must declarer take?

Exercise Ten *Answers* — A Repeated Finesse

The Bidding

- East opens 1 ♦ .

- South overcalls 1NT.

- North can see that the partnership belongs in a game in notrump and bids 3NT.

- Pass, pass, pass. The contract is 3NT. South is the declarer.

The Play

- West leads the ♦ 8, the top of a doubleton in partner's suit.

- To take nine tricks, declarer must try the spade finesse. Declarer must be careful to use dummy's high cards wisely so spades can be led twice toward declarer's hand.

Exercise Eleven — Finessing Against Two Cards

(E–Z Deal Cards: #3, Deal 3 — Dealer, South)

Turn up all of the cards on the third pre-dealt deal and arrange them as in the previous deal.

The Bidding

What is South's opening bid?

What bid does West make to compete?

North passes. How does East advance the bidding after West's overcall?

South passes. How many points is East showing? Does West bid again? What will the contract be? Who'll be the declarer?

```
Dealer:      ♠ 9 6 2
South        ♥ 10 7 6 2
             ♦ Q J 6
             ♣ Q 7 5
♠ A K J 10 8        ♠ Q 4 3
♥ 8 5 4       N     ♥ A 9 3
♦ 7 2       W   E   ♦ K 5 4 3
♣ A J 10      S     ♣ 8 6 2
             ♠ 7 5
             ♥ K Q J
             ♦ A 10 9 8
             ♣ K 9 4 3
```

The Play

Which player makes the opening lead? What will the opening lead be? Why?

Declarer starts by making a PLAN. After going through the four steps, how does declarer plan to eliminate one of the club losers? To do this, what precaution must declarer take?

Exercise Eleven *Answers* — Finessing Against Two Cards

The Bidding

- South opens 1♦.
- West overcalls 1♠.
- East responds 2♠ to West's overcall.
- East is showing 8 or 9 points, so West doesn't bid again. The contract is 2♠. West is the declarer.

The Play

- North leads the ♦Q, the top of touching honors in partner's suit.
- To make the contract, declarer must try the club finesse twice, using the ♠Q and the ♥A as entries. The first finesse of the ♣10 loses to North's ♣Q, but the second finesse of the ♣J wins, since South has the ♣K.

Exercise Twelve — Leading a High Card

(E–Z Deal Cards: #3, Deal 4 — Dealer, West)

Turn up all of the cards on the fourth pre-dealt deal and arrange them as in the previous deal.

The Bidding

West doesn't have enough to open the bidding. What will North bid?

East has a good suit and an opening bid. What will East bid?

Does South have support for partner's major suit? What will South respond?

West passes. Does North have a minimum, medium or maximum hand? What will North's rebid be?

```
Dealer:        ♠ A 4
West           ♥ A Q J 9 6 5
               ♦ 9 5 4
               ♣ A K
♠ 10 9 6 5 2              ♠ K J 8
♥ K 8 4          N        ♥ 7
♦ 8          W     E      ♦ K Q J 10 3 2
♣ 10 9 8 2       S        ♣ Q J 4
               ♠ Q 7 3
               ♥ 10 3 2
               ♦ A 7 6
               ♣ 7 6 5 3
```

How will the auction proceed from there? What will the contract be? Who'll be the declarer?

The Play

Which player makes the opening lead? What will the opening lead be?

Declarer starts by making a PLAN. After going through the four steps, how will declarer play the hand? How does declarer plan to avoid losing a trump trick? Which card must declarer be careful to lead from dummy? Why?

Exercise Twelve *Answers* — Leading a High Card

The Bidding

- North opens 1♥.
- East overcalls 2♦.
- South supports North's major by bidding 2♥.
- North has a maximum hand and bids 4♥.
- Pass, pass, pass. The contract is 4♥. North is the declarer.

The Play

- East leads the ♦K.
- To make the contract, declarer must try the heart finesse. Declarer needs to be careful to lead the ♥10 from dummy on the first trick and to play low if West plays low. Now declarer leads another heart from dummy, and West's ♥K is trapped.

CHAPTER 4

Eliminating Losers –
Ruffing and Discarding

As you saw in the previous two chapters, a number of techniques are available to help create extra winners in notrump contracts or eliminate extra losers in trump contracts. They are: promotion of high cards, development of long suits and leading toward high cards (the finesse). In this chapter, we will look at two techniques that are useful only in trump contracts. They are: *ruffing* (winning the lead of a suit other than the trump suit with a trump card) *losers in dummy* and *discarding losers on extra winners in dummy.* Both methods take advantage of the unique power of the trump suit.

RUFFING LOSERS IN DUMMY

One advantage of playing in a trump contract is the tremendous power of the trump suit. Even an ace in another suit can fall to the lowliest trump. The ability to ruff the opponents' winners is the key to one of the most common techniques for eliminating losers.

Ruffing in Dummy

Having played in some trump contracts, you are familiar with using the trump suit to stop the opponents from taking tricks in other suits. However, ruffing in declarer's hand does not eliminate any of the losers you started with. For example, suppose that hearts is the trump suit, and look at the following layout of your heart and club suits:

DUMMY
♥ 4 3 2
♣ 4 3 2

DECLARER (YOU)
♥ A K Q J 10
♣ 5

When counting your losers, concentrate on declarer's hand — count none in hearts and one in clubs. If the opponents try to take tricks in clubs, you will lose the first trick but ruff the next trick. You have gained nothing since you still have the one loser you originally counted.

Nothing is gained by ruffing dummy's clubs in your hand other than to prevent losing a trick. You still end up with the same five heart tricks that you started with. You shouldn't go out of your way to ruff dummy's clubs. Eventually, you may run out of trumps in your hand and that would make it impossible for you to draw the opponents' trumps or stop the opponents from taking their winners in other suits.

Suppose we change the layout of the club suit:

DUMMY
♥ 4 3 2
♣ 5

DECLARER (YOU)
♥ A K Q J 10
♣ 4 3 2

This time, you have three club losers in your hand. If the opponents try to take tricks in clubs, you'll lose the first trick but you can ruff the next trick with one of dummy's trumps. In this case, you have gained something since you have eliminated one of your losers by ruffing in dummy. You'll win one trick with dummy's trump and still have five heart tricks left in your hand, for a total of six.

You want to go out of your way to ruff a club in dummy, since that will allow you to eliminate a loser. If you can maneuver to ruff another club with one of dummy's hearts, you will eliminate another loser. Now, you'll end up taking seven tricks in all, rather than the five you originally had.

In general, you *eliminate a loser by ruffing in dummy;* you do not eliminate a loser by ruffing in your own hand.

Sometimes, ruffing your losers in dummy takes careful planning. Look for the following conditions to ruff your losers in dummy successfully:

- More cards in the suit (with losers) in your hand than in dummy;
- Enough trumps in dummy so you can ruff your losers;
- High cards in other suits to get to your hand so you can lead the suit you want to ruff in dummy.

Let's look at each of these conditions in turn.

The Opportunity for Ruffing Losers

Side suits equally divided between your hand and dummy provide no opportunity to ruff losers:

DUMMY:	9 4 3	8 2	7
DECLARER:	A 8 2	10 9	3

Even though dummy may have only a doubleton or singleton, declarer can't ruff a loser because declarer also has shortness. For there to be an opportunity to ruff losers, the cards in a side suit must be unevenly divided, with declarer having more cards than dummy.

DUMMY: A 4

DECLARER: K 3 2

Declarer's hand has more cards than dummy. This provides a good opportunity to ruff a loser. Plan to start by playing the high card from the short side, the ace, and then lead the 4 to the king. Now, lead your remaining low card and ruff it in dummy.

DUMMY: —

DECLARER: 8 4 2

Since dummy is void in the suit, you have the opportunity to ruff your losers. You need trumps in dummy (at least three if you plan to eliminate all three losers) and transportation — some way of getting back to your hand after ruffing in order to lead the suit again.

DUMMY: 4

DECLARER: A 9 3

Since dummy has a singleton, the conditions are right to ruff both of your losers.

DUMMY: A 9 3

DECLARER: 4

When dummy has more cards in the suit than declarer, you have no opportunity to ruff losers.

Let's see how ruffing a loser in dummy works with a complete deal.

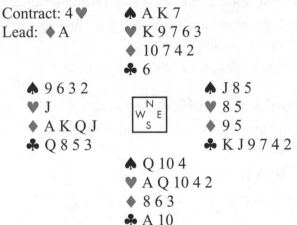

Contract: 4 ♥
Lead: ♦ A

In a contract of 4 ♥, you can afford three losers. You have three diamond losers and one club loser. You need to eliminate one of your losers. When you *Analyze your alternatives*, you can't do much about the diamond losers. West is poised to take the first three tricks, but the club suit provides an opportunity to ruff your loser in dummy. Draw trumps, play the ♣A and ruff the ♣10 in dummy to make your contract.

Creating the Opportunity to Ruff Losers

In the previous example, declarer could ruff a club loser without losing a club trick. Sometimes, declarer has some work to do before the conditions are right for ruffing losers in the dummy.

DUMMY: 6

DECLARER: 9 7 5

You'd like to ruff your losers in dummy but can't immediately since dummy isn't void in the suit. Concede a trick to the opponents. When you regain the lead, dummy will be void, and the opportunity will be there to ruff both of your losers.

DUMMY: 7 4

DECLARER: 10 8 2

This time you can still ruff a loser in dummy because the suit is unevenly divided — declarer has more cards than dummy. You'll have to give up the lead twice before the conditions are right to ruff your remaining loser.

It can be nerve-wracking to give up the lead, since you may wonder what the opponents will do when they get the lead. The reward for your efforts, however, is that you eliminate one or more of your losers and frequently make your contract.

Consider this deal:

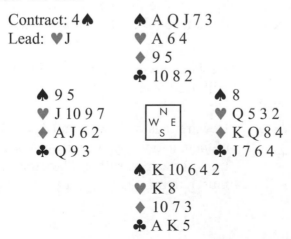

Contract: 4♠
Lead: ♥J

♠ A Q J 7 3
♥ A 6 4
♦ 9 5
♣ 10 8 2

♠ 9 5
♥ J 10 9 7
♦ A J 6 2
♣ Q 9 3

♠ 8
♥ Q 5 3 2
♦ K Q 8 4
♣ J 7 6 4

♠ K 10 6 4 2
♥ K 8
♦ 10 7 3
♣ A K 5

In a contract of 4♠, you can afford three losers. You have three diamond losers and one club loser. You need to eliminate one of your losers. When you *Analyze your alternatives,* you can see the opportunity to ruff one of your diamond losers in dummy since dummy has fewer diamonds than you.

Some work, however, must be done. When putting your plan together, decide to give up two diamond tricks, creating the right conditions to ruff your loser in dummy. As you have seen, you generally want to take your losses early. Give up the diamond tricks (after drawing trumps) while you still have some trumps left in dummy (and some winners left in the other side suits so you can regain the lead).

Managing Dummy's Trumps

Managing the trump suit is a very important part of your PLAN when you get to the fourth step, *Now put it all together.* We'll discuss it in more detail in Chapter 7. Since trump management is also important when ruffing losers in dummy, we'll look at that aspect now.

It is generally a good idea to draw the opponents' trumps — however small. If you are not careful and the opponents have some outstanding trumps, they may turn some of your winners into unexpected losers. Declarer sometimes needs dummy's trumps, however, to take care of losers and can't afford to draw all of the trumps right away.

Let's look at declarer's considerations when deciding whether to draw the opponents' trumps right away. The first consideration is how many trump cards are needed in dummy to take care of the losers in declarer's hand.

DUMMY: —

DECLARER: A 3

Declarer has one loser to eliminate, so dummy will need one trump to take care of it.

DUMMY: 4 2

DECLARER: A 6 3

Declarer has two losers and can ruff only one of them in dummy. A trick must be lost before the loser can be ruffed. Therefore, one trump must remain in dummy when declarer is ready to ruff the loser.

DUMMY: 5	Declarer has a chance to ruff two losers, so
DECLARER: A 9 7	declarer will need two trumps in dummy.
DUMMY: —	Declarer needs three trumps in dummy to ruff
DECLARER: 8 6 5	all three losers.

Declarer must consider if enough trumps will be left in dummy if trumps are drawn first. If enough trumps will be left, declarer can start by drawing trumps.

Contract: 4♠
Lead: ♥K

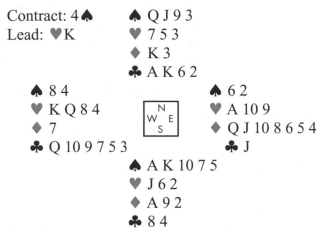

♠ Q J 9 3
♥ 7 5 3
♦ K 3
♣ A K 6 2

♠ 8 4
♥ K Q 8 4
♦ 7
♣ Q 10 9 7 5 3

♠ 6 2
♥ A 10 9
♦ Q J 10 8 6 5 4
♣ J

♠ A K 10 7 5
♥ J 6 2
♦ A 9 2
♣ 8 4

You can afford three losers. You have three heart losers and one diamond loser, one too many. To eliminate your extra loser, plan to ruff your diamond loser in dummy. To do this, you need only one of dummy's trumps.

Suppose the opponents win the first three heart tricks and then lead a diamond. Win dummy's ♦K (high card from the short side). Should you draw trumps first or ruff your losing diamond? Since you need only one trump in dummy, start drawing the trumps. Since the opponents' trumps divide 2–2, this takes only two rounds, and you have two trumps left in dummy, more than enough. You can now play the ♦A safely and ruff your diamond loser in dummy, making your contract.

Notice what happens if you don't draw trumps first. When you play your ♦A, West ruffs it, and you are defeated. A little unlucky perhaps, but this is what you are trying to guard against by drawing trumps first.

Suppose we change the opponents' hands slightly:

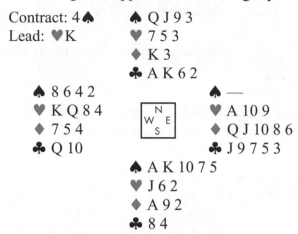

Contract: 4♠
Lead: ♥K

          ♠ Q J 9 3
          ♥ 7 5 3
          ♦ K 3
          ♣ A K 6 2

♠ 8 6 4 2   ♠ —
♥ K Q 8 4   ♥ A 10 9
♦ 7 5 4   ♦ Q J 10 8 6
♣ Q 10   ♣ J 9 7 5 3

          ♠ A K 10 7 5
          ♥ J 6 2
          ♦ A 9 2
          ♣ 8 4

From your perspective, it looks the same. The opponents take the first three heart tricks and lead a diamond. Win the ♦K. Needing only one trump in dummy, you start to draw trumps so that the opponents can't ruff one of your winners.

This time, however, the missing trumps are divided 4–0 — you will need four rounds to draw them all. If you draw all of the trumps first, dummy will have none left to ruff your loser. Once you realize this (East discards when you lead a spade), stop drawing the missing trumps. Play your ♦A and ruff your diamond loser. Now you can finish drawing West's trumps and make your contract.

Of course, the possibility exists that West started with only one diamond and will ruff your ♦A. However, you have no alternative but to take that risk. Your PLAN tells you that you need to ruff a loser in dummy and you need at least one trump to do so. You can't afford to draw all of the trumps first.

Here is another example where declarer can't afford to draw trumps first:

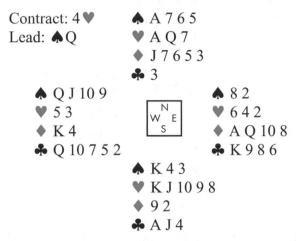

Contract: 4♥
Lead: ♠Q

```
            ♠ A 7 6 5
            ♥ A Q 7
            ♦ J 7 6 5 3
            ♣ 3
♠ Q J 10 9               ♠ 8 2
♥ 5 3          N         ♥ 6 4 2
♦ K 4       W   E        ♦ A Q 10 8
♣ Q 10 7 5 2   S         ♣ K 9 8 6
            ♠ K 4 3
            ♥ K J 10 9 8
            ♦ 9 2
            ♣ A J 4
```

You can afford to lose three tricks in your 4♥ contract. You have one spade loser, two diamond losers and two club losers — two too many. There appears to be a good opportunity to ruff two club losers in dummy. Should you draw trumps immediately after winning the first trick?

You are missing five trumps, and hopefully they are divided 3–2. You will need three rounds of hearts to draw them all, leaving no hearts in dummy. Since you need two of dummy's trumps to ruff your club losers, you must delay drawing trumps until your other work is done.

Win the ♠A, play the ♣A and ruff a club in dummy. Come back to your hand (perhaps using one of your trumps for this purpose — we will discuss this shortly) and ruff your remaining club loser in dummy. Now you are ready to draw trumps and make your contract.

Be careful about the number of trumps left in dummy if you must give up the lead to ruff a loser. When the opponents get the lead, they have an opportunity to lead the trump suit themselves. If they see that you're planning to ruff losers in dummy, they may try to prevent this.

Consider this example:

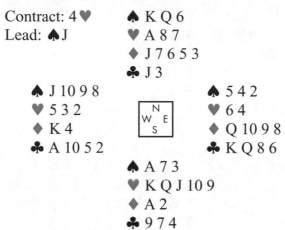

Contract: 4 ♥
Lead: ♠J

♠ K Q 6
♥ A 8 7
♦ J 7 6 5 3
♣ J 3

♠ J 10 9 8
♥ 5 3 2
♦ K 4
♣ A 10 5 2

♠ 5 4 2
♥ 6 4
♦ Q 10 9 8
♣ K Q 8 6

♠ A 7 3
♥ K Q J 10 9
♦ A 2
♣ 9 7 4

In your contract of 4 ♥, you have one diamond loser and three club losers, one more than you can afford. The club suit offers the opportunity to ruff your third club loser in dummy. To do this, you must give up two club tricks.

You need only one heart in dummy to ruff your loser. It would seem safe enough to draw two rounds of trumps before going to work on the club suit. You must let the opponents in the lead twice, however, before dummy is ready to ruff the club loser. At either opportunity, the opponents, seeing your plan, can lead a heart themselves, getting rid of dummy's last trump.

Even one round of trumps is too many. Since the opponents will get the lead twice, they could lead trumps at both opportunities. By the time you are ready to ruff your loser, dummy will have no trumps left. You need to start early and lead a club as soon as you win the first trick. Another example of taking your losses early!

Avoiding an Overruff

Don't send a boy to do a man's job (or a girl to do a woman's job). When you ruff a loser in dummy, don't forget that the opponents can also play a trump if they have no cards in the same suit. Consider this deal:

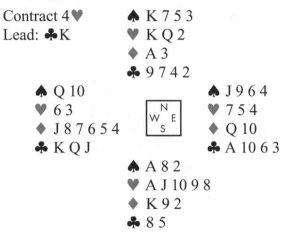

Contract 4♥
Lead: ♣K

You can afford three losers in your contract of 4♥. You have one spade loser, one diamond loser and two club losers. You need to eliminate one of your losers. This looks simple enough, since the situation is ripe for ruffing your diamond loser in dummy.

You need to leave a trump in dummy in order to ruff your diamond loser. For that reason, you can't afford to draw all of the opponents' trumps right away. Suppose the opponents take the first two club tricks and play another club, which you ruff in your hand. If you play the ♦A and the ♦K and then ruff your diamond loser with dummy's ♥2, look what happens. East can overruff your ♥2 with the ♥4, since East is also out of diamonds.

You must be careful to ruff your loser with as high a trump as you can afford. In this hand, you can afford to ruff with the king or the queen since you have all of the other high trumps. This play avoids the possibility of an overruff and still leaves you with enough high trumps to draw the opponents' trumps.

Using Your High Cards Wisely

To ruff a loser in dummy, you must first get to your (declarer's) hand to lead the loser. Remember to take transportation into account when making your PLAN. Look at this example:

Contract: 2♠
Lead: ♣Q

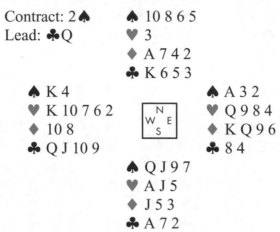

```
              ♠ 10 8 6 5
              ♥ 3
              ♦ A 7 4 2
              ♣ K 6 5 3
♠ K 4                          ♠ A 3 2
♥ K 10 7 6 2      N            ♥ Q 9 8 4
♦ 10 8         W     E         ♦ K Q 9 6
♣ Q J 10 9        S            ♣ 8 4
              ♠ Q J 9 7
              ♥ A J 5
              ♦ J 5 3
              ♣ A 7 2
```

You can afford five losers in a contract of 2♠. You must lose the ♠A and the ♠K, and you also have two heart losers, two diamond losers and a club loser — a total of seven losers. Ruffing your heart losers in dummy looks like the best way to eliminate the extra losers.

Does it matter whether you win the first trick with dummy's ♣K or your ♣A? Suppose you win it with the ♣A. You can play the ♥A and ruff one of your heart losers in dummy, but how do you get back to your hand to lead your other heart loser? No matter which suit you lead, the opponents will win the trick. Now, seeing that you are trying to ruff losers in dummy, they may play the ♠K, the ♠A and another spade to eliminate dummy's remaining trumps.

It is important to look ahead — you will need to get back to your hand to ruff your other heart loser. Win the first trick with dummy's ♣K. Then you can lead a heart to your ♥A and ruff one of your heart losers. Next you can lead a club to your preserved ♣A and be in the right hand to ruff your remaining heart loser. Once this is done, you can start drawing the opponents' trumps by driving out their ace and king. You end up just making your contract.

We will discuss other examples of the careful utilization of your high cards in the next chapter.

The Crossruff

Sometimes you have so many losers to ruff that you never get around to drawing trumps at all. Consider the following deal:

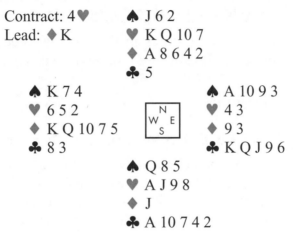

Contract: 4♥
Lead: ♦K

♠ J 6 2
♥ K Q 10 7
♦ A 8 6 4 2
♣ 5

♠ K 7 4
♥ 6 5 2
♦ K Q 10 7 5
♣ 8 3

♠ A 10 9 3
♥ 4 3
♦ 9 3
♣ K Q J 9 6

♠ Q 8 5
♥ A J 9 8
♦ J
♣ A 10 7 4 2

In a contract of 4♥, you can afford only three losers. You have three losers in spades and four losers in clubs — far too many. Dummy's singleton club, however, offers some potential. You can plan to ruff all four of your club losers with dummy's trumps.

You can't afford to draw any trumps since you will need all of dummy's trumps for your losers. After winning the ♦A, start right away to ruff your club losers. Lead a club to your ♣A, lead another club and ruff it in dummy. Now you need to get back to your hand to lead another club. Since you have no high cards in your hand other than trumps, make use of the trump suit. You can't lead one of dummy's trumps since you need all of them to ruff your club losers. However, you can lead a diamond from dummy and ruff it in your hand.

Now you can lead another club and ruff it in dummy. To get back to your hand, you lead a diamond again and ruff it. You ruff another club loser in dummy, lead another diamond and ruff it. You lead your last club loser and ruff it with dummy's last heart. The only trump you have left is the ace in your hand, but it is your 10th trick — your only remaining cards are the three spade losers. You have made your contract without ever drawing trumps.

Because you ruffed losers in both hands, crossing back and forth, this play is called a *crossruff*. This is one occasion when you do benefit from ruffing losers in your hand.

DISCARDING LOSERS

When you can't ruff your losers in the dummy, another method of eliminating them is to discard losers on extra winners available in dummy.

Let's see how this works.

Discarding Losers on Extra Winners in Dummy

When you're looking for alternative ways of disposing of losers in a trump contract, look to see if dummy has additional winners in a side suit (*i.e.*, other than trumps) on which you can throw (discard) your losers. It often happens that weakness in one area is compensated for by extra strength somewhere else.

There is a distinct advantage to discarding side-suit losers on winners. It allows you to take advantage of your trump suit to prevent the opponents from taking tricks in that side suit. Obviously, this technique isn't useful in a notrump contract. When you don't have a trump suit, you can't use your trumps to prevent the opponents from taking tricks in the suit you discarded.

To discard a loser, you must have a side suit that is divided with more cards in dummy than in your hand. The suit also must contain more winners than you need to take care of your losers in that suit.

Here are some examples:

DUMMY: A K 4   You have one low card in your hand but
DECLARER: 2   dummy's ace will take care of it. So you have
               no losers in the suit. Dummy also has the king.
This is an extra winner that you can use to take care of a loser in another side suit.

DUMMY: A K Q

DECLARER: 3

Dummy has two extra winners. You can discard two of your losers in another side suit.

DUMMY: A Q 3

DECLARER: K 4

Dummy has a surplus winner in this suit. Start by playing the king (high card from the short side) and then lead the 4 to dummy's ace. Now the queen can be played, allowing you to discard a loser.

Let's see how discarding a loser works in a complete deal.

Contract: 4♥
Lead: ♦ K

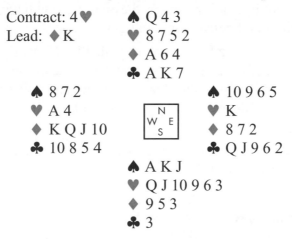

♠ Q 4 3
♥ 8 7 5 2
♦ A 6 4
♣ A K 7

♠ 8 7 2
♥ A 4
♦ K Q J 10
♣ 10 8 5 4

♠ 10 9 6 5
♥ K
♦ 8 7 2
♣ Q J 9 6 2

♠ A K J
♥ Q J 10 9 6 3
♦ 9 5 3
♣ 3

You are in 4♥ and can afford three losers. When you count your losers, you find that you have two in hearts, since you are missing the ♥ A and the ♥ K, and two in diamonds, since dummy's ♦ A will take care of only one of your low diamonds. That's a total of four, one loser too many.

When analyzing your alternatives, you can see that dummy has an extra club winner — only the ♣ A is needed to take care of the low club in your hand. Use this extra winner to discard one of your diamond losers. After winning the ♦ A, play the ♣ A and then the ♣ K, throwing a diamond from your hand. Now you are left with only one diamond loser in your hand. If the opponents lead diamonds, you'll ruff after losing just one trick. Combined with your two heart losers, you're left with just three losers. Now you can make your contract.

To Draw or not to Draw

Should you draw trumps before discarding your losers? In general, you want to draw the opponents' trumps as soon as possible. However, if you look at the previous deal, you can see that this won't always be the case.

In the previous deal, the opponents have led the ♦ K, driving out your ♦ A. Now you have two quick losers in diamonds. As soon as the opponents regain the lead, they'll be able to take two diamond tricks. To draw trumps, you must lose the lead, since you are missing the ♥ A and the ♥ K. If you start by leading trumps, the opponents will win, take their two diamond tricks and defeat your contract.

When you come to the fourth step of your PLAN, *Now put it all together,* consider whether to draw trumps before discarding your losers. If your losers are quick (as in the above example) and you must lose the lead to draw trumps, delay drawing trumps until you have disposed of your extra losers.

If you can draw trumps without giving up the lead, then it's safer to do so before discarding your losers.

Look at this example:

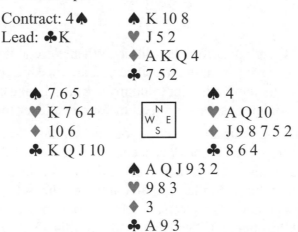

```
            Contract: 4♠     ♠ K 10 8
            Lead: ♣K         ♥ J 5 2
                             ♦ A K Q 4
                             ♣ 7 5 2
        ♠ 7 6 5                              ♠ 4
        ♥ K 7 6 4         N                  ♥ A Q 10
        ♦ 10 6         W       E             ♦ J 9 8 7 5 2
        ♣ K Q J 10         S                 ♣ 8 6 4
                             ♠ A Q J 9 3 2
                             ♥ 9 8 3
                             ♦ 3
                             ♣ A 9 3
```

You can afford three losers in your contract of 4♠. You have three heart losers and two club losers — two too many. Dummy has two extra diamond winners on which you can discard two of your losers. Discarding two losers will allow you to make your contract.

Should you draw trumps first or discard your losers first? Once the ♣K has driven out your ace, all your losers are quick. However, since you can draw trumps without giving up the lead, you should do so before discarding your losers. Once the opponents' trumps are drawn, you can play the ♦ A, the ♦ K and the ♦ Q, and discard two of your losers.

Notice what happens if you don't draw trumps first. When you play the ♦ A, the ♦ K and the ♦ Q, West ruffs the ♦ Q. That's unlucky, but it can be prevented if you draw trumps first.

If your losers are slow — that is, the opponents can't take their winners in the suit right away when they get the lead — it is generally true that you can afford to draw trumps first, even if you must give up the lead.

Take a look at this deal:

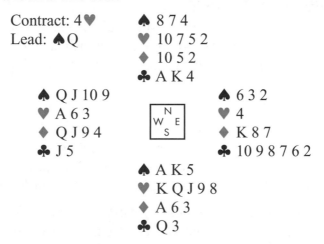

```
Contract: 4♥        ♠ 8 7 4
Lead: ♠Q            ♥ 10 7 5 2
                    ♦ 10 5 2
                    ♣ A K 4

♠ Q J 10 9                      ♠ 6 3 2
♥ A 6 3          N              ♥ 4
♦ Q J 9 4      W   E            ♦ K 8 7
♣ J 5            S              ♣ 10 9 8 7 6 2

                    ♠ A K 5
                    ♥ K Q J 9 8
                    ♦ A 6 3
                    ♣ Q 3
```

In your 4♥ contract, you can afford three losers. You have one loser in spades, one in hearts and two in diamonds. Your club holding provides the opportunity to discard a loser on dummy's extra winner.

Should you draw trumps first? If you do, you have to drive out the opponents' ♥A, giving up the lead. Your losers are slow, however, not quick. When you win the first trick with your ♠K, you will still have the ♠A. You can give up the lead in the trump suit and the opponents won't be able to take their winners right away. Whatever they lead, you can win the trick and draw the remaining trumps. Now it's safe to play the ♣Q (high card from the short side) and lead the ♣3 to dummy's ♣A and ♣K. On the last club, you can discard one of your losers.

If you don't draw trumps first, you'll be defeated on this deal. When you play the third round of clubs, discarding your loser, West ruffs it. Now one of your winners has been turned into a loser.

What if West leads the ♦Q instead of the ♠Q? After you win with the ♦A, you have two quick losers left in diamonds. When the opponents get the lead with their ♥A, they'll be able to take their two diamond winners. However, that's not enough to defeat your contract. You still have a slow loser in spades, and this is the loser you will discard after drawing trumps. You must be careful not to give up the lead too soon only when you have too many quick losers.

Developing Extra Winners

Sometimes dummy doesn't have an immediate extra winner on which to discard your loser. It may be possible to establish an extra winner by using one of the techniques you have seen earlier: promotion, length or the finesse.

Consider these examples:

DUMMY: K Q J   Dummy has no sure winners, but you can pro-
DECLARER: 4 2   mote two tricks by driving out the opponents'
                              ace. Since you have two low cards in your hand,
you can use dummy's extra winner to discard one of your losers.

DUMMY: A K 8 6 2   If the missing cards are divided 3–2, you can
DECLARER: 5 4 3   develop two extra winners by giving up a trick.
                              You can use these winners to discard some of
                              your losers.

DUMMY: A Q J   With this combination, you can take a finesse
DECLARER: 7 3   and hope the opponent on your left has the
                              king. If your finesse is successful, you can
                              come back to your hand and repeat the finesse.
Then you'll have an extra winner in dummy on which you can discard one of your losers. Even if the finesse loses, you still have an extra winner on which you can discard a loser.

Here is a complete deal that illustrates how to promote an extra winner on which to discard a loser.

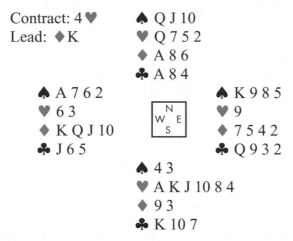

Contract: 4 ♥
Lead: ♦ K

```
                 ♠ Q J 10
                 ♥ Q 7 5 2
                 ♦ A 8 6
                 ♣ A 8 4
  ♠ A 7 6 2                    ♠ K 9 8 5
  ♥ 6 3          N             ♥ 9
  ♦ K Q J 10   W   E           ♦ 7 5 4 2
  ♣ J 6 5          S           ♣ Q 9 3 2
                 ♠ 4 3
                 ♥ A K J 10 8 4
                 ♦ 9 3
                 ♣ K 10 7
```

You can afford three losers. You have two in spades, one in diamonds and one in clubs — one too many. Since you can't ruff any losers in dummy, you must consider whether you can discard one of them. Dummy has no immediate extra winners, but the spade suit offers an extra trick if you drive out the opponents' ♠A and ♠K.

After winning the first trick, you can afford to draw trumps since you don't have to give up the lead. Then play a spade and use dummy's ♠10 (or ♠J or ♠Q) to drive out the opponents' ♠K. They can take their diamond winner. If they lead another diamond, you can ruff it and lead another spade, using dummy's ♠J to force out their ♠A. Now you have established dummy's remaining spade as a winner and can use it to discard your club loser.

Here is an example of establishing an extra winner using length.

Contract: 4 ♥
Lead: ♦ 4

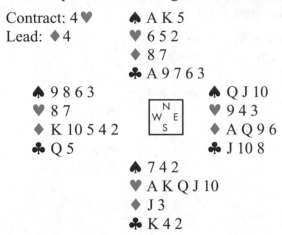

You can afford to lose three tricks in 4 ♥. You have one spade loser, two diamond losers and one club loser. You can't do much about the diamond losers, since the opponents are poised to take the first two tricks. You can't ruff your club loser, and there is nowhere to discard it. You must concentrate on eliminating your spade loser.

The length in clubs offers an opportunity to develop extra winners. You have eight clubs and the opponents have five. If the missing clubs divide 3–2, your remaining clubs will be winners once you have given up a trick. You can use one of these extra winners to discard your spade loser.

Suppose the opponents win the first two diamond tricks and then lead a spade, driving out your ♠ K. You can draw trumps, and then you can play the ♣ K, the ♣ A and another club to establish your remaining clubs as winners. If the opponents lead another spade, driving out your ♠ A, you can play one of your club winners and discard your remaining low spade. Then you have the rest of the tricks and you'll make the contract.

Here is an example of establishing an extra winner using the finesse.

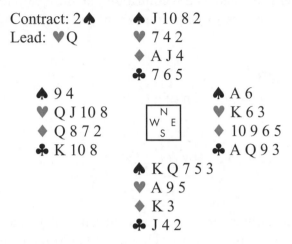

Contract: 2♠
Lead: ♥Q

In your partscore of 2♠, you can afford five losers. You have one spade loser, two heart losers and three club losers — one too many. Since the opponents will drive out your ♥A with their opening lead, all of your losers are quick. You can't afford to start drawing trumps because the opponents will win with the ♠A and take two heart tricks and three club tricks.

How can you eliminate one of your losers? The only hope is to discard one of them on an extra winner in dummy. Dummy has no sure winners you can use, but a winning diamond finesse is possible. You can play the ♦K and lead your ♦3 toward dummy's ♦A and ♦J. When West follows with a low diamond, you finesse dummy's ♦J. Since East doesn't have the ♦Q, you'll win the trick. Now you can play dummy's ♦A and discard one of your losers. You're down to five losers. Now you can safely start to play trumps and you'll make your contract.

What if East held the ♦Q? In that case, your finesse would lose, and you would be defeated two tricks. The opponents would take their heart tricks, three club tricks and the ♠A in addition to the ♦Q. That's the chance you have to take sometimes if you are going to try to make your contract — double or nothing!

GUIDELINES FOR DEFENSE

If your partner is on lead, you'll contribute the third card to the trick. Here are some guidelines to help you when you're the third hand to play.

Third Hand High

Consider the following layout of a suit:

```
              7 6 5
                 N
K J 8 4 3     W     E     Q 9 2
                 S
              A 10
```

Suppose your partner leads the 4 and dummy plays the 5. Which card should you play? You're the third hand to play. You are also the last person to play for your side. A good guideline for this situation is third hand high. If it looks as though partner's card won't win the trick, play a high card and try to win the trick for your side.

In this case, play the highest card you can afford, the queen. Since declarer has the ace, your queen won't win the trick, but it will drive out declarer's ace and promote your partner's king and jack into winners. If you play the 2, or a halfhearted 9, declarer will win the trick with the 10 and still have the ace left. You will not have promoted any winners for your side.

The objective of the guideline *third hand high* is to win the trick for your side or promote other cards in the suit. You don't need to play third hand high if partner's card will win the trick or if second hand has played a card higher than any you have.

For example:

```
              K 6 5
                 N
Q J 10 9     W     E     A 4 2
                 S
              8 7 3
```

If partner leads the queen and dummy plays a low card, you don't need to play your ace since partner's queen is going to win the trick. Of course, if dummy plays the king, you would play your ace.

Only as High as Necessary

The principle of third hand high doesn't always require you to play your highest card. You need to play only as high a card as is necessary. Look at this layout:

<pre>
              Q 6 3
                ┌─────┐
                │ N │
10 7 4 2   │W   E│   K J 9
                │ S │
                └─────┘
               A 8 5
</pre>

Suppose your partner leads the 2 and the 3 is played from dummy. You don't need to play your king since you can see the queen in dummy. Instead, play the jack. If your partner has the ace, your jack will win the trick. If declarer has the ace, the jack will force out the ace and you will have promoted your king into a winner.

The concept of *only as high as necessary* also applies in this situation.

<pre>
               9 6
                ┌─────┐
                │ N │
K 10 8 5 2   │W   E│   Q J 3
                │ S │
                └─────┘
               A 7 4
</pre>

If your partner leads the 5 and the 6 is played from dummy, your queen and jack are equals. Either card can be used to force out declarer's ace. In such a case, play the jack rather than the queen, following the principle of playing only as high a card as is necessary. When your jack forces out declarer's ace, your partner will know that you have the queen. Declarer would have won the trick with the queen holding both the ace and the queen (keeping the ace for a second trick). If you play the queen in such situations, your partner won't know who holds the missing jack (and probably should assume that declarer has it).

BIDDING REVIEW

The Takeout Double

One way to compete in the auction is by making a takeout double. You can tell when a double is for takeout by using the following guideline:

- If you and your partner have done nothing except pass at your first or second turn to bid and the doubled contract is a partscore suit contract, the double is for takeout.
- If either you or your partner has bid or the doubled contract is a game, the double is for penalty.

Requirements for a Takeout Double

To make a takeout double, you need a hand that satisfies the following criteria:

- A takeout double promises at least three-card support for all unbid suits with 13 to 17 total points *or* any hand with 18 or more total points (*i.e.*, a hand too strong for an overcall).

Advancing after a Takeout Double

The takeout double is forcing, and responder must reply unless the right-hand opponent bids. You choose your response using the following guidelines:

With a minimum hand (0 to 8 points):

- Bid a four-card or longer major suit at the cheapest level.
- Bid a four-card or longer minor suit at the cheapest level.

With a medium hand (9 to 11 points):

- Jump in a four-card or longer major suit.
- Jump in a four-card or longer minor suit.

With a maximum hand (12 or more points):

- Jump to game in a four-card or longer major suit.
- Cuebid the opponent's suit to ask the doubler for assistance in finding the best game contract.

Notrump Advances

- 1NT shows 8 to 10 HCP and at least one stopper in the opponents' suit.
- 2NT shows 11 or 12 HCP and at least one stopper in the opponents' suit.
- 3NT shows 13 or more HCP with at least one stopper in the opponents' suit.

Rebids by the Takeout Doubler

Once you've made a takeout double, don't bid again unless partner shows a better than minimum hand or unless you have a better than minimum hand. Use the following guidelines:

With a minimum hand (13 to 15 points):

- Pass if partner bids at the cheapest level.
- Pass with 13 or 14 points if partner jumps a level.
- Invite a Golden Game with 15 points if partner jumps a level.

With a medium hand (16 to 18 points):

- Raise one level if partner bids at the cheapest level.
- Bid a Golden Game if partner jumps a level.

With a maximum hand (19 to 21 points):

- Jump raise if partner bids at the cheapest level.
- Bid a Golden Game if partner jumps a level.

SUMMARY

When you're playing in a trump contract and come to the third step in your PLAN, *Analyze your alternatives,* you may consider two techniques to eliminate losers:

- Ruff losers in dummy.
- Discard losers on extra winners in dummy.

When planning to ruff losers in dummy, make certain that sufficient trumps are left in dummy to accomplish your purpose. Sometimes you must delay drawing trumps until you have ruffed your losers. Use your high cards wisely — make certain you're in the correct hand at the correct time.

When discarding losers, you must also be careful about drawing trumps. If you must give up the lead while drawing trumps and you have too many losers, delay drawing trumps until you have discarded your extra losers.

Sometimes, you must establish the extra winners you need in dummy using the techniques of promotion, development of long suits and the finesse.

A useful guideline when defending is **third hand high.** Play **only as high a card as necessary,** however, either to win the trick or to promote winners for your side.

Exercise One — Ruffing Losers in Dummy

These are your holdings in various side suits in a trump contract. Which of them provide an opportunity to ruff losers in dummy?

DUMMY:	1) 8	2) 10 9 8 7	3) 4 2	4) —	5) A K 6
DECLARER:	A 4 2	A K	Q J	9 6 5	5

_____   _____   _____   _____   _____

Exercise Two — Managing Trumps

In each of the following examples, decide how many trumps declarer needs to keep in dummy to take care of the losers in declarer's hand?

DUMMY:	1) K 4	2) —	3) A	4) Q 2	5) Q J
DECLARER:	A 8 5	10 5 3	7 5 4	A K 4	5 4 2

_____   _____   _____   _____   _____

Exercise Three — Preparing to Ruff Losers

In each of the following examples, determine how many times declarer has to give up the lead before declarer can ruff losers in dummy?

DUMMY:	1) A 4	2) J	3) 7 4	4) —	5) 5
DECLARER:	9 8 3	10 9 8	9 8 3	6 4 3	A 4 2

_____   _____   _____   _____   _____

Exercise One **Answers** — Ruffing Losers in Dummy

1) With more cards in declarer's hand than dummy, declarer has the opportunity to ruff two losers.

2) With only two cards in declarer's hand and more than two in dummy, there is no opportunity to ruff losers.

3) With an equal number of cards in declarer's hand and dummy, there is no opportunity to ruff losers.

4) Since there are three more cards in declarer's hand than dummy, declarer could ruff three losers.

5) There is no opportunity to ruff losers in dummy because dummy has more cards than declarer.

Exercise Two **Answers** — Managing Trumps

1) One	2) Three	3) Two
4) None	5) One	

Exercise Three **Answers** — Preparing to Ruff Losers

1) One	2) One	3) Two
4) None	5) None	

Exercise Four — Discarding Losers

Each of the following side suits provides an opportunity for declarer to discard losers by throwing them on extra winners in dummy. How many losers can be discarded? What must declarer do to get the side suit ready for discarding losers?

DUMMY:	1) A K Q	2) K Q J	3) A K 7 6 4	4) A Q J	5) Q J 10 9
DECLARER:	9 8	7 4	9 8 3	8 3	6 5

_____   _____   _____   _____   _____

Exercise Five — Third Hand High

Your partner leads the 5 against a 3NT contract and the 3 is played from dummy. Which card do you play in each of the following examples?

1)	DUMMY	2)	DUMMY	3)	DUMMY
	8 4 3		Q 6 3		9 3
PARTNER ▮ YOU		PARTNER ▮ YOU		PARTNER ▮ YOU	
5	K 10 6	5	K J 2	5	K Q 4

_____   _____   _____

Exercise Six — Review of Takeout Doubles

The opponent on your right opens the bidding 1 ♦. What do you say with each of the following hands?

1) ♠ A J 6 3
♥ A J 7 5
♦ 4
♣ K 9 4 2

2) ♠ A K 7
♥ 9 3
♦ A J 7 3
♣ J 9 7 2

3) ♠ A Q J 8 3
♥ A 7
♦ 3 2
♣ K 8 5 2

_____   _____   _____

4) ♠ K 10 9 3
♥ Q J 8 2
♦ —
♣ A 10 7 6 2

5) ♠ K J 10
♥ A Q 3
♦ A Q J
♣ 10 9 7 2

6) ♠ J 8 3
♥ 5 2
♦ A K J 9 8
♣ A 7 3

_____   _____   _____

Exercise Four *Answers* — Discarding Losers

1) One loser can be discarded. After the ace and the king have been played, declarer has no cards left and can discard a loser on the queen.

2) One loser can be discarded. After the suit is played twice, losing the first trick to the ace, declarer has no cards left in the suit.

3) Assuming the suit is divided 3–2, two losers can be discarded after the suit has been played three times, giving up a trick. Declarer can discard on dummy's two remaining winners.

4) One loser could be discarded after two winning finesses. Even after a losing finesse, one loser could be discarded.

5) Two losers could be discarded after the suit is played twice and the opponents take the ace and the king.

Exercise Five *Answers* — Third Hand High

1) King   2) Jack   3) Queen

Exercise Six *Answers* — Review of Takeout Doubles

1) Double   2) Pass   3) 1♠

4) Double   5) 1NT   6) Pass

Exercise Seven — Review of Advances After Takeout Doubles

The opponent on your left opens the bidding 1♦. Your partner doubles, and the opponent on your right passes. How do you advance the bidding with each of the following hands?

1) ♠ 7 6 4
   ♥ J 9 8 3
   ♦ J 8 7 2
   ♣ 10 8

2) ♠ A 9 8 4
   ♥ 10 2
   ♦ 9 4 3
   ♣ Q J 8 5

3) ♠ 7 4
   ♥ A Q 10 9 7
   ♦ 10 6 3
   ♣ K J 4

4) ♠ K 10 8
   ♥ 8 5
   ♦ K 8 2
   ♣ K Q 10 9 7

5) ♠ J 10 8
   ♥ J 9 4
   ♦ K Q 10 8
   ♣ A J 2

6) ♠ A 10
   ♥ Q J 8 6 3
   ♦ 9 4 2
   ♣ A Q 4

Exercise Eight — Review of Rebids by the Takeout Doubler

The opponent on your right opens the bidding 1♥ and you double. The opponent on your left passes, partner advances to 1♠ and opener passes. What do you rebid with each of the following hands?

1) ♠ K J 9 3
   ♥ 4
   ♦ K Q 8 2
   ♣ K 9 6 2

2) ♠ A K 10 8
   ♥ 9 5
   ♦ K Q J
   ♣ A 10 8 2

3) ♠ K Q 9 5
   ♥ 2
   ♦ A K J 3
   ♣ K J 10 9

Exercise Seven *Answers* — Review of Advances After Takeout
Doubles

1) 1♥ 2) 1♠ 3) 2♥

4) 2NT 5) 2NT 6) 4♥

Exercise Eight *Answers* — Review of Rebids by the Takeout
Doubler

1) Pass 2) 2♠ 3) 3♠

Exercise Nine — Discarding a Loser

(E–Z Deal Cards: #4, Deal 1 — Dealer, North)

Turn up all of the cards on the first pre-dealt deal. Put each hand dummy-style at the edge of the table in front of each player.

The Bidding

What is North's opening bid?

With an opening bid and support for all of the unbid suits, what call does East make?

Can South support partner's major suit? What does South respond?

Does West have to advance after partner's takeout double when South bids? What does West call?

```
Dealer:        ♠ Q 10 9 7 6 3
North          ♥ A K
               ♦ Q 3
               ♣ A 8 2
♠ K 5                          ♠ A
♥ 8 7 5 2         N            ♥ Q 9 6 3
♦ 10 9 8 4      W   E          ♦ J 7 5 2
♣ 10 4 3          S           ♣ K Q J 6
               ♠ J 8 4 2
               ♥ J 10 4
               ♦ A K 6
               ♣ 9 7 5
```

With a medium-strength hand, what rebid does North make to invite partner to carry on to game?

East passes. Does South accept North's invitation? What will the contract be? Who will be the declarer?

The Play

Which player makes the opening lead? What will the opening lead be?

Declarer starts by making a PLAN:
1. **P**ause to consider your objective
2. **L**ook at your winners and losers
3. **A**nalyze your alternatives
4. **N**ow put it all together

How many losers can declarer afford? How many losers does declarer have? How can declarer eliminate one of the losers? Should declarer draw trumps first? Why not?

Exercise Nine *Answers* — Discarding a Loser

The Bidding

- North opens 1♠.
- East doubles.
- South responds 2♠.
- West does not have to bid after South bids. West passes.
- With a medium hand of 17 points, North bids 3♠.
- South accepts the invitation and bids 4♠. The contract is 4♠. North is the declarer.

The Play

- East leads the ♣ K.
- Declarer can afford three losers, but has four.
- Declarer can eliminate a club loser by discarding a club on the diamonds but must do so before drawing trumps. Once the opponents gain the lead — which they would do if declarer tried to draw trumps — they can take four quick tricks.

Exercise Ten — More Discards

(E–Z Deal Cards: #4, Deal 2 — Dealer, East)

Turn up all of the cards on the second pre-dealt deal and arrange them as in the previous deal.

The Bidding

East doesn't have enough to open the bidding. What will South's opening bid be?

West has an opening bid and support for the unbid suits. How does West describe the hand?

North passes. With a medium hand of 11 points, how does East show the hand's strength?

```
Dealer:        ♠ 6 4
East           ♥ Q 9 4 3
               ♦ 8 7 4
               ♣ 7 4 3 2
♠ J 10 8 2              ♠ Q 9 7 5 3
♥ 10 6          N       ♥ A J
♦ K Q J 5     W   E     ♦ 10 9 6 2
♣ A Q J         S       ♣ K 9
               ♠ A K
               ♥ K 8 7 5 2
               ♦ A 3
               ♣ 10 8 6 5
```

South passes. Counting dummy points, does West have enough to accept East's invitation to bid on to game? What does West bid? What will the contract be? Who will be the declarer?

The Play

Which player makes the opening lead? Assuming South chooses to lead a heart, which heart will be led? When dummy plays a low card, which card will North play? Why?

Declarer starts by making a PLAN. How can declarer eliminate an extra loser? Should declarer draw trumps first?

Exercise Ten *Answers* — More Discards

The Bidding

- South opens 1 ♥.

- West doubles.

- East shows a medium hand of 11 points by jumping to 2 ♠.

- With 15 dummy points, West invites game by bidding 3 ♠. East will accept the invitation and bid game. The contract is 4 ♠. East is the declarer.

The Play

- South leads the ♥5. North plays the ♥Q, third hand high.

- Declarer can eliminate the extra heart loser, the jack, by throwing it on the extra club winner. Declarer must do this before drawing trumps, because the opponents have enough tricks to defeat the contract if they gain the lead.

Exercise Eleven — Ruffing a Loser

(E–Z Deal Cards: #4, Deal 3 — Dealer, South)

Turn up all of the cards on the third pre-dealt deal and arrange them as in the previous deal.

The Bidding

South passes. What is West's opening bid?

How does North describe the hand?

East doesn't have enough to respond. Can South pass partner's takeout double? What does South bid?

West passes. What rebid does North make to show a medium-strength hand?

Dealer:	♠ A K Q 2
South	♥ A 10 6 2
	◆ 7 3
	♣ A 9 5

♠ J 8
♥ K J 3
◆ A K 10 6 5
♣ Q 7 2

N
W E
S

♠ 10 7 5 3
♥ Q 8
◆ Q 9 8
♣ J 10 8 4

♠ 9 6 4
♥ 9 7 5 4
◆ J 4 2
♣ K 6 3

East passes. Knowing North has a medium-strength hand (16 to 18 points), does South bid again? What will the contract be? Who will be the declarer?

The Play

Which player makes the opening lead? What will the opening lead be?

Declarer starts by making a PLAN. Assuming the missing trumps are divided 3–2, how many losers does declarer have? How can declarer eliminate one of the diamond losers? How does declarer plan to play the trump suit?

Exercise Eleven *Answers* — Ruffing a Loser

The Bidding

- West opens 1 ♦.

- North doubles.

- When East passes, South must bid and chooses 1 ♥.

- With a medium-strength hand, North raises to 2 ♥.

- With only 4 points, South passes. The contract is 2 ♥. South is the declarer.

The Play

- The opening lead is the ♦ A by West.

- Declarer has six losers if the missing trumps divide 3–2. One of the losers can be eliminated by ruffing a diamond in dummy when the suit is led a third time. Declarer must give up the lead twice in the trump suit, hoping the missing trumps divide 3–2.

Exercise Twelve — More Losers to Ruff

(E–Z Deal Cards: #4, Deal 4 — Dealer, West)

Turn up all of the cards on the fourth pre-dealt deal and arrange them as in the previous deal.

The Bidding

West doesn't have enough to open the bidding. Does North have enough to open? Which suit will North bid?

How can East compete in the auction?

What does South advance after North's opening bid?

Once South bids, West is no longer obliged to advance after partner's takeout double. How-

```
Dealer:     ♠ Q J 5 4
West        ♥ Q J 3
            ♦ A 10 6
            ♣ K 6 3
♠ 9 7 2              ♠ A 8 6 3
♥ 9 8 6 2    N       ♥ A K 7 5
♦ K J 8    W   E     ♦ Q 9 2
♣ A 9 2      S       ♣ 10 7
            ♠ K 10
            ♥ 10 4
            ♦ 7 5 4 3
            ♣ Q J 8 5 4
```

ever, with 8 points, West should bid if possible since partner has invited West to compete. What does West bid?

With a minimum-opening bid, North passes. Does East have a minimum, medium or maximum hand? What does East rebid? What will the contract be? Who will be the declarer?

The Play

Which player makes the opening lead? What will the opening lead be? Assuming North leads a low club, which card will South play to the first trick? Why?

Declarer starts by making a PLAN. Assuming the missing trumps divide 3–2, how many losers does declarer have? How can one of the losers be eliminated?

Exercise Twelve *Answers* — More Losers to Ruff

The Bidding

- Playing five-card majors, North can't bid a four-card major suit and therefore opens 1♣, the lower-ranking of two three-card minor suits.

- East doubles.

- South responds 2♣.

- West bids 2♥.

- With a minimum hand, East passes. West is the declarer in 2♥.

The Play

- North leads the ♣3, the partnership's suit. South should play the ♣J to the first trick, third hand high (only as high as necessary).

- Declarer has six losers and can eliminate a club loser by ruffing a club in dummy.

CHAPTER 5
Watching Out for Entries

If declarer doesn't have enough tricks to make the contract in notrump or has too many losers in a trump contract, declarer goes through the third step of the PLAN, *Analyze your alternatives.* Declarer looks at the opportunities in each suit for developing extra winners or eliminating losers.

Next, declarer moves on to the fourth step, *Now put it all together,* to develop an overall strategy for playing. Declarer considers the overall picture, not just the individual suits. The best play in a particular suit may not be the best play for the entire deal. Declarer may have to choose between the available alternatives or consider in which order to play the suits.

Many of the techniques for developing extra winners or eliminating losers require declarer to lead from one hand or the other. For example, declarer may need to lead toward a high card to take a finesse. When declarer plans the strategy for the play, careful attention must be given to being able to shift the lead from one side of the table to the other as necessary. In this chapter, we will look at declarer's strategy for dealing with transportation problems.

ENTRIES

A card which allows the shifting of the lead from one hand to the other is called an entry. In some hands, declarer has all of the entries necessary. At other times, declarer must create the entries needed.

Sure Entries

A sure entry is a winner on one side of the table accompanied by a low card on the other side. This combination allows declarer to cross over to the winner.

Look at these examples:

DUMMY: A 8 3   Dummy's ace is an entry. Declarer can play
DECLARER: 7 4 2   any low card to dummy's winner.

DUMMY: A K Q

DECLARER: —

Dummy has plenty of winners, but declarer has no low cards in the suit. This suit doesn't provide a sure entry to the dummy. In fact, declarer will need an entry in another suit to get to dummy to take the winners in this suit.

DUMMY: —

DECLARER: 6 5

Declarer has low cards in this suit but dummy has no winners. The suit itself doesn't provide an entry to dummy. If this is a side suit in a trump contract, however, declarer may be able to lead one of the low cards and ruff it in dummy. This play would eliminate a loser while providing an entry to dummy.

DUMMY: Q 5 3

DECLARER: A K 4

An entry doesn't need to be the highest card in the suit. In this example, the queen is an entry since declarer has the ace and the king. Declarer can play the 4 to dummy's queen. The ace and the king serve as entries to declarer's hand.

DUMMY: 9 2

DECLARER: A K Q J 10 4

Even a low card can provide a useful entry. Declarer can play the 4 to dummy's 9 to get to the dummy.

DUMMY: K Q J 10

DECLARER: A

Having a low card in the opposite hand is important. Declarer has lots of winners in dummy but no entry because there aren't any low cards in declarer's hand.

DUMMY: A 4 2

DECLARER: K 5

This is a useful suit since it provides an entry to either hand. If the lead is in dummy, playing a low card to the king would provide transportation to declarer's hand. Leading the 5 from declarer's hand to dummy's ace would provide transportation the other direction. If the opponents lead this suit, declarer must decide where to win the trick. Declarer's strategy will identify the hand which will need an entry later in the play. Based on the PLAN, declarer would take the trick with either the king in hand or the ace in dummy.

Creating an Entry

When dummy has no sure entry, it may be possible to create one through promotion, length or the use of the finesse. Declarer may have to depend on the favorable location of a missing high card or a favorable division of a suit. Look at these examples:

DUMMY: K Q

DECLARER: 8 4

Declarer has no quick entry to dummy in this suit, but one can be created by force. If the 4 is led to dummy's queen and the opponents take their ace, the king becomes a sure entry. If the opponents don't take their ace, declarer is in dummy right away.

DUMMY: K 5 3

DECLARER: 7 6 2

The king is a possible entry to dummy, depending on which opponent has the ace. Declarer can lead a low card toward dummy. If the opponent on declarer's left has the ace and plays it, the king will be an entry to the dummy. If the ace isn't played, declarer can win dummy's king immediately. If the ace is on declarer's right, the king will be taken by the ace. In this case, declarer won't have an entry in the suit.

Here is a similar example.

DUMMY: Q 4

DECLARER: A 6 2

Declarer can lead a low card toward dummy's queen. If the king is on declarer's left, dummy's queen will become an entry. If the king is on declarer's right, the queen won't be an entry.

DUMMY: 8 6 4 2

DECLARER: A K 5 3

Dummy has no ready entry in this suit. If the missing cards are divided 3–2, however, declarer can establish an entry by playing the ace and the king and then leading the suit again. If the opponent's cards divide 3–2, dummy's 8 is a winner, and it will provide an entry since declarer has the 5 (or 3) left.

Preserving Entries when Playing a Suit

To help preserve entries for when they are needed, declarer must use some of the guidelines we looked at earlier: play the high card from the short side first and take your losses early.

Here are some examples:

DUMMY: A Q 9 8   When a suit is divided evenly between declarer
DECLARER: K J 6 3   and dummy, declarer can take the tricks in any
                       order. Declarer can start by taking dummy's ace
                       and queen or declarer's king and jack.

DUMMY: Q 3   When the suit is unevenly divided between
DECLARER: A K J 2   the two hands, declarer must be more careful.
                       When taking the winners in this suit, declarer
                       starts by leading the 2 to dummy's queen
— high card from the short side first.

The 3 in dummy can be led back to the ace, the king and the jack.
When the first trick is won with a high card in declarer's hand and then
the 2 is led to dummy's queen, declarer will need an entry in another suit
to get back to take the rest of the winners.

DUMMY: K Q 10 3   When promoting tricks in this suit, declarer
DECLARER: J 2   starts with the jack, the high card from the
                       short side. If the opponents don't take the
                       ace, declarer can continue by leading the
2 to dummy's high cards. Declarer will need only one entry in another
suit to get to the winners in dummy. If declarer starts by leading the 2 to
dummy, two outside entries may be needed to take all three of the tricks
in dummy.

DUMMY: A K 8 6 3   If declarer plays the ace and the king and then
DECLARER: 5 4 2   leads the suit a third time, giving up a trick,
                       dummy's remaining two low cards will be win-
                       ners if the opponents' cards divide 3–2.

However, declarer will need an entry to dummy to get to them. Instead,
declarer should give up (duck or lose) the first or second trick (take your
losses early) to preserve the high cards as entries to dummy once the
winners are established.

Now let's put it all together and use these carefully preserved entries
in a complete deal.

USING ENTRIES

Entries are important when using any of the techniques discussed in earlier chapters: promoting high cards, developing long suits, finessing, ruffing losers and discarding losers.

Promoting High Cards

Take a look at the following deal. You are in a 3NT contract and West leads the ♣Q.

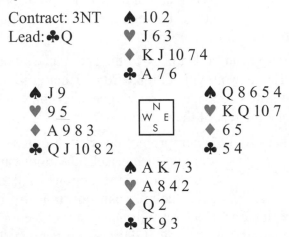

Contract: 3NT
Lead: ♣Q

♠ 10 2
♥ J 6 3
♦ K J 10 7 4
♣ A 7 6

♠ J 9
♥ 9 5
♦ A 9 8 3
♣ Q J 10 8 2

♠ Q 8 6 5 4
♥ K Q 10 7
♦ 6 5
♣ 5 4

♠ A K 7 3
♥ A 8 4 2
♦ Q 2
♣ K 9 3

You need nine tricks. You have two sure tricks in spades, one in hearts and two in clubs. Four more tricks need to be developed. When you *Analyze your alternatives,* the diamond suit appears to offer an excellent opportunity for all four.

In the fourth step of the PLAN, *Now put it all together,* you must consider exactly how you will play the hand, watching your entries carefully. You want to promote diamond winners in dummy. Once they have been established, you will need an entry to get to them. The ♣A looks like dummy's only entry, so you want to preserve it by winning the first trick with the ♣K in your hand. Next, you must be careful to start the diamonds by playing the ♦Q from your hand — high card from the short side first. Whether or not West wins the first trick with the ♦A, you can establish the diamonds and have the ♣A to get to them.

Developing Long Suits

You need to develop a long suit to make your contract, and you must be careful to watch your entries.

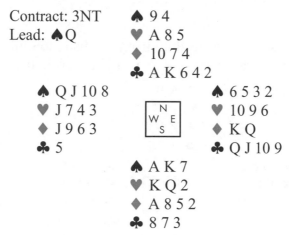

Contract: 3NT
Lead: ♠Q

♠ 9 4
♥ A 8 5
♦ 10 7 4
♣ A K 6 4 2

♠ Q J 10 8
♥ J 7 4 3
♦ J 9 6 3
♣ 5

♠ 6 5 3 2
♥ 10 9 6
♦ K Q
♣ Q J 10 9

♠ A K 7
♥ K Q 2
♦ A 8 5 2
♣ 8 7 3

You need nine tricks in a 3NT contract and you have eight. There are two spade winners, three hearts, one diamond and two clubs. You need one more. The diamond suit offers some chance. You have seven diamonds and the opponents have six. You need the missing diamonds to divide exactly 3–3, but they are more likely to divide slightly unevenly, 4–2. A more promising alternative is the club suit in which you have eight cards. If the missing clubs divide 3–2, you can give up one trick and establish two extra winners, more than enough to fulfill the contract.

With the ♥A in dummy, you seem to have no entry problems, but don't be lulled into carelessness. Suppose you play the ♣A and the ♣K, intending to give up the next trick and establish your remaining two clubs as winners. That play works if the missing clubs divide 3–2. You would still have the ♥A as an entry to dummy. On this deal, however, the missing clubs break 4–1. You can get to dummy one time with the ♥A to lead the suit again and establish your remaining club, but then you have no way to get back to it.

Instead, take your losses early. Win the first trick, and give up a club trick right away by playing a low club from both hands. You have to lose at least one club trick anyway. (You could also win the first club trick and give up the second club trick.) Whatever the opponents lead, you win (be-

ing careful to keep the ♥A in dummy if the opponents lead hearts) and
lead clubs again. When the suit breaks 4–1, give up a second trick. You
still have the ♥A left in dummy as an entry to your established winner.

Finessing

Taking a finesse involves leading from one hand toward a high card
in the other hand. Entries, therefore, play a vital part in the PLAN.

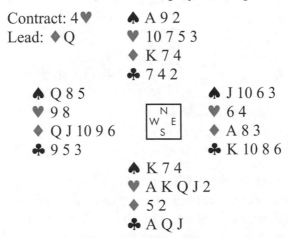

Contract: 4♥
Lead: ♦Q

	♠ A 9 2	
	♥ 10 7 5 3	
	♦ K 7 4	
	♣ 7 4 2	

♠ Q 8 5		♠ J 10 6 3
♥ 9 8	N W E S	♥ 6 4
♦ Q J 10 9 6		♦ A 8 3
♣ 9 5 3		♣ K 10 8 6

	♠ K 7 4	
	♥ A K Q J 2	
	♦ 5 2	
	♣ A Q J	

You can afford three losers in a contract of 4♥. You have one spade
loser, two diamond losers and one club loser. You can't do anything about
the spade loser, but you do have a good chance to avoid a loser in both
diamonds and clubs. You have the ♦K in dummy. If West has the ♦A,
you will have only one diamond loser. Admittedly, things do not look
good since West has led the ♦Q — it is quite likely that East has the ♦A.
In clubs, you have the opportunity to take a repeated finesse against the
king. If East has the ♣K, you can eliminate your club loser.

When you put your plan together, you must lead twice from dummy
toward your hand. This means that you will need two entries into the
dummy. What will they be? The ♠A is one entry. If East has the ♦A,
the ♦K won't be an entry. You do, however, have the ♥10 in dummy that
can serve as a second entry. Since you have all of the other high hearts,

plan to play the ♥2 to dummy's ♥10. This will allow you to take two club finesses.

Once again, be careful. The opening lead is the ♦Q. Suppose you play the ♦K from dummy at the first trick, hoping West started with the ♦A. It turns out that East has the ♦A and wins the first trick. East returns partner's suit, and West wins a second diamond trick. West leads another diamond which you ruff in order to avoid a third loser in the suit — but which card do you ruff with? Having made your PLAN beforehand, you know that you will need the ♥2 to lead to dummy's ♥10 later so that you can lead a low club toward your hand. For that reason, you can't afford to use the ♥2 to ruff West's diamond lead. Instead, ruff with one of your higher hearts, the ♥J, for example.

Now you can draw the opponents' trumps with your high hearts. They break 2–2, and you can lead your carefully preserved ♥2 to dummy's ♥10 in order to lead a low club toward your hand. When East plays low, finesse with your ♣J. It wins the trick since West does not have the ♣K. You can get back to dummy by playing a low spade to dummy's ♠A. Then lead another club. When East plays low, repeat the finesse by playing your ♣Q. This wins the trick, and you have avoided losing a club trick. You end up making your contract, losing only two diamond tricks and one spade trick.

This hand shows the importance of pausing to make your PLAN at the beginning of play. If you didn't think ahead, you might ruff the third round of diamonds with your ♥2 and no longer be able to make the contract. Dummy's winner would be stranded. The PLAN alerted you to the fact that the ♥2 was a very important card.

Ruffing Losers in Dummy

When you want to ruff a loser in dummy, you must be able to get to your hand to lead the loser. The more losers you have, the more entries you need. Look at this example:

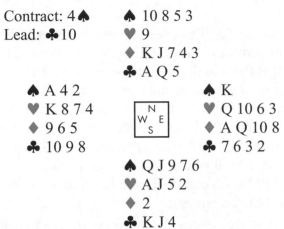

Contract: 4♠
Lead: ♣10

♠ 10 8 5 3
♥ 9
♦ K J 7 4 3
♣ A Q 5

♠ A 4 2
♥ K 8 7 4
♦ 9 6 5
♣ 10 9 8

♠ K
♥ Q 10 6 3
♦ A Q 10 8
♣ 7 6 3 2

♠ Q J 9 7 6
♥ A J 5 2
♦ 2
♣ K J 4

You can afford three losers. You have two losers in spades, three in hearts and one in diamonds. When you *Analyze your alternatives,* you see that nothing can be done about the spade and diamond losers. Concentrate on eliminating the three heart losers. With a singleton heart in dummy, this looks like the perfect opportunity to ruff your losers.

Since you plan to ruff three losers in dummy, you'll need to get to your hand three times. One entry is the ♥A. Where will you find the other two? You can't use the spade suit since the opponents have the ace and the king. You also don't want to lead spades early because you need to leave three trumps in dummy to ruff your losers.

You might consider giving up a diamond trick — then you could ruff one of dummy's diamonds to get to your hand. If you give up a diamond trick, however, the opponents may lead spades and remove some of dummy's trumps. That would leave you with too few to ruff all of your heart losers. The best suit to provide the entries you need is clubs.

Be careful to preserve your entries until you need them. If you win the first trick in your hand with the ♣J or the ♣K, you use up one of your entries too soon. Even winning the first trick with dummy's ♣Q won't be good enough — dummy's clubs aren't low enough to lead to your hand twice. You must win the first trick with dummy's ♣A. Once again we can see the importance of making a PLAN.

After winning the ♣A, lead dummy's ♥9 to the ♥A and ruff one of your heart losers in dummy. Now lead dummy's ♣5 to your ♣J so you can ruff another heart in dummy. Cross your fingers and play dummy's ♣Q to the remaining ♣K in your hand. Now you can ruff your last heart in dummy. Why cross your fingers? You started with six clubs and the opponents with seven. You must hope the missing clubs divide 4–3, otherwise one of the opponents could ruff one of your club winners and defeat the contract.

After the clubs divide nicely and you ruff your last heart loser, you are home free. Lead trumps, driving out the missing ace and king and make your contract. You lose only the ♠A, the ♠K and the ♦A.

Discarding Losers

Another way to eliminate losers in a trump contract is by discarding them on extra winners in dummy. If this is your PLAN, remember to watch those entries.

Consider the following deal. You are in a partscore of 2♥ and the opening lead is the ♦Q.

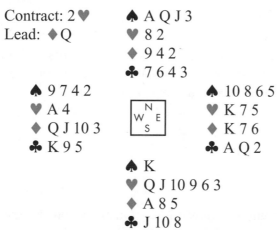

Contract: 2♥
Lead: ♦Q

♠ A Q J 3
♥ 8 2
♦ 9 4 2
♣ 7 6 4 3

♠ 9 7 4 2
♥ A 4
♦ Q J 10 3
♣ K 9 5

♠ 10 8 6 5
♥ K 7 5
♦ K 7 6
♣ A Q 2

♠ K
♥ Q J 10 9 6 3
♦ A 8 5
♣ J 10 8

You can afford five losers. You are missing the ♥A and the ♥K, and you have two diamond losers and three club losers. Since all of the losers are quick, you can't start by leading trumps. You must eliminate two of your losers before giving up the lead.

The extra spade winners in dummy will provide discards for some of your losers, but an entry to dummy is the problem. After winning the ♦A and taking a trick with your ♠K, how do you get to dummy's ♠A, ♠Q and ♠J to discard your losers?

The key comes from your PLAN. You can afford five losers, so you need to discard only two of your losers on dummy's spades. The spade suit itself can provide an entry if you *overtake* your ♠K with dummy's ♠A. This may seem wasteful but it gets you to dummy. It will allow you to play the ♠Q and the ♠J and discard two of your losers. Now you can draw trumps by driving out the opponents' ♥A and ♥K and make your contract.

GUIDELINES FOR DEFENSE

If a card is led from declarer's hand or dummy and you are next to play, you will be contributing the second card to the trick. Here are some guidelines that will help you decide what to play when you are in second position.

Second Hand Low

Consider the following situation. You (West) are defending with dummy on your left — you can't see declarer's cards and you can't see partner's cards. Here are the cards in one suit that you are able to see. Declarer leads the 4 towards dummy's king:

K 8 3

A 10 6 2

	N	
W		E
	S	

4

Which card should you play? Since you are second to play, your partner will have the opportunity to play last for your side. A good guideline for this situation is *second hand low*. It may not seem like it will make much difference. You'll get only one trick with your ace, and declarer, having followed the principle of leading toward a high card, will get a trick with dummy's king.

Let's see how it can make a difference. Suppose the complete layout of the suit is:

```
                    K 8 3
                   ┌─────┐
                   │  N  │
        A 10 6 2   │W   E│   J 9 5
                   │  S  │
                   └─────┘
                    Q 7 4
```

If you play the ace, declarer will play a low card from dummy. Later, declarer will get a trick with the queen as well as the king.

Instead, suppose you play low. Declarer will play dummy's king and win the first trick. However, if declarer tries to get a second trick by leading toward the queen, you'll win the trick. Since your side has the remaining high cards in the suit, declarer will get only one trick.

The objective of the guideline *second hand low* is to avoid using your high cards when declarer is playing low cards. In the above example, if you play the ace when declarer leads the 4, you capture two low cards. It is better to wait to capture one of declarer's high cards with your ace.

Your partner, rather than declarer, may hold the queen, but you'll lose nothing by playing second hand low. Declarer is entitled to one trick with the king once declarer plays a card toward it.

When Not to Play Low

The guideline second hand low should not be followed blindly. It is good advice only if you clearly have nothing better to do. In many situations, you should not play low.

Let's look again at our earlier example:

```
                    K 8 3
                   ┌─────┐
                   │  N  │
        A 10 6 2   │W   E│   ? ? ?
                   │  S  │
                   └─────┘
                    ? ? 4
```

If you are defending against a trump contract and this is a side suit, the possibility exists that declarer may have a singleton. The complete layout could be:

```
                    K 8 3
                   ┌───────┐
                   │   N   │
        A 10 6 2   │ W   E │   Q J 9 7 5
                   │   S   │
                   └───────┘
                      4
```

If you play low, declarer can win the king — declarer will ruff if you later try to take a trick with your ace. Declarer started with one loser in the suit but ended up with no losers! In such a situation, you must use the bidding and your holdings in other suits to guide you. Don't blindly play second hand low when it looks like declarer has a singleton or when you can see enough tricks to defeat the contract if you win your ace.

If you aren't sure, playing low is usually correct. Even if declarer is leading a singleton and you don't take your ace, it may cost nothing. Declarer may use the king later to discard another loser if you do play the ace.

Let's take another look at an earlier example:

```
                    K 8 3
                   ┌───────┐
                   │   N   │
        A 10 6 2   │ W   E │   J 9 5
                   │   S   │
                   └───────┘
                    Q 7 4
```

If the queen rather than a low card is played from declarer's hand, this would not be a time for you to play low. You have an opportunity to win one of declarer's high cards with your ace, and you should do it. Declarer will get only one trick with the king. If you play low, declarer wins the queen, and then declarer can lead toward the king in dummy and get a second trick.

This situation falls under another, seemingly conflicting, guideline: *cover an honor with an honor.* The idea here is to promote the lower cards your side holds in a suit by playing your high cards on top of declarer's high cards. In this example, by covering the queen with your ace, you promote partner's jack into a trick after declarer takes a trick with dummy's king.

Even if you exchange your ace with dummy's king, it's right to cover declarer's queen with your king rather than play low:

A 8 3

K 10 6 2 | N W E S | J 9 5

Q 7 4

By covering declarer's queen with your king, you make declarer use dummy's ace to win the trick. In effect, you eliminate two of declarer's high cards for one of your own. Now you've promoted your side's jack and 10 into winners. (As we saw in Chapter 3, declarer should lead *toward* the queen to try for a trick, hoping your partner has the king. That wouldn't work in this layout.)

Here is another situation where second hand low clearly would not be the best play:

A J

K Q 10 9 2 | N W E S |

4

If declarer leads the 4 toward dummy and you play low, declarer may play dummy's jack and win the trick. Instead, you should play your queen to make declarer play dummy's ace. Now, your king has been promoted into a winner, and declarer will not get a trick with dummy's jack.

This situation is called *splitting your honors*. You split your honors, rather than play second hand low, to avoid letting declarer win an undeserved trick with a lower-ranking card.

The advice to play second hand low in second position is very useful. Remember, however, to use it only when you clearly have no better alternative.

BIDDING — THE STAYMAN CONVENTION

In *Bidding*, the first book in this series, we introduced some new ideas to improve your ability to reach the best contract and add a new dimension to your game. In this chapter, we will review an artificial, or conventional, bid that is very useful when responding to an opening bid of 1NT, the Stayman convention.

The Stayman Convention

When partner opens the bidding with 1NT, responder, as captain, decides the level and strain of the contract. When selecting the strain, responder wants to determine if the combined hands have a *Golden Fit* — eight or more cards — in a major suit. The Stayman convention helps responder uncover a Golden Fit in a major suit.

The *Stayman convention* is a response of 2♣ to an opening bid of 1NT. It asks if opener has a four-card major suit. With a four-card (or longer) major suit, opener bids it. Without a four-card major suit, opener rebids 2♦. The 2♣ response and the 2♦ rebid are conventional calls that do not relate in any way to the club and diamond suits respectively.

Here are some examples of the 1NT opener's rebid when responder bids 2♣:

♠ A 8 7 3   Rebid 2♠ to show the four-card spade suit.
♥ Q J 10
♦ A Q 8
♣ K 8 5

♠ A K   Rebid 2♥ to show the four-card heart suit. Re-
♥ 10 9 7 3   sponder is not interested in how good a suit you have,
♦ K Q 9 2   merely whether you have four of them.
♣ A J 10

♠ K 10 2   With no four-card major, rebid 2♦. This says noth-
♥ A K 5   ing about your diamond holding. It's a conventional
♦ 8 2   (artificial) response saying that you don't have a
♣ A Q 10 6 3   four-card major suit. Responder will bid again.

Let's see how the Stayman convention is used when responder has enough for a game contract.

When Responder Has 10 or More Points

With 10 or more points, responder knows that the partnership belongs in a game contract, since opener has at least 15 HCP. The only thing in question is the strain. If there is a Golden Fit in a major suit, the partnership belongs in 4♥ or 4♠; otherwise, the partnership belongs in 3NT.

With a six-card major suit, responder knows that a Golden Fit exists since opener has a balanced hand. Responder can bid game in the appropriate major suit. With a five-card major suit, responder can make a forcing response of 3♥ or 3♠ to tell opener to bid 4♥ or 4♠ with three-card or longer support; otherwise, to bid 3NT. But what if responder has only four cards in a major suit? Look at this hand:

♠ K 7 6 4   With 11 HCP, responder wants to be in game when
♥ A J 7 3   opener bids 1NT — but which game? If opener has
♦ 6 2   four spades, the partnership has a Golden Fit in that
♣ K 8 3   suit and belongs in 4♠. Similarly, if opener has
                 four hearts, the partnership belongs in 4♥. Finally,
if opener doesn't have four cards in either major, the contract should be 3NT.

Responder can determine the best contract by using the Stayman convention. Responder starts by responding 2♣, asking opener to show a four-card major. If opener rebids 2♠, showing a four-card spade suit, responder can place the contract in 4♠. Similarly, if opener rebids 2♥, responder can raise to 4♥. Finally, if opener rebids 2♦, denying four cards in either major, responder can jump to 3NT, knowing there is no Golden Fit in a major suit.

Responder doesn't need four cards in both majors to use the Stayman convention. Suppose responder's hand is:

♠ Q J 7 4   Opener bids 1NT, and responder bids 2♣ to ask if
♥ 9 3   opener has a four-card major. If opener rebids 2♠,
♦ 7 2   responder puts the partnership in 4♠. If opener rebids
♣ A K 8 4 3   2♦, showing no four-card major, or 2♥, showing
                 four hearts, responder places the contract in 3NT.

This raises an interesting point. Suppose opener started with four hearts and four spades. When responder bids 2♣, asking for a major suit, opener has to pick one of them to bid. Holding both four-card majors, opener rebids the heart suit first, going up the line. Opener would rebid 2♥. Responder, with the above hand, would jump to 3NT, since responder isn't interested in hearts.

Now opener must wonder: "Why did responder bid 2♣ and then

show no interest in hearing about my heart suit?" The answer must be that responder was interested only in spades. Thus, opener should bid 4♠ with a four-card spade suit when responder jumps to 3NT over a 2♥ rebid. This puts the partnership in its Golden Fit.

Clearly, responder must be careful to bid 2♣ only if there is interest in finding a Golden Fit in a major suit. Once the partnership agrees to use 2♣ as the Stayman convention, responder can't suddenly decide to use that bid to show clubs — opener will be confused. A *conventional* bid is one that has a special (artificial) meaning for the partnership. Conventions, such as Stayman, can be very useful, but both partners must be on the same wavelength.

Here are some examples of responding to 1NT when you and your partner have agreed to use the Stayman convention:

♠ 6 4 ♥ 9 7 5 3 ♦ A K 8 3 ♣ A J 5	Respond 2♣. You are interested in finding a Golden Fit in hearts. If opener rebids 2♥, raise to 4♥. If opener rebids 2♦ or 2♠, jump to 3NT.
♠ 9 6 2 ♥ 7 4 ♦ Q 7 2 ♣ A K J 8 6	Respond 3NT. Don't bid 2♣, since you aren't interested in a major suit.
♠ A Q J 9 3 ♥ K 5 ♦ J 7 4 ♣ 10 9 4	Respond 3♠. With a five-card suit, you don't need to ask if opener has a four-card spade suit; three-card support will be sufficient. 3♠ asks opener to choose between 4♠ and 3NT.
♠ A 9 6 4 ♥ A 8 6 3 ♦ 4 ♣ Q 10 9 4	Use the Stayman convention, 2♣, to find out if opener has a four-card major. If opener rebids 2♥ or 2♠, raise to game. If opener rebids 2♦, jump to 3NT.

When Responder Has 8 or 9 Points

The Stayman convention can also be used when responder has a hand of invitational strength and is interested in finding a Golden Fit in a major suit. Consider this hand as responder when opener bids 1NT:

♠ 10 4
♥ K J 8 3
♦ 9 6 2
♣ A 10 8 3

With 8 HCP, responder is not sure whether the partnership belongs in partscore or game. If opener has a minimum, 15 HCP, there isn't enough combined strength for game. If opener has a maximum, 17 HCP, there is enough for game. Responder could invite opener to bid on to game by responding 2NT, but this would lose the opportunity to find a Golden Fit in hearts.

Instead, responder can start by using the Stayman convention, 2♣. If opener rebids 2♥, showing a four-card heart suit, responder can invite game by raising to 3♥. With a maximum, opener bids 4♥; otherwise, opener passes 3♥. If opener rebids 2♦ or 2♠, responder can bid 2NT, again inviting opener to bid game with a maximum or pass with a minimum. The Stayman convention gives responder the best of both worlds — responder can invite opener to bid a game and look for a Golden Fit in a major suit along the way.

The Stayman convention is useful on another type of invitational hand. Consider the following hand when opener bids 1NT:

♠ A J 9 7 4
♥ 8 3
♦ 9 6 2
♣ K 10 7

With 9 points — 8 HCP plus 1 point for the five-card suit — responder again wants to invite opener to carry on to game. At the same time, responder is interested in finding out whether there is a Golden Fit in spades. Responder can't bid 2♠ since that's a signoff showing 0 to 7 points, and opener will pass. Responder also can't bid 3♠, since that's a forcing bid showing 10 or more points, and opener will bid either 4♠ or 3NT.

The solution is to start with 2♣, the Stayman convention. If opener rebids 2♠, showing four spades, responder raises to 3♠, showing the Golden Fit and inviting game. If opener rebids 2♦ or 2♥, responder bids 2♠. This tells opener that responder has an invitational hand (8 or 9 points) with a five-card or longer suit. How does opener know this? With a weak hand (0 to 7 points), responder would have signed off in

2♠ (and would not have bid 2♣ first). With a strong hand (10 or more points), responder would have bid 3♠ with a five-card spade suit or 4♠ with a six-card or longer suit. Responder must have an invitational hand (8 or 9 points). With only a four-card spade suit, responder would have rebid 2NT rather than 2♠. Responder must have five or more spades. Opener can pass with a minimum hand, bid 3NT with a maximum hand and only two spades or bid 4♠ with a maximum hand and three spades. Once again, the partnership has the best of all possible worlds.

Here are some examples of responding to an opening bid of 1NT when you hold 8 or 9 points.

♠ Q 9 7 4   Respond 2♣. You're interested in finding a Golden
♥ 5 3   Fit in spades. If opener rebids 2♠, raise to 3♠, in-
♦ K Q 8 3   viting game with a maximum. If opener rebids 2♦
♣ J 10 3   or 2♥, bid 2NT, again inviting game.

♠ 10 8 3   Respond 2NT to invite opener to bid game with a
♥ 10 5   maximum. Don't bid 2♣, since you aren't interested
♦ Q J 4   in a major suit.
♣ A J 8 6 3

♠ 9 5   Respond 2♣. With 7 HCP plus 2 points for the six-
♥ K J 8 7 6 3   card suit, you are too strong to sign off in 2♥ but
♦ 7 4   not strong enough to bid 4♥. If opener rebids 2♥,
♣ K 8 2   raise to 3♥. If opener rebids 2♦ or 2♠, you can
             bid your heart suit showing an invitational hand with
             at least five hearts.

♠ 10 8 5 4   Use the Stayman convention, 2♣, to find out if
♥ K 8 6 5   opener has a four-card major. If opener rebids 2♥,
♦ A J 5   raise to 3♥. If opener rebids 2♠, raise to 3♠. If
♣ 3 2   opener rebids 2♦, bid 2NT.

When Responder Has Fewer Than 8 Points

Suppose opener bids 1NT and responder holds this hand:

♠ Q 10 8 3   With 4 HCP, responder wants to play in a partscore.
♥ Q 6 4 2   Since responder is interested in playing in a Golden
♦ 8 4   Fit, should responder bid 2♣ to find out if opener
♣ 7 5 3   has a four-card major? At first glance, this looks
reasonable. If opener rebids 2♥ or 2♠, responder
passes and plays a partscore in the Golden Fit. But what if opener rebids
2♦? Responder can't pass because opener's bid isn't showing a diamond
suit. Opener is only denying a four-card major suit. Responder also can't
bid 2NT, since this would show an invitational hand (8 or 9 points), and
opener might bid on to 3NT. The solution is to pass 1NT.

♠ K 9 8 3   With 7 points, responder is not strong enough to use
♥ Q 6 4   the Stayman convention. The Bidding Scale leaves
♦ Q 8 6   no room to go exploring. With a five-card suit, re-
♣ 7 5 3   sponder can sign off in 2♦ or 2♥ or 2♠, but with
a hand such as this one, responder must pass and
play in 1NT.

Note, also, that responder can't sign off in 2♣ holding a weak hand
with a long club suit. Opener would interpret the 2♣ bid as the Stayman
convention and bid something.

SUMMARY

An entry is a way of getting from one hand to the other.

When you come to the fourth step of the PLAN, *Now put it all together,* you must be careful to watch out for the entries between your hand and dummy. Entries are important when using the techniques for establishing winners and eliminating losers:

- Promoting high cards,
- Developing long suits,
- Finessing,
- Ruffing,
- Discarding losers.

Sometimes, you will need to create an entry to a particular hand. At other times, you will be concerned with preserving an entry to one of the hands.

When you are defending, a useful guideline is **second hand low,** but don't follow it blindly. For example, if declarer leads a high card and you have a higher card, you should **cover an honor with an honor** if doing so will promote tricks for your side.

When responding to an opening bid of 1NT, you can use the conventional (artificial) response of 2♣, **the Stayman convention,** to find out if opener has a four-card major. With a four-card (or longer) major suit, opener bids it; otherwise, opener rebids 2♦, a **conventional** (artificial) rebid showing no four-card major. Holding both majors opener will bid 2♥, going up the line. Responder can use this information to help determine the partnership's best contract.

Exercise One — Recognizing Entries

How many entries to dummy do each of the following examples contain?

DUMMY:	1) A Q 7	2) A K 3	3) 10 4	4) K 10 9	5) K Q J
DECLARER:	K 9 2	5	A K Q J 3	A Q J 3 2	A

_____   _____   _____   _____   _____

Exercise Two — Creating Entries

How could you try to create an entry to dummy in each of the following suits?

DUMMY:	1) K Q 6	2) K 8	3) Q 7 4	4) Q J 10	5) 9 7 5 4
DECLARER:	7 4 2	9 3	A 8 2	8 5 4	A K 3 2

_____   _____   _____   _____   _____

Exercise One Answers — Recognizing Entries

1) Two — the ace and queen.

2) One — since you have only one low card in declarer's hand.

3) One — the 10, by playing the 3 from declarer's hand to dummy's 10.

4) Three — the king, the 10 and the 9. Play the low cards from declarer's hand and win them with the 10 and the 9. The king can also be an entry by overtaking the queen or the jack.

5) No entries. Declarer doesn't have a card lower than those in dummy.

Exercise Two Answers — Creating Entries

1) Lead toward the king–queen combination. You have two entries if the ace is on your left.

2) Lead toward the king, hoping for one entry if the ace is on your left.

3) Lead toward the queen, hoping the opponent on your left has the king.

4) Play the suit twice, driving out the ace and the king to get an entry to dummy.

5) Play the suit three times, giving up a trick and keeping the 9 in dummy. By that time, the opponents won't have any cards left in the suit if the missing cards divide 3–2. Now you can lead your remaining low card to dummy's 9.

Exercise Three — Preserving Entries

How would you play each of the following suits to avoid needing entries in other suits to take all of your tricks?

DUMMY: 1) K 5   2) K 8 7 5 4   3) A K 7 4   4) A 7 6 3 2   5) A K J 10
DECLARER: A Q J 6   A 9 3   Q J 2   8 5 4   Q

———   ———   ———   ———   ———

Exercise Four — Estimating the Number of Entries Needed

How many entries to dummy would you need in other suits to try the finesse(s) in each of the following side suits?

DUMMY: 1) 8 5   2) 8 6 3   3) 6 5 2   4) 9 6 3   5) A 6 3
DECLARER: A Q 4   A Q J   K Q 3   A Q 10   Q 5 4

———   ———   ———   ———   ———

Exercise Three *Answers* — Preserving Entries

1) Win the first trick with the king. Then lead low toward the winners in declarer's hand.

2) Play the ace and then a low card from both hands (or vice versa), losing a trick. This leaves the king in dummy as an entry to the established winners.

3) Win the first two tricks with the queen and the jack. Then lead low to the ace and the king in the dummy.

4) Lose two tricks and win the third round with the ace in dummy.

5) Win the first trick by overtaking the queen with a high card in dummy, the ace or the king.

Exercise Four *Answers* — Estimating the Number of Entries Needed

1) One   2) Two   3) Two

4) Two   5) None (use the ace)

Exercise Five — Second Hand Low

Which card do you play in each of the following examples when declarer leads the indicated card toward the dummy?

1) DUMMY	2) DUMMY	3) DUMMY	4) DUMMY
Q 4 3	A Q 10	K Q 5	A 6 3
YOU ■	YOU ■	YOU ■	YOU ■
A 6 5	K J 3	A J 9	K 10 9
DECLARER	DECLARER	DECLARER	DECLARER
2	5	6	Q

_____   _____   _____   _____

Exercise Six — Using the Stayman Convention

Your partner opens the bidding 1NT. What do you respond with each of the following hands?

1) ♠ A J 7 3	2) ♠ A 5	3) ♠ 10 5
♥ K 10 8 6	♥ J 10 7 3	♥ J 3
♦ 10 5 2	♦ A Q J 6	♦ A 8 4
♣ Q 8	♣ 9 6 3	♣ K Q 10 8 6 3

_____   _____   _____

4) ♠ Q 9 8 5	5) ♠ 4 2	6) ♠ K 8 6 3
♥ K 2	♥ Q J 9 7 3	♥ 10 9 6 4
♦ K 10 8 4	♦ A 8 4	♦ 10 5
♣ 9 8 4	♣ J 10 5	♣ 8 7 5

_____   _____   _____

Exercise Five *Answers* — Second Hand Low

    1) 5

    2) 3

    3) 9

    4) King

Exercise Six *Answers* — Using the Stayman Convention

1) 2♣	2) 2♣	3) 3NT
4) 2♣	5) 2♣	6) Pass

Exercise Seven — Responding to the Stayman Convention

You open the bidding 1NT and your partner responds 2♣, the Stayman convention. What do you rebid with each of the following hands?

1) ♠ K 9
   ♥ A Q 8 3
   ♦ J 9 4
   ♣ K Q J 2

2) ♠ 9 7 4 2
   ♥ A K 3
   ♦ A J 8
   ♣ K Q 5

3) ♠ A J 9
   ♥ A K 7
   ♦ J 7
   ♣ K 10 9 8 2

_____   _____   _____

Exercise Eight — Responder's Rebid after Using Stayman

Your partner opens 1NT and you respond 2♣, the Stayman convention. Opener rebids 2♥. What do you rebid with each of the following hands?

1) ♠ K 9 7 3
   ♥ A J 7 4
   ♦ 8 4
   ♣ A 5 4

2) ♠ A K 5 3
   ♥ 10 9 3
   ♦ J 10 8 6
   ♣ Q J

3) ♠ Q 10
   ♥ Q J 3 2
   ♦ K 10 6 4
   ♣ 9 6 2

_____   _____   _____

4) ♠ A Q 7 4
   ♥ J 2
   ♦ 10 6 3
   ♣ Q 9 8 6

5) ♠ K J 10 7 3
   ♥ 3
   ♦ A 9 8 5
   ♣ 10 7 5

6) ♠ K Q 7 6 3
   ♥ J 10 9 4
   ♦ A 10 5
   ♣ 5

_____   _____   _____

Exercise Seven *Answers* — Responding to the Stayman
Convention

1) 2♥   2) 2♠   3) 2♦

Exercise Eight *Answers* — Responder's Rebid after Using
Stayman

1) 4♥   2) 3NT   3) 3♥

4) 2NT   5) 2♠   6) 4♥

Exercise Nine — Using Entries for a Finesse

(E–Z Deal Cards: #5, Deal 1 — Dealer, North)

Turn up all of the cards on the first pre-dealt deal. Put each hand dummy-style at the edge of the table in front of each player.

The Bidding

With a balanced hand and 17 HCP, what is North's opening bid?

East passes. South has 10 points. Does the partnership belong in game or partscore? Does South know if there is a Golden Fit in a major suit? How can South find out?

West passes. With a four-card spade suit, which rebid does North make?

```
Dealer:     ♠ K Q 7 3
North       ♥ Q 5 2
            ♦ 9 4
            ♣ A K Q J
♠ A J 9              ♠ 10 5
♥ 10 7 3      N      ♥ J 9 4
♦ A 7 6     W   E    ♦ Q J 10 8 3
♣ 8 5 4 2     S      ♣ 9 7 3
            ♠ 8 6 4 2
            ♥ A K 8 6
            ♦ K 5 2
            ♣ 10 6
```

East passes. Now that South has found a Golden Fit, at which level and in which strain does the partnership belong? Which bid does South make?

What will the contract be? Who will be the declarer?

The Play

Which player makes the opening lead? What will it be?

```
Declarer starts by making a PLAN:
  1. Pause to consider your objective
  2. Look at your winners and losers
  3. Analyze your alternatives
  4. Now put it all together
```

How many losers can declarer afford? How many losers does declarer have? How can declarer avoid losing two trump tricks? Which suit provides entries to dummy? When declarer leads the first spade from dummy, which card should West play? Why?

Exercise Nine *Answers* — Using Entries for a Finesse

The Bidding

- North opens 1NT.

- The partnership belongs in game. South bids 2♣, the Stayman convention, to find out if there is a major-suit fit.

- North shows the four-card major suit by bidding 2♠.

- South now bids 4♠.

- The contract is 4♠. North is the declarer.

The Play

- East leads the ♦Q.

- Declarer has four losers, one too many. If the opponents' trumps break 3–2, the number of losers in the trump suit can be held to only one by leading twice toward the king-queen. The heart suit provides the entries to dummy, so declarer can lead toward declarer's hand twice. When declarer first leads spades, West should play low rather than the ace. This is second hand low. Although it may not matter on this deal, it does make things more difficult for declarer.

Exercise Ten — Watching Entries While Promoting Winners

(E–Z Deal Cards: #5, Deal 2 — Dealer, East)

Turn up all of the cards on the second pre-dealt deal and arrange them as in the previous deal.

The Bidding

With a balanced hand of 16 HCP, what is East's opening bid?

South passes. West has 9 points. Does West know whether the partnership belongs in game or partscore? Is West interested in finding a Golden Fit in a major suit? What does West respond?

North passes. How can East tell partner that the hand doesn't have a four-card major suit?

```
Dealer:        ♠ A 9 7 2
East           ♥ 7 5
               ♦ J 10 8 6
               ♣ A 9 8
♠ K J 6 5              ♠ Q 10 3
♥ A 8 6 3      N        ♥ K 2
♦ 9 5        W   E      ♦ A K Q 4
♣ J 4 2        S        ♣ Q 7 6 3
               ♠ 8 4
               ♥ Q J 10 9 4
               ♦ 7 3 2
               ♣ K 10 5
```

South passes. Since opener doesn't have a four-card major suit, what does West rebid to invite opener to bid game?

North passes. Does East have enough to accept West's invitation to bid game? What will the contract be? Who will be the declarer?

The Play

Which player makes the opening lead? What will the opening lead be?

Declarer starts by making a PLAN. Which suit offers the best potential for developing extra tricks? How does declarer plan to play the suit? What can North do to make life difficult for declarer? In which hand, should declarer win the first trick? Why?

If declarer were to play a club from either hand, which card should the defender play? Why?

Exercise Ten *Answers* — Watching Entries While Promoting
                      Winners

The Bidding

- East opens 1NT.

- West doesn't know what level or what strain until there is more information from the opener. West responds 2♣ (Stayman convention) to start to get some answers.

- East rebids 2♦, announcing no four-card or longer major suit.

- West now bids 2NT to invite East to game with maximum values.

- East doesn't have a maximum and passes. The contract is 2NT. East is the declarer.

The Play

- The opening lead by South is the ♥Q.

- The spade suit offers the best chance to get the extra tricks declarer needs. Declarer tries to win the first trick with the high card from the short side, the queen.

- North can make things difficult by refusing to play the ♠A until the third round of spades.

- Declarer should win the first trick with the ♥K and keep the ♥A in dummy so the established spades won't be stranded.

- If declarer were to lead a club from either hand, the next defender would play second hand low. On this deal, it would prevent declarer from establishing a third club trick.

Exercise Eleven — Entries When Developing a Long Suit

(E–Z Deal Cards: #5, Deal 3 — Dealer, South)

Turn up all of the cards on the third pre-dealt deal and arrange them as in the previous deal.

The Bidding

With a balanced 18 points, what is South's opening bid?

West passes. With 9 points, does North know if the partnership belongs in game or a partscore? Is North interested in finding a Golden Fit in a major suit? What does North respond?

East passes. What does South rebid?

```
Dealer:      ♠ J 9 6 2
South        ♥ 10 4
             ♦ 7 3
             ♣ A K 8 6 3
♠ 8 4 3                    ♠ Q 10 7 5
♥ K J 5          N         ♥ Q 9 8 2
♦ Q 10 8 6 5   W   E       ♦ J 9
♣ J 9            S         ♣ Q 10 5
             ♠ A K
             ♥ A 7 6 3
             ♦ A K 4 2
             ♣ 7 4 2
```

West passes. What should North rebid?

What will the contract be? Who will be the declarer?

The Play

Which player makes the opening lead? What will the opening lead be?

Declarer starts by making a PLAN. Which suit does declarer plan to establish to make the contract? What will declarer have to hope for? How does declarer make certain that dummy has an entry to the established winners?

Exercise Eleven *Answers* — Entries When Developing a
Long Suit

The Bidding

- South opens 1 ♦.

- North doesn't know if the partnership belongs in a partscore
  or game and is interested in finding a major-suit fit. North
  responds 1 ♠ and waits to hear South's rebid..

- South rebids 2NT.

- North carries on to game and rebids 3NT.

- The contract is 3NT. South is the declarer.

The Play

- West leads the ♦ 6.

- Declarer needs to establish clubs to get the extra tricks needed
  to make the contract and must hope they divide 3–2.

- To make sure dummy has an entry to the established winners,
  South will duck the first or second club and hold a low card
  which is needed to get to the winners. South must lose a club
  trick and make sure it is early in the play.

Exercise Twelve — Creating an Entry

(E–Z Deal Cards: #5, Deal 4 — Dealer, West)

Turn up all of the cards on the fourth pre-dealt deal and arrange them as in the previous deal.

The Bidding

With a balanced hand and 15 HCP, what is West's opening bid?

North passes. Does East have enough for game? Is East interested in finding a Golden Fit in a major suit? What does East respond?

South passes. Does West have a major suit? What does West respond?

```
Dealer:        ♠ 10 8 4 2
West           ♥ K 3
               ♦ 8 7 4
               ♣ Q J 10 9
♠ A K                        ♠ Q 7 5
♥ J 9 6 5 4      N           ♥ Q 10 8 7
♦ 10 9 5      W   E          ♦ K Q J
♣ A K 3          S           ♣ 8 6 2
               ♠ J 9 6 3
               ♥ A 2
               ♦ A 6 3 2
               ♣ 7 5 4
```

North passes. Does East know the level and strain in which the partnership belongs? What does East bid?

What will the contract be? Who will be the declarer?

The Play

Which player makes the opening lead? What will the opening lead be?

Declarer starts by making a PLAN. How many losers can declarer afford? How many losers does declarer have? How does declarer plan to eliminate the extra loser?

Does declarer have an immediate entry to dummy? How does declarer plan to get to dummy? Can declarer start by drawing trumps? Why not?

Exercise Twelve *Answers* — Creating an Entry

The Bidding

- West opens 1NT.

- East has enough for game and bids 2♣, the Stayman convention, to investigate for a major-suit fit.

- Yes. West rebids 2♥.

- East bids 4♥.

- The contract is 4♥. West is the declarer.

The Play

- The opening lead by North is the ♣Q.

- Declarer has one too many losers but plans to discard a club on the ♠Q. The problem is that there is no immediate entry to that card. An entry must be developed in diamonds. As soon as declarer gets the lead, declarer plays the ♠A K and then leads a diamond to create an entry to dummy.

- Declarer can't try to draw trumps because the opponents will gain the lead in the process. They will lead another club, getting rid of declarer's last club winner. If declarer then tries to create an entry in diamonds, the opponents will take the ♦A and their club winner.

CHAPTER 6
Watching Out for the Opponents

While you are working to develop the extra tricks you need to make the contract, the defenders are trying to prevent you from succeeding. When you consider the fourth step of the PLAN, *Now put it all together,* you must take into account what the defenders may do to interfere with your strategy.

The defenders can do things such as take tricks in their long suit once they have driven out your high cards, capture your high cards and make you use your entries before you are ready. Let's see what you can do about this when you are the declarer.

THE HOLD-UP PLAY

Against a notrump contract, the defenders usually try to establish a long suit by driving out declarer's high cards. When the defenders regain the lead, they take their winners in that suit. The defenders have the advantage of making the opening lead. They can choose the suit they want to attack.

Although declarer may not be able to prevent the defenders from driving out the high cards in a suit, declarer can sometimes make it more difficult for them to take their tricks when they regain the lead. Let's look at how declarer does this.

Holding Up the Ace

Timing is an important aspect of playing a hand. In the previous chapter, we saw how declarer could create an entry to a suit by ducking a trick (letting the opponents win a trick that declarer could have won). Declarer doesn't lose anything by ducking. Declarer is still entitled to the winner(s) in the suit and has to lose one or more tricks sooner or later. However, declarer may gain by choosing exactly the right moment to win the trick.

When the opponents are trying to establish their suit, choosing the right time to take a winner can also make a difference.

Consider this layout:

```
              7 5
              ┌─────┐
KQJ 10 9      │  N  │      8 3 2
              │W   E│
              │  S  │
              └─────┘
              A 6 4
```

West leads the king against declarer's notrump contract. Declarer has only one sure trick, the ace, whether it's played on the first, second or third round of the suit. When declarer takes the ace, however, may make a big difference in the number of tricks the opponents get in the suit.

First, suppose declarer wins the first trick with the ace. The remaining cards in the suit are:

```
              7
              ┌─────┐
Q J 10 9      │  N  │      8 3
              │W   E│
              │  S  │
              └─────┘
              6 4
```

Unless declarer has enough winners to make the contract, declarer must establish extra tricks. To do this, declarer may have to give up the lead. No matter which opponent takes the trick, the opposing side will take all four of their winners in the above suit.

If declarer wins the second trick with the ace, the result will be the same. If East obtains the lead, East will still have a low card left to lead back to West's remaining winners. The opponents will take four tricks in the suit.

Suppose, however, that declarer waits until the third time the suit is led before taking the ace. Now the remaining cards are:

```
              —
              ┌─────┐
10 9          │  N  │      —
              │W   E│
              │  S  │
              └─────┘
              —
```

If declarer has to lose a trick to West, West will take the two remaining winners — the opponents once again get four tricks in the suit. However, if declarer loses a trick to East, East has no low card(s) left to lead to partner. Unless West has some other way to gain the lead, these winners are stranded. The opponents would take only two tricks in the suit instead of four.

Declarer can make it difficult for the opponents to take all of their winners by holding up the ace until one opponent has no cards left in the suit. Here is an example of the hold-up play in action:

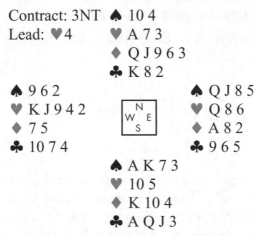

```
Contract: 3NT   ♠ 10 4
Lead: ♥4        ♥ A 7 3
                ♦ Q J 9 6 3
                ♣ K 8 2

♠ 9 6 2                      ♠ Q J 8 5
♥ K J 9 4 2      N           ♥ Q 8 6
♦ 7 5          W   E         ♦ A 8 2
♣ 10 7 4           S         ♣ 9 6 5

                ♠ A K 7 3
                ♥ 10 5
                ♦ K 10 4
                ♣ A Q J 3
```

Declarer needs nine tricks. There are two spade tricks, one heart and four clubs — a total of seven. Two more tricks need to be developed. Four diamond tricks can be developed by driving out the opponents' ace. That is more than enough to make the contract, but when putting it all together, declarer must watch out for the opponents.

The opponents have led hearts and will drive out declarer's only high card in hearts. If the hearts are divided 5–3, as is likely, the opponents will have four heart winners. The heart tricks plus the ♦ A will be enough to defeat the contract.

Declarer's best chance to make the contract is to use the hold-up play. Declarer can play a low heart from dummy on the first trick, letting East win with the ♥ Q. When East returns partner's suit, declarer ducks again, holding up the ace. West leads hearts once more to establish two winners in the suit, and now declarer wins dummy's ♥ A.

Hoping for the best, declarer plays the ♦K, high card from the short side, to drive out the ♦A. When East wins, East doesn't have a heart to lead back to West's established winners. Whatever East leads, declarer wins the trick and takes the remaining winners. Declarer ends up with an overtrick.

Why does declarer need to hope for the best? If West had the ♦A instead of East, West would win the diamond trick and take two heart winners to defeat the contract. Declarer needs luck on this deal but luck combined with an element of skill. If declarer doesn't hold up the ♥A, the contract will be defeated no matter which defender has the ♦A. The hold-up play gives declarer a 50% chance.

Holding Up the King

The hold-up play involves letting the opponents win the trick instead of taking a sure winner. Sometimes the hold-up play can be used when the sure winner is a king.

Consider this situation:

```
              10 4
            ┌─────┐
            │  N  │
  Q 9 7 6 3 │ W  E│  A J 2
            │  S  │
            └─────┘
              K 8 5
```

West leads the 6 to East's ace, and East leads back the jack. Declarer's king is now a sure winner. Declarer can hold up by playing the remaining low card. If East leads the suit again, declarer wins the king. Now East has no cards left in the suit to lead to West's winners if East later regains the lead.

If the ace hasn't been played, the king isn't a sure winner — declarer can't afford to hold up.

Look at this layout:

```
              10 4
            ┌─────┐
            │  N  │
  A Q 9 6 3 │ W  E│  J 7 2
            │  S  │
            └─────┘
              K 8 5
```

West leads the 6 and East plays the jack. If declarer lets East win the trick, East will lead the suit back — now the king is trapped by West's ace and queen. The opponents will take the first five tricks in the suit, and declarer gets no tricks. In this case, declarer should take the king when it's possible to do so.

Here's an example of holding up with the king:

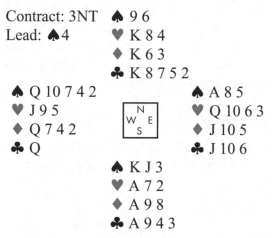

Contract: 3NT ♠ 9 6
Lead: ♠4 ♥ K 8 4
♦ K 6 3
♣ K 8 7 5 2

♠ Q 10 7 4 2   ♠ A 8 5
♥ J 9 5   ♥ Q 10 6 3
♦ Q 7 4 2   ♦ J 10 5
♣ Q   ♣ J 10 6

♠ K J 3
♥ A 7 2
♦ A 9 8
♣ A 9 4 3

West leads the ♠4 to East's ♠A, and East returns the ♠8. Should declarer win the trick with the ♠K? Declarer needs nine tricks. The ♠K is now a sure winner, and there are two tricks each in hearts, diamonds and clubs — a total of seven. Where will the two extra tricks come from?

The club suit looks promising. Declarer has nine clubs, the opponents have four. If the missing clubs divide 2–2, declarer's remaining three clubs will be winners after taking the ♣A and the ♣K. If, as is more likely, the clubs break 3–1, declarer must give up a trick to establish the remaining two low clubs as winners.

Since declarer may have to lose a trick, declarer doesn't want the opponents to take four spade tricks as well. Declarer should hold up the ♠K and play the ♠J instead. This play loses to West's ♠Q, and West can lead the suit again to drive out the king. The hold-up play has the desired effect, however. When the clubs break 3–1, declarer must give up a trick to East to establish the suit. Since East has no spades left to lead to West's winners, declarer makes the contract.

How Long to Hold Up

Earlier we examined this layout:

```
              7 5
                 ┌───┐
K Q J 10 9       │ N │      8 3 2
             W   │W E│   E
                 │ S │
                 └───┘
              A 6 4
```

When the king was led, declarer held up twice, winning the ace on the third round. East was left with no cards in the suit, and provided West never got the lead, the opponents took two winners rather than four.

Suppose, instead, that the missing cards are divided in this fashion:

```
              7 5
                 ┌───┐
K Q J 10         │ N │      9 8 3 2
             W   │W E│   E
                 │ S │
                 └───┘
              A 6 4
```

If the eight missing cards divide 4–4, it doesn't help declarer to hold up the ace, but it also doesn't do any harm. East still has a low card left, and whichever opponent gets the lead, the opponents get one more trick. Since the suit breaks 4–4, however, the opponents get only three tricks in all.

When deciding how long to hold up, consider how many tricks you can afford to lose. If you are in 3NT, you can afford to lose four tricks. If you must give up a trick in another suit, you can afford to lose three tricks in the suit the opponents are trying to establish. In the above example, holding up the ace until the third round ensures that you will still make the contract if East, rather than West, gets the lead. If the suit was originally divided 5–3, East will have no cards left in the suit. If it was divided 4–4, East will have one left, but the opponents can take only three winners in the suit.

When deciding whether to hold up, declarer must take into consideration the possibility that the opponents may switch to another suit. That could be more dangerous.

Look at this example:

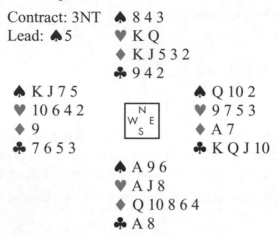

Contract: 3NT ♠ 8 4 3
Lead: ♠5   ♥ K Q
            ♦ K J 5 3 2
            ♣ 9 4 2

♠ K J 7 5   ♠ Q 10 2
♥ 10 6 4 2   ♥ 9 7 5 3
♦ 9   ♦ A 7
♣ 7 6 5 3   ♣ K Q J 10

            ♠ A 9 6
            ♥ A J 8
            ♦ Q 10 8 6 4
            ♣ A 8

Declarer has one sure spade trick, three sure heart tricks and one sure club trick. Declarer can get the four extra tricks required to make the contract by driving out the opponents' ♦ A. The ♠5 has been led and East plays the ♠Q. Should declarer hold up?

Since declarer must let the opponents in the lead with the ♦ A, it may seem like a good time to employ the hold-up play. However, declarer's holding in the club suit is not very strong. If declarer lets East win the first trick, East may decide to try another suit and switch to clubs. Once declarer's ♣A is driven out, the defenders will have more than enough tricks to defeat the contract.

Declarer can't afford to use the hold-up play. Instead, declarer wins the first trick with the ♠A and drives out the ♦ A to establish the extra winners needed to make the contract. When the opponents win with the ♦ A, declarer must hope the missing spades are divided so that the opponents can't take more than three tricks in the suit.

Holding Up with Two High Cards

If there is no danger of the opponents switching to another suit, declarer sometimes holds up even with two winners.

Consider this example:

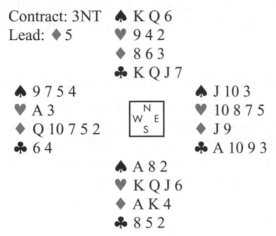

Contract: 3NT
Lead: ♦ 5

North:
♠ K Q 6
♥ 9 4 2
♦ 8 6 3
♣ K Q J 7

West:
♠ 9 7 5 4
♥ A 3
♦ Q 10 7 5 2
♣ 6 4

East:
♠ J 10 3
♥ 10 8 7 5
♦ J 9
♣ A 10 9 3

South:
♠ A 8 2
♥ K Q J 6
♦ A K 4
♣ 8 5 2

Declarer starts with three spade tricks and two diamond tricks. Four more tricks are needed to make 3NT. Neither the club suit nor the heart suit alone will provide all of the necessary tricks. Declarer must promote tricks in both suits by driving out the missing aces. This means declarer will have to give the opponents the lead twice.

The ♦ 5 is led to East's ♦ J. Since declarer has both the ♦ A and ♦ K, it may not seem necessary to hold up — but look what happens! Suppose declarer wins the first trick with the ♦ K and leads a club to dummy's ♣ J to drive out the ace. East wins with the ♣ A and leads back the ♦ 9. Declarer may try holding up the ♦ A, but it is too late.

West wins the trick and leads another diamond to drive out declarer's ace. Since declarer still doesn't have enough winners, declarer must lead a high heart to drive out the ace. West wins the ♥ A and takes the established diamonds to defeat the contract. Declarer loses three diamond tricks and two aces.

Let's see what happens if declarer doesn't win the first diamond trick, holding up the ace and the king. East wins and leads another diamond, which declarer wins with the ♦ K. Next, declarer leads a club and drives out East's ♣A. Now the effect of the hold-up play becomes apparent. East has no more diamonds and can't drive out declarer's remaining ♦A.

Suppose East leads a spade. Declarer wins and drives out West's ♥A. When West wins, another diamond can be played to drive out declarer's ♦A, but it's too late for the defense. Declarer has established the necessary number of tricks — declarer can take enough winners to make the contract.

When the Defenders Try to Take Away Declarer's Entries

It isn't only the declarer who can make use of the hold-up play. The defenders don't have to win the first round of a suit declarer is trying to establish, and a hold-up play by a defender can give declarer entry problems. We saw some examples of this in the previous chapter when declarer had to be careful to watch the entries.

Here is another deal:

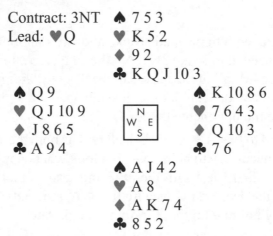

```
Contract: 3NT   ♠ 7 5 3
Lead: ♥Q        ♥ K 5 2
                ♦ 9 2
                ♣ K Q J 10 3
    ♠ Q 9                      ♠ K 10 8 6
    ♥ Q J 10 9      N          ♥ 7 6 4 3
    ♦ J 8 6 5    W     E       ♦ Q 10 3
    ♣ A 9 4         S          ♣ 7 6
                ♠ A J 4 2
                ♥ A 8
                ♦ A K 7 4
                ♣ 8 5 2
```

Declarer has one spade trick, two heart tricks and two diamond tricks. Declarer needs four more tricks. These can come from the club suit by driving out the opponents' ♣A. Declarer must be careful, however.

The opponents have led hearts, so declarer first needs to consider whether to use the hold-up play. Since the opponents will get the lead only once, with the ♣A, and declarer has two heart tricks, it isn't necessary to hold up.

Next declarer must decide in which hand to win the first trick. Because the defenders may hold up their ♣A, declarer must win the first trick with the ♥A, keeping the ♥K as an entry to dummy. Now it is a simple task to drive out the ♣A and end up with nine tricks.

If declarer doesn't watch out for the opponents, the result may be different. Suppose declarer wins the first trick with dummy's ♥K and leads the ♣K to drive out the ace. West, seeing that declarer is trying to develop club tricks, holds up the ♣A, refusing to take the first trick. When declarer continues with the ♣Q, West can hold up again. If declarer persists by leading another club, West must win the ace — but now there are no clubs left in declarer's hand and no entry to dummy. Dummy's club winners are stranded.

Declarer can't always prevent the opponents from successfully holding up in a suit. Sometimes, declarer must use a countermeasure. Consider this deal:

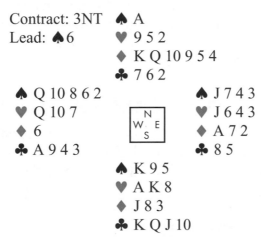

```
Contract: 3NT    ♠ A
Lead: ♠6         ♥ 9 5 2
                 ♦ K Q 10 9 5 4
                 ♣ 7 6 2

♠ Q 10 8 6 2              ♠ J 7 4 3
♥ Q 10 7        N        ♥ J 6 4 3
♦ 6          W     E      ♦ A 7 2
♣ A 9 4 3         S       ♣ 8 5

                 ♠ K 9 5
                 ♥ A K 8
                 ♦ J 8 3
                 ♣ K Q J 10
```

West leads the ♠6. You have no choice but to win the first trick with dummy's ♠A. Your only sure entry to dummy has been driven out at trick one. You have two sure spade tricks and two sure heart tricks. You must develop five more tricks. The diamond suit looks like it can provide the tricks you need once the ♦A is driven out.

After winning dummy's ♠A, suppose you lead a diamond to your jack (high card from the short side) and a diamond back to dummy's queen, trying to drive out the ace. East realizes what you are doing and refuses to take the ♦ A. Should you lead another diamond to drive out the ace?

Leading another diamond wouldn't do any good. You could establish dummy's remaining three diamonds but you have no entry to them. After winning the ♦ A, East would lead another spade, driving out your ♠ K. Now if you try to set up the club tricks, West would win and take enough spade tricks to defeat the contract.

Instead, you must abandon the diamond suit and switch your attention to clubs. You already have two diamond tricks, so all you need is three club tricks. After winning the second diamond trick, lead a club and drive out the opponents' ace. You'll end up with two spade tricks, two heart tricks, two diamond tricks and three club tricks — a total of nine.

East's hold-up play made you change your tactics. The diamond suit was no longer able to provide all of the extra tricks you needed. Fortunately, you had another option.

Sometimes, of course, you'll have no suitable countermeasure to the opponents' defense. In those cases, congratulate the opponents on their excellent defense and go on to the next deal. If you make every contract you bid, you're not bidding enough!

AVOIDING THE DANGEROUS OPPONENT

Sometimes, it's dangerous to let one particular opponent have the lead. In such cases, you want to avoid giving the lead to the *dangerous opponent*. If you must lose a trick, try to lose it to the non-dangerous opponent.

The Dangerous Opponent

How do you know which opponent is the dangerous one? Let's return to the layout of a suit we examined earlier:

```
              7 5
                  ┌─────┐
                  │  N  │
K Q J 10 9        │W   E│     8 3 2
                  │  S  │
                  └─────┘
              A 6 4
```

West leads the king against your notrump contract. You use the hold-up play, winning your ace on the third round.

The remaining cards are:

$$
\begin{array}{ccc}
 & \text{---} & \\
10\ 9 & \boxed{\begin{array}{c}\text{N}\\ \text{W}\quad\text{E}\\ \text{S}\end{array}} & \text{---} \\
 & \text{---} &
\end{array}
$$

West is clearly the dangerous opponent. If West gains the lead, West can take the two remaining winners. If East gains the lead, East doesn't have any cards left in the suit and isn't a threat.

Dangerous opponents don't crop up only in notrump contracts. Suppose an opponent's opening lead is a singleton against your suit contract. The opener hopes to ruff the suit the next time it's led. Until the trumps are drawn, *the opening leader's partner is the dangerous opponent.* That's the player who can lead back the suit led by the opening leader who can ruff it.

Here's another suit combination that creates a dangerous opponent in either a notrump contract or a suit contract:

$$
\begin{array}{ccc}
 & 7\ 5\ 2 & \\
\text{A}\ 9\ 8\ 3 & \boxed{\begin{array}{c}\text{N}\\ \text{W}\quad\text{E}\\ \text{S}\end{array}} & \text{Q}\ \text{J}\ 10 \\
 & \text{K}\ 6\ 4 &
\end{array}
$$

If declarer can't afford to lose several tricks in this suit, which opponent is dangerous? There wouldn't be any danger if East held the ace, since declarer would get a trick with the king whichever opponent led the suit. (Declarer could even lead the suit himself, taking a finesse by leading toward the king.) But in the actual layout, West holds the ace.

East is the dangerous opponent. If West gains the lead, West can take the ace but now declarer gets a trick with the king. If East gains the lead, however, East can lead the queen. Whether declarer plays the king on the first trick or a subsequent trick, declarer never gets a trick with that card — the opponents trap the king and take all of the tricks in the suit.

Here is a similar case. West leads the 5 against your notrump contract. You play dummy's 2 and East plays the jack:

7 2

A 10 8 5 3   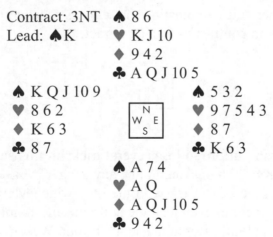   J 9 6

K Q 4

If you win with the queen (or the king), who is the dangerous opponent? It's East. After winning a trick, East can lead the suit and your remaining king is trapped. If West gains the lead, West can take the ace but you'll get a trick with the king.

Avoiding the Dangerous Opponent

Once you have identified the dangerous opponent, how do you avoid giving that player the lead? Sometimes it won't be possible; at other times, you can control your own destiny.

Consider the following deal:

Contract: 3NT   ♠ 8 6
Lead: ♠K   ♥ K J 10
                 ♦ 9 4 2
                 ♣ A Q J 10 5

♠ K Q J 10 9   ♠ 5 3 2
♥ 8 6 2   ♥ 9 7 5 4 3
♦ K 6 3   ♦ 8 7
♣ 8 7   ♣ K 6 3

                 ♠ A 7 4
                 ♥ A Q
                 ♦ A Q J 10 5
                 ♣ 9 4 2

West leads the ♠K. You have one spade trick, three hearts, one diamond and one club, for a total of six tricks. Either the club suit or the diamond suit will provide the extra tricks you need. In either suit, you can finesse for the missing king. If the finesse works, you'll take five tricks in the suit. If it loses, you'll still end up with four tricks, enough for your contract.

Which finesse should you take? West has led a spade. If the missing spades divide 5–3 or worse, the danger is that you will lose four or more tricks in the suit. Use the hold-up play and try to leave East without any spades. Duck the first two rounds and win the third round. Now West is the dangerous opponent if West holds two good spade winners.

Next try the club finesse. You don't mind if it loses to East's ♣K, since East isn't a threat. Without a spade to lead to West's winners, it doesn't matter if East gains the lead.

If East wins the ♣K and leads back a diamond, don't take the finesse. Win the ♦A and take your nine tricks. You don't want to lose a trick to West, the dangerous opponent, if you can avoid it.

Sometimes you have a choice of which way to finesse in a suit. This is called a *two-way finesse.* You want to proceed so that if a finesse loses, the dangerous opponent doesn't gain the lead. Here's an example:

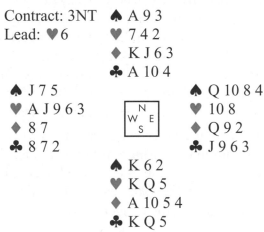

```
Contract: 3NT    ♠ A 9 3
Lead: ♥6         ♥ 7 4 2
                 ♦ K J 6 3
                 ♣ A 10 4
   ♠ J 7 5                    ♠ Q 10 8 4
   ♥ A J 9 6 3      N         ♥ 10 8
   ♦ 8 7         W     E      ♦ Q 9 2
   ♣ 8 7 2          S         ♣ J 9 6 3
                 ♠ K 6 2
                 ♥ K Q 5
                 ♦ A 10 5 4
                 ♣ K Q 5
```

You start with two spade tricks, two diamonds and three clubs. You'll get at least one trick from the heart suit since you hold both the king and queen. Where will your ninth trick come from if you are to make your 3NT contract?

In the diamond suit, you have all of the high cards except the queen. You can develop another trick in this suit simply by playing the ace and the king and then driving out the queen, or you can finesse for the missing queen. If you think West has the ♦ Q, win a trick with the ♦ A and lead a low diamond toward dummy, finessing the ♦ J if West plays a low card. If you think East has the ♦ Q, win a trick with dummy's ♦ K and lead a low diamond toward your hand, finessing the ♦ 10 if East plays low. Since you have a choice of finessing either West or East for the ♦ Q, this is called a two-way finesse.

Before deciding how to play the diamond suit, you need to think about the whole deal. West has led the ♥ 6, and when you play low from dummy, East plays the ♥ 10. When you win this trick with the ♥ Q, who is the dangerous opponent? In this case, it's East. When on lead, East can lead a heart, and your remaining ♥ K will be trapped. However, if West gains the lead, your ♥ K can't be trapped.

This piece of information tells you how to play the diamond suit. After winning the ♥ Q in your hand, lead a small diamond toward dummy's ♦ K. Next lead a low diamond from dummy and finesse with the ♦ 10 when East plays low. If the finesse works, you make the contract with an overtrick. If the finesse loses, you're still safe — West can't take more than one heart trick without giving you a trick with the ♥ K. If West leads anything else, you've established the extra diamond winner you need.

On the actual layout of the cards, you're rewarded with an overtrick by playing the diamond suit in this fashion. If you had finessed in the other direction, East would have won the ♦ Q and led back a heart, trapping your king. West would have taken four heart tricks to defeat the contract. It pays to know about avoiding the dangerous opponent!

Here is an example of watching out for the opponents in a suit contract:

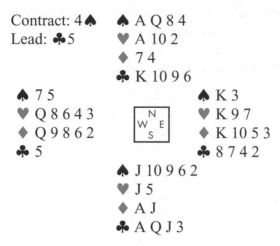

Contract: 4♠
Lead: ♣5

North:
♠ A Q 8 4
♥ A 10 2
♦ 7 4
♣ K 10 9 6

West:
♠ 7 5
♥ Q 8 6 4 3
♦ Q 9 8 6 2
♣ 5

East:
♠ K 3
♥ K 9 7
♦ K 10 5 3
♣ 8 7 4 2

South:
♠ J 10 9 6 2
♥ J 5
♦ A J
♣ A Q J 3

West, hoping to ruff some of your winners, leads a singleton club. When you look at your losers, you see one in spades, since you are missing the ♠K, one in hearts and one in diamonds. There doesn't appear to be a problem, but you must not get careless.

The spade suit offers an opportunity to finesse. You could win the first trick with a high club in your hand and lead the ♠J. If West plays a low spade, you could play low from dummy. If West has the ♠K, your finesse will work and you'll end up with an overtrick. If the finesse loses — well, you could afford to lose one spade anyway.

On this hand, however, when the spade finesse loses, East leads back a club. West ruffs your winner and down you go, losing two trumps instead of one — unfortunate but avoidable.

Since you can afford one trump loser but not two, you should avoid letting the dangerous opponent, East in this case, gain the lead until trumps are drawn. Instead of taking a finesse, play the ♠A and another spade to drive out the ♠K, drawing trumps as quickly as possible. When East wins with the king, all of the trumps are gone and the danger is past. If West started with the king, West would win a trick with it, but there would no longer be any danger of a club ruff. Safety first!

As we will see in the next chapter, you can't always draw all of the missing trumps right away because of other considerations. When you can afford to draw trumps, draw them as quickly as possible to avoid letting a dangerous opponent jeopardize the contract.

When Both Opponents Are Dangerous

On some deals, you can't afford to let either opponent win a trick since they are both dangerous. In such cases, you will have to look for a way of making the contract without giving up the lead.

Here is an example:

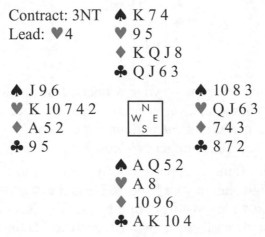

In 3NT, you have three spades, one heart and four clubs — eight tricks in all. It looks easy enough to develop extra tricks by driving out the ♦A, but you must watch out for those opponents! West has led a heart, and even if you hold up with the ♥A, you can do so for only one round. If you give up the lead, even if the missing hearts divide 5–4, the opponents will get four heart tricks to go along with the ♦A.

Is there an alternative to conceding the ♦A? The spade suit does provide some potential. You have seven spades and the opponents have six. If the missing spades divide 3–3, your remaining low spade will be a winner after you take the ♠A, the ♠K and the ♠Q. This goes against the odds, since you expect an even number of missing cards to divide slightly unevenly, 4–2, and they could divide 5–1 or 6–0. However, when it is your only legitimate chance, go for it!

In such a situation, it does no harm to take your four club winners first. This gives you the added chance that an unsuspecting opponent who started with four spades may discard a spade when declarer plays the third and/or fourth round of clubs. Even though the spade suit started out breaking 4–2, it might suddenly become 3–2. It's not always easy for the defenders to know which cards to keep when declarer is taking tricks in a long suit.

GUIDELINES FOR DEFENSE

During the play, the defenders will have many decisions to make. Should they win this trick or hold up? If they win the trick, what should they do next? Many of declarer's techniques are just as useful to the defenders: the hold-up play, ducking to keep an entry and leading toward the high card. The difficulty comes from recognizing when they apply, since the defenders can't see each other's hands. Here are a couple of techniques we have discussed presented from the defenders' point of view.

Defensive Hold-up Play

The hold-up play is not solely the prerogative of declarer. The defenders can also put it to good use.

Consider the following layout of a suit in a notrump contract:

Q J 10 8 7 5

2     $\begin{array}{c} \text{N} \\ \text{W} \quad \text{E} \\ \text{S} \end{array}$ A 9 3

K 6 4

If you hold the ace of this suit, and dummy has no entries outside of the suit, choosing when to win your ace is very important. Suppose declarer starts by leading the king (high card from the short side), trying to drive out the ace and establish the remaining cards in dummy. If you take the ace, declarer will still have two low cards left to use as entries to dummy's winners.

Use the hold-up play instead and refuse to win the first trick. If declarer leads the suit again, hold up again. How do you know declarer still has a low card left without peeking? Partner will have to discard. You can see all of the cards in dummy and your own hand, and each suit has 13 cards, so declarer must still have one left. If declarer leads the suit again, you must win the ace. Your hold-up play has done its job. Declarer has no low cards left in hand, and dummy's winners are stranded. Declarer gets only two tricks rather than five.

The principle is the same as when declarer holds up. Declarer hopes a defender won't have any cards left in the suit when that defender gains the lead. Just as declarer can't see the exact division of the cards in the defenders' hands, you can't see how many cards declarer has in the suit. However, you will often be able to tell, as in the above example.

Suppose we change the layout of the suit slightly:

Q J 10 8 7 5

6 2   N W E S   A 9 3

K 4

Again, declarer leads the king and you hold up. This time, when declarer leads the suit again, your partner follows suit. Since you can see all 13 cards in the suit, it's safe to win the ace on the second round. Declarer gets only one trick, and four winners are stranded in the dummy.

Let's take a look at the defensive hold-up play in action:

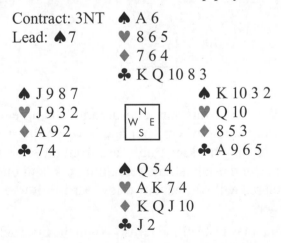

Contract: 3NT   ♠ A 6
Lead: ♠7   ♥ 8 6 5
           ♦ 7 6 4
           ♣ K Q 10 8 3

♠ J 9 8 7   ♠ K 10 3 2
♥ J 9 3 2   N   ♥ Q 10
♦ A 9 2   W   E   ♦ 8 5 3
♣ 7 4   S   ♣ A 9 6 5

        ♠ Q 5 4
        ♥ A K 7 4
        ♦ K Q J 10
        ♣ J 2

Your partner leads the ♠7.The ♠6 is played from dummy and you win with the ♠K. Being a good partner, you return partner's lead — declarer wins with dummy's ♠A. Declarer now leads a low club to the ♣J. You play low, holding up your ace. Declarer leads another club to dummy's ♣K. What do you do?

With five clubs originally in dummy and four in your hand, only four clubs are missing. You've seen two in declarer's hand and two from your partner. Win the ♣A since declarer doesn't have any clubs left. Three club winners are left in dummy, but they are stranded. Now you can lead another spade, driving out declarer's queen — eventually, declarer goes down to defeat. Declarer gets two spade tricks, two heart tricks and three diamond tricks (by driving out partner's ace), but only one club trick.

Had you won the first club trick, declarer would have ended up with four club tricks. Had you held up with your ♣A until the third round, declarer would have gotten two club tricks. In either case, declarer would have made the contract. Well defended!

Ducking to Keep an Entry

In an earlier chapter, we saw how declarer can preserve an entry within a suit by using the idea of taking losses early and giving up a trick. The defenders can also use this technique.

Look at the following layout:

```
          Q J 8
               ┌─────┐
               │  N  │
A 9 7 3 2      │W   E│      K 6 4
               │  S  │
               └─────┘
          10 5
```

You lead the 3 against a notrump contract, and your partner wins the first trick with the king. Partner then leads the suit back. Do you win the second trick with the ace?

If you have an entry in another suit, it's all right to win the ace and lead the suit again, establishing your remaining cards as winners. If partner subsequently gets the lead, partner can lead the suit in which you have an entry, and you can take your winners.

But what if you don't have an entry in another suit? If you win the ace and lead the suit again, you set up two winners but they are stranded. If partner gains the lead, partner won't have any low cards in this suit to lead. Instead, duck the second trick, keeping the ace as an entry. Declarer is entitled to one trick anyway. If your partner subsequently gains the lead, partner can lead the remaining low card back to your ace, and you can take your other two winners.

Again, this is identical to the way declarer would handle this suit if declarer had to watch out for entries.

Let's see how the defenders make use of this technique in an actual deal:

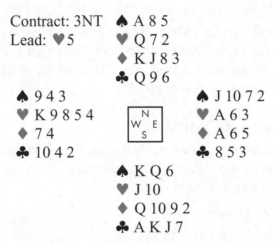

Contract: 3NT ♠ A 8 5
Lead: ♥ 5 ♥ Q 7 2
       ♦ K J 8 3
       ♣ Q 9 6

♠ 9 4 3   ♠ J 10 7 2
♥ K 9 8 5 4   ♥ A 6 3
♦ 7 4   ♦ A 6 5
♣ 10 4 2   ♣ 8 5 3

       ♠ K Q 6
       ♥ J 10
       ♦ Q 10 9 2
       ♣ A K J 7

You lead the ♥ 5. Your partner wins the first trick with the ♥ A and leads back a heart. Do you win the trick with the ♥ K?

Since you don't have another entry to your heart winners and can see declarer will always win one heart trick, duck this trick. Declarer has three spade tricks and four club tricks to go along with the heart trick. Sooner or later, declarer will have to lead a diamond to try to establish a ninth trick. Your partner can win with the ♦ A and lead back a heart. You'll win with the ♥ K and take your remaining two heart winners to defeat the contract.

BIDDING – STRONG OPENING BIDS

Opening suit bids at the one level are used with hands in the range of 13 to 21 points. Responder passes with fewer than 6 points, since it is unlikely that there is enough combined strength for a game contract. With a very strong hand of 22 or more points, opener wants responder to bid, even with fewer than 6 points. In this chapter, we will look at how opener and responder handle such hands.

Strong hands are designated by two different opening bids:

1. A 3NT opening bid promises between 25 and 27 HCP and a balanced hand.

2. A 2♣ opening bid is used for all other hands with 22 or more total points.

The first rule is very logical. We have learned that 25 HCP are usually sufficient to make 3NT (or 4♠ or 4♥). By opening 3NT you are telling partner that you have enough points in your own hand for game.

The second rule does not relate to anything you have learned so far. The 2♣ opening bid is an example of an artificial forcing bid. The artificial part means that the bid says nothing about the club suit. The forcing part means that partner cannot pass. The 2♣ opening bid is used for all hands with 22 or more points that cannot be opened with 3NT.

BALANCED HANDS

We have just learned to open 3NT with 25-27 HCP and a balanced hand. Let's look at what we knew before and how this new bid will fit into a complete balanced hand bidding system.

- With a balanced 13-14 HCP, open 1 of a suit and make a non-jump rebid in notrump.

- With a balanced 15-17 HCP, open 1NT.

- With a balanced 18-19 HCP, open 1 of a suit and make a jump rebid in notrump.

With hands greater than 19 HCP, you will use the following structure.

- With a balanced 20-21 HCP, open 2NT.
- With a balanced 22-24 HCP, open 2♣ and make a non-jump rebid in notrump (2NT).
- With a balanced 25-27 HCP, open 3NT.

As you can see, the solution to showing balanced hands in the 22-24 HCP range is to start by opening 2♣. The bid of 2♣ indicates a strong hand of 22 or more points that is unsuitable for a 3NT opening bid. We will learn more about 2♣ in the following section. It's possible that you may have a balanced hand containing more than 27 HCP. To see the complete notrump structure and learn more about opening notrump at higher levels read *The Finer Points* at the end of the bonus chapter on *Jacoby Transfers*.

Here are some balanced hand examples:

♠ K Q 8 3   With a balanced hand and 20 HCPs, open 2NT.
♥ A Q 3
♦ K Q 8 4
♣ A 10

♠ A Q J   You have 26 HCPs with a balanced hand. Open
♥ K Q   3NT to show a balanced hand in the 25 to 27 HCP
♦ A K J 8 2   range.
♣ K Q J

♠ A K J   You have 22 HCPs and a balanced hand. Begin
♥ A 10 9   with 2♣. Your rebid will be 2NT.
♦ K J 8 7
♣ K Q J

♠ K J 8   Although this is a balanced hand, you have only 19
♥ A Q J   HCPs. While this hand is too strong to open 1NT, it's
♦ K 10 9 7   too weak to open 2NT. Instead, open 1♦. You intend
♣ K Q 10   to jump in notrump at your next opportunity to show
             a balanced hand in the 18-19 HCP range.

Responding to a 2NT Opening Bid

If your partner opens 2NT (20-21 HCP), you are the captain and responsible for determining the level and strain in which the partnership belongs. Use the following guidelines. Remember you need much less in your own hand to go to game since partner has 20 or 21 HCPs.

- Pass with less than 4 points and no five-card major.
- Use Stayman to uncover a four-card major-suit fit with a game-going hand.
- Bid 3 ♥ or 3 ♠ with less than a game-going hand and a five-card suit (signoff).
- Bid 3NT with more than four points and no four-card major.
- Bid 4♥ or 4♠ with a six-card suit and a game-going hand.

When partner opens a hand with 2NT, you can still use Stayman. Look at this auction.

Partner	You
2NT	3♣ (Stayman)
3♥	3NT
4♠	Pass

Partner is showing a hand with 20-21 HCP that contains both a four-card heart suit and a four-card spade suit. You have shown enough points to go to game along with a four-card major by bidding Stayman.

Unbalanced Hands

A 2♣ opening bid is used for all hands with 22 or more total points that are unsuitable for a 3NT opening bid (a balanced hand with 25-27 HCP).

Suppose, for example, you are dealt this amazing hand:

♠ A K Q J 10 8 4   This hand contains 24 total points (21 HCP and 3
♥ A K   distribution points for the extra spades). According
♦ 5   to the above rule, the correct opening bid with this
♣ A 7 4   hand is 2♣.

Is this really true? What if your partner passes? This hand has game all by itself without any help from partner. As we mentioned before, the 2♣ opening bid is an example of an artificial forcing bid. The artificial part means that the bid says nothing about clubs. The forcing part means that partner cannot pass.

You may be wondering why we are going to open almost all of our strong hands with 2♣. It wasn't always this way. In Charles Goren's original Standard American system, 2♣, 2♦, 2♥ and 2♠ opening bids were all used to describe very strong hands. These were all natural bids. This approach became known as Strong Two Bids.

Over the years, it became apparent that it was quite rare to be dealt a hand strong enough to qualify for a strong two-bid. The idea of opening 2♣ on all such hands was born. This approach frees up other two-level opening bids to describe other types of hands (more on this in Chapter 8). The concept of using 2♣ as the only strong two-level opening bid worked so well in practice that today it is more or less the standard among bridge players in North America.

Responding to a 2♣ Opening Bid

2♣ is perhaps the easiest of all opening bids to respond to. Despite this fact, there are many conventional variations for responses available to partnerships. You can read about some other alternatives in *The Finer Points* at the end of this chapter.

- When partner opens 2♣ and you have less than 8 total points, always respond 2♦. This 2♦ bid is an artificial negative that denies the ability to make a positive response. The nice thing about the negative 2♦ response to a 2♣ opening is that it sends the opener an immediate warning that responder is quite weak. Opener knows at once to proceed with caution.

- The 2♥, 2♠, 3♣ and 3♦ responses are positive responses. These bids show a good five-card (or longer) suit with two of the top three honors. (With strong spot cards and/or extra length beyond the five cards, it is okay to relax this restriction.) Note that the 3♦ positive is a jump bid since we use 2♦ as an artificial negative.

- With enough total points to make a positive response, but without a long enough or strong enough suit for a 2♥, 2♠, 3♣ or 3♦ response, make the positive response of 2NT.

A positive response sends an immediate slam suggestion to the 2♣ opener. The opener can then focus on making sure the values for a small slam exist, finding the best strain and possibly exploring for a grand slam.

Here are some examples of responses when opener bids 2♣.

♠ 6 5 4
♥ 5 4 3
♦ 7
♣ 9 8 5 4 3 2

Respond 2♦. Do not even think about passing. There might be game in partner's hand. Don't worry about having only one diamond – remember, your bid says nothing about your diamond holding.

♠ 4 3 2
♥ A Q J 4 3
♦ 5 4 3
♣ 7 5

Respond 2♥. This bid is natural showing a positive response in hearts.

♠ K 5 4 2
♥ K 9 8 7
♦ 8 4 3
♣ 5 2

Although this is a nice hand, it doesn't have the required 8 points for a positive response. So, you would respond 2♦. If opener rebids 2NT, showing a hand with 22-24 HCPs, you can use Stayman to discover whether there is an eight-card heart or spade fit. If there isn't, 3NT will be a great contract.

OPENER'S REBIDS

After opener bids 2♣ and hears partner's response, opener will either bid some level of notrump or the best suit in the hand.

Opener	Partner
2♣	2♦
2NT	

Opener's 2NT rebid shows 22-24 HCP with a balanced hand.

Opener	Partner
2♣	2♦
2♥	

Opener's 2♥ rebid shows an unbalanced hand with 22 or more total points.

The bidding will continue based upon the strength of the combined hands. While game is reached almost all of the time, on occasion the bidding may stop below the game level. In addition, slams also can be bid. We will learn more about slam bidding in the next chapter.

SUMMARY

When going through the fourth step of the PLAN, *Now put it all together,* you often must watch out for the opponents. If you have to give up the lead, you don't want the opponents to be in a position to take enough tricks to defeat your contract.

One such technique is the **hold-up play.** If the opponents lead a suit in which you have only one winner, you may not have to play it at the first opportunity. By holding up (delaying taking your winners), you may get the opponents into the position where one of them has no more cards in the suit. If that opponent subsequently gains the lead, there will be no low cards left to lead back to partner's winners.

Sometimes it is advantageous to hold up even with two winners in the suit. Don't hold up your winners any longer than necessary, however, and be careful to check and see that you can afford to hold up at all. The opponents may be able to do even more damage in another suit.

If you have to give up the lead, it's often dangerous to give up the lead to one opponent rather than the other. One opponent may have winners to take or be able to lead a suit, trapping one of your high cards. In such cases, you want to avoid the **dangerous opponent.** If you must lose a trick, try to arrange your play so that you lose the trick to the non-dangerous opponent.

When defending, you can make use of the same techniques declarer employs. A defender can use a hold-up play to make it difficult or impossible for declarer to take all of the winners in a suit. The defenders can also duck a trick, letting declarer win it, if ducking will maintain entries between their two hands.

Strong hands are shown as follows:

    2NT   Balanced hand with 20-21 HCP.

    3NT   Balanced hand with 25-27 HCP.

    2♣   22 or more total points with an unbalanced hand or A balanced hand with 22-24 HCP.

2♣ is an artificial, forcing bid. With 0 to 7 total points, responder bids 2♦, an artificial negative. Any other bid by responder is a positive response.

THE FINER POINTS

Responses to a 2♣ Opener

In this chapter, we looked at one way for responder to show the 2♣ opener what type of hand responder holds. Here are a couple of other popular options that you and your partner could choose to play:

- One of the most common treatments revolves around the use of 2♦ as a *waiting bid*. If you cannot made a positive response of 2♠, 2♥, 3♣ or 3♦, you would make the conventional response of 2♦, essentially *waiting* for partner to describe the hand. This bid includes all hands with fewer than 8 points as well as those with 8 or more that are unsuitable for a positive response. This bid is not forcing to game.

- Another treatment is designed to show the 2♣ opener how many controls responder holds. Each king equals one control and each ace equals two controls. Here are the responses to the opening 2♣ bid:

  2♦ — 0 controls
  2♥ — 1 control (one king)
  2♠ — 2 controls (one ace or two kings)
  2NT — 3 controls (three kings, specifically)
  3♣ — 3 controls (exactly one ace and one king)
  3♦ — 4 controls (two aces or one ace and two kings or four kings)
  3♥ — 5 controls (two aces and one king or one ace and three kings)

- The *2♥ super negative response* is another option. Here are the responses:

    2♦ — Waiting response, artificial, says nothing about diamonds, semi-positive in that responder promises at least a king.

    2♥ — Super negative response, artificial, says nothing about hearts, denies holding any ace or king.

    2♠ — Positive response, natural, five-card suit or longer headed by at least two of the top three honors.

    3♣/♦/♥ — Positive response, natural, six-card suit or longer headed by at least two top honors.

Exercise One — Holding Up

Your left-hand opponent leads the following suit against your notrump contract. If you don't take your ace until you have to, how many cards will your right-hand opponent have left in the suit if it divides as you expect?

DUMMY:	1) 8 6	2) 7 4 3	3) 7 6 4 2
DECLARER:	A 9 2	A 6 5	A 3

———————   ———————   ———————

DUMMY:	4) 9 7 4	5) 10 7
DECLARER:	A 8	A 6

———————   ———————

Exercise Two — How Long to Hold Up

The hold-up play is such an exciting concept that it's tempting to use it whenever you get the chance. West leads the ♥K against your 3NT contract. Should you hold up? State the reason for your answer.

Contract: 3NT   ♠ 8 6 2
Lead: ♥K   ♥ 7 4
                 ♦ K 9 7 3
                 ♣ A Q J 5

♥K
```
        N
      W   E
        S
```

♠ Q 3
♥ A 6 5
♦ A Q J 10
♣ K 9 4 2

Exercise One *Answers* — Holding Up

1) The opponents have eight cards, which you expect to divide 5–3. If you take your ace on the third round, your right-hand opponent shouldn't have any left.

2) The opponents have seven cards, which you expect to divide 4–3. If you take your ace on the third round, the opponent on your right shouldn't have any left.

3) The opponents have seven cards. When you take the ace on the second round, your right-hand opponent will still have one card left.

4) The opponents have eight cards, which you expect to divide 5–3. When you take the ace on the second round, your right-hand opponent will still have one card left.

5) The opponents have nine cards, which you expect to divide 5–4. When you take your ace on the second round, your right-hand opponent will still have two cards left.

Exercise Two *Answers* — How Long to Hold Up

You need nine tricks to make the contract and have nine, so there is no advantage to holding up your ace. Indeed, there may be a disadvantage — the opponents could shift to spades and defeat your contract.

Exercise Three — The Dangerous Opponent

Who is the dangerous opponent in each of the examples in Exercise One? If you can't afford to lose three tricks in the following suits, which opponent is the dangerous one?

DUMMY:	1) K 8 4	2) 5 4 2
DECLARER:	7 5 2	K 7 3

_____   _____

Exercise Four — Avoiding the Dangerous Opponent

The opponent on your right is the dangerous opponent. How would you play each of the following suits to avoid giving up the lead to the dangerous opponent whenever possible?

DUMMY:	1) A J 10 5	2) 10 7 5 3	3) J 10 3
DECLARER:	K 9 8 3	A Q J 8	A K 8 7 2

_____   _____   _____

DUMMY:	4) A 9 7 5 2	5) A Q J 8 3
DECLARER:	K J 3	10 7 6 4

_____   _____

Exercise Three *Answers* — The Dangerous Opponent

In each example in Exercise One, the dangerous opponent is the one on your left, who has led the suit and presumably has the greatest length. However, when you can't hold up enough times to exhaust your right-hand opponent of cards, then both opponents become dangerous.

1) The opponent on declarer's left is dangerous because that opponent might lead a high card to trap dummy's king.

2) The opponent on delcarer's right is dangerous because that opponent might lead a high card to trap declarer's king.

Exercise Four *Answers* — Avoiding the Dangerous Opponent

1) Play the ace and then lead the jack (or the 10). If the opponent on your right plays the queen, play the king and you win all of the tricks; otherwise, take the finesse. You don't mind if it loses to the opponent on your left.

2) Lead the 10 from dummy. If it is covered with the king, play the ace; otherwise, play low. You don't mind losing a trick to the opponent on your left, who is not dangerous.

3) Lead the jack from dummy and take the finesse if your right-hand opponent doesn't play the queen. You don't mind if your left-hand opponent wins a trick with the queen.

4) Lead low from dummy toward your hand and finesse the jack. You don't mind losing a trick to the queen on your left. If the suit divides 3–2, you take the rest of the tricks without letting the dangerous opponent win a trick.

5) If you try the finesse and it doesn't work, the dangerous opponent gains the lead. Play the ace in case your right-hand opponent has the singleton king. You don't mind if your left-hand opponent eventually wins a trick with the king, but you want to prevent your right-hand opponent from winning a trick whenever possible.

Exercise Five — Defensive Hold-up

If dummy has no outside entries, when should you win your ace in each of the following examples if your partner has one card in the suit? What if your partner has two cards in the suit?

1)   DUMMY
       K Q J 10 9
       ■   YOU
             A 7 5 2

2)   DUMMY
       K Q J 10 9 8
       ■   YOU
             A 6 2

Exercise Six — Strong Opening Bids

What would your opening bid be with each of the following hands?

1) ♠ K J 10
   ♥ A K J
   ♦ K Q J 9 4
   ♣ A J

2) ♠ A K
   ♥ A Q J 8
   ♦ K Q J
   ♣ A Q 10 5

3) ♠ A K J 10 9 7
   ♥ A
   ♦ K Q J 7
   ♣ K J

Bid: _____   Bid:_____   Bid: _____

Exercise Five *Answers* — Defensive Hold-up

1) You can see nine cards. If partner has only one (partner will discard on the second round), you know declarer has three. You should wait until the third round to take your ace, leaving declarer with no low cards. If partner has two cards (following suit both times), you can win the second trick with the ace since declarer won't have any low cards left.

2) You can see nine cards. If partner discards on the second round, you must hold up your ace until the third round since declarer started with three cards. If partner follows suit on the second round, you can safely win the trick on the second round since declarer won't have any low cards left.

Exercise Six *Answers* — Strong Opening Bids

1) 2♣ followed by 2NT

2) 3NT

3) 2♣ followed by 2♠

Exercise Seven — Responding to 2NT

Your partner opens the bidding 2NT. What do you respond with each of the following hands?

1) ♠ J 7 3
   ♥ Q 9 8 6 4 3
   ♦ 5
   ♣ Q 9 3

   Response: _____

2) ♠ J 10 8 6 2
   ♥ 7 3
   ♦ J 6 5
   ♣ 9 7 6

   Response: _____

3) ♠ 10 5
   ♥ K J 8 3
   ♦ Q 8 4 2
   ♣ 10 7 3

   Response: _____

4) ♠ J 9 5
   ♥ 8 4 2
   ♦ 10 7 6
   ♣ K J 8 5

   Response: _____

5) ♠ 10 4 2
   ♥ 10 7 3
   ♦ 9 8 5
   ♣ 10 6 5 2

   Response: _____

6) ♠ J 5
   ♥ 6 4
   ♦ 10 5 3
   ♣ Q J 8 6 4 2

   Response: _____

Exercise Eight — Responding to a 2♣ Opening Bid

Your partner opens 2♣, a strong bid. What do you respond with each of the following hands?

1) ♠ 7 3
   ♥ J 9 7 6 3
   ♦ 10 8 4
   ♣ 7 5 2

   Response: _____

2) ♠ K Q 6 3 2
   ♥ 10 9 7
   ♦ 8 5
   ♣ K 9 3

   Response: _____

3) ♠ 6 4
   ♥ 3 2
   ♦ K Q 10 6 4
   ♣ K 9 8 4

   Response: _____

Exercise Seven *Answers* — Responding to 2NT

    1) 4♥   2) 3♠   3) 3♣, Stayman

    4) 3NT   5) Pass   6) 3NT

Exercise Eight *Answers* — Responding to a 2♣ Opening Bid

    1) 2♦   2) 2♠   3) 3♦

Exercise Nine — The Hold-up Play

(E–Z Deal Cards: #6. Deal 1 — Dealer, North)

Turn up all of the cards on the first pre-dealt deal. Put each hand dummy-style at the edge of the table in front of each player.

The Bidding

North and East pass. With a balanced hand and 22 HCP, what is South's opening bid?

West passes. North has 5 points. Does the partnership belong in game or in a partscore? What does North respond?

How would the auction proceed? What will the contract be? Who will be the declarer?

```
Dealer:        ♠ 8 5 3
North          ♥ 7 4
               ♦ K 9 6 2
               ♣ Q 7 5 2
♠ 7 4                        ♠ A 10 9 6
♥ K Q J 10 8    N            ♥ 6 5 2
♦ Q 7 4       W   E          ♦ J 10 5 3
♣ 6 4 3         S            ♣ 10 9
               ♠ K Q J 2
               ♥ A 9 3
               ♦ A 8
               ♣ A K J 8
```

The Play

Which player makes the opening lead? What will the opening lead be?

Declarer starts by making a PLAN:
1. **P**ause to consider your objective
2. **L**ook at your winners and losers
3. **A**nalyze your alternatives
4. **N**ow put it all together

How many tricks does declarer need? How many winners does declarer have? How can declarer develop the extra winners needed? Is there any danger? What can declarer do to minimize the danger?

Exercise Nine *Answers* — The Hold-up Play

The Bidding

- South, holding a balanced hand and lots of points, would like to open notrump. With 22 HCP, however, South first must open 2♣ and then rebid notrump to show this point-count.

- The partnership belongs in game. North responds 2♦.

- South rebids 2NT. Since North isn't interested in a major-suit fit, North bids 3NT. The final contract is 3NT. South is the declarer.

The Play

- West leads the ♥K.

- Declarer needs nine tricks and has seven. Declarer can get the extra tricks needed in the spade suit. The danger is that when the opponents gain the lead, they may take enough heart tricks to defeat the contract.

- South holds up the ♥A until the third round. Now East has no hearts left, and West's heart winners are stranded when East gains the lead.

Exercise Ten — Holding up with a King

(E–Z Deal Cards: #6. Deal 2 — Dealer, East)

Turn up all of the cards on the second pre-dealt deal and arrange them as in the previous deal.

The Bidding

With an unbalanced hand of 23 points, what is East's opening bid?

South passes. West has 5 points. Can West pass? How does West show a weak hand?

North passes. How does East describe the hand?

South passes. Can West pass? With no known Golden Fit, what looks like the best contract? What does West bid?

```
Dealer:        ♠ 4 2
East           ♥ Q 9 7 4 3
               ♦ 8 7 4 2
               ♣ K 8
♠ 6 5                      ♠ A K Q J 3
♥ K 10 5        N          ♥ J 2
♦ 10 6 5      W   E        ♦ A Q J 9
♣ J 10 9 4 2    S          ♣ A 5
               ♠ 10 9 8 7
               ♥ A 8 6
               ♦ K 3
               ♣ Q 7 6 3
```

North passes. Does East have any reason to disagree with West's decision? What will the contract be? Who will be the declarer?

The Play

Which player makes the opening lead? What will the opening lead be? Which card will the leader's partner play to the first trick? To the second trick?

Declarer starts by making a PLAN. Which suit offers the best potential for developing extra tricks? How does declarer plan to play the suit? Is there any danger? How can declarer minimize the danger?

Exercise Ten *Answers* — Holding up with a King

The Bidding

- East opens 2♣.

- West can't pass and shows a weak hand by responding 2♦.

- East describes the hand by bidding 3♠.

- West can't pass. Without a known Golden Fit, the best game contract looks like notrump. West bids 2NT to see what East will do.

- East is happy with notrump and bids 3NT.

- The contract is 3NT. West is the declarer.

The Play

- North makes the opening lead of the ♥4. South plays third hand high, the ♥A, and leads back a heart, returning partner's suit.

- Declarer can seek extra tricks in the diamond suit by finessing for the ♦K. If South wins a trick with the ♦K and still has a heart left to lead back to North, the opponents will take enough tricks to defeat the contract. When the heart is returned, therefore, declarer should hold up the ♥K for one round. South won't have any hearts left if South wins a trick with the ♦K.

Exercise Eleven — Defensive Hold-up

(E–Z Deal Cards: #6. Deal 3 — Dealer, South)

Turn up all of the cards on the third pre-dealt deal and arrange them as in the previous deal.

The Bidding

South and West pass. With a balanced hand and 26 HCP, what is North's opening bid?

East passes. What does South do? What will the contract be? Who will be the declarer?

```
Dealer:        ♠ A K Q
  South        ♥ A K 8 3
               ♦ K J 5
               ♣ K Q J
♠ 5 2                        ♠ J 10 9 7 4
♥ J 10 9 5      N            ♥ Q 6 2
♦ A 8 6 2    W     E         ♦ 9
♣ 10 9 4        S            ♣ A 7 6 2
               ♠ 8 6 3
               ♥ 7 4
               ♦ Q 10 7 4 3
               ♣ 8 5 3
```

The Play

Which player makes the opening lead? What will the opening lead be?

Declarer starts by making a PLAN. Which suit can provide the extra tricks declarer needs to make the contract? How does declarer plan to play the suit? What can West do to make things difficult for declarer? What can declarer do to counter West's effort?

Exercise Eleven *Answers* — Defensive Hold-up

The Bidding

- North opens 3NT.
- South passes. The contract is 3NT. North is the declarer.

The Play

- The opening lead by East is the ♠J.
- The diamonds could provide all of the tricks declarer needs. Declarer plays the ♦K and the ♦J, but West can make things difficult by holding up the ♦A.
- There isn't any point in continuing diamonds — any established diamond winners would be stranded. Instead, declarer shifts to the club suit and establishes the remaining two tricks needed by driving out the ♣A.

Exercise Twelve — Creating an Entry

(E–Z Deal Cards: #6. Deal 4 — Dealer, West)

Turn up all of the cards on the fourth pre-dealt deal and arrange them as in the previous deal.

The Bidding

With a balanced hand and 22 HCP, what is West's opening bid?

North passes. What does East bid? What does West rebid? What does East know after hearing West's rebid? What does East respond?

How does the auction proceed? What will the contract be? Who will be the declarer?

```
Dealer:        ♠ K 8 4
  West         ♥ 9
               ♦ J 10 9 7 5
               ♣ Q J 10 2
♠ A Q 5                      ♠ 7 2
♥ A K 7         N            ♥ Q 10 8 6 4 2
♦ A K Q 6     W   E          ♦ 8 4
♣ 9 8 4         S            ♣ K 7 3
               ♠ J 10 9 6 3
               ♥ J 5 3
               ♦ 3 2
               ♣ A 6 5
```

The Play

Which player makes the opening lead? What will the opening lead be?

Declarer starts by making a PLAN. How many losers can declarer afford? How many losers does declarer have? What are declarer's alternatives for eliminating a loser?

Is there a dangerous opponent? Should declarer take the spade finesse? If not, why not? How should declarer play the suit?

Exercise Twelve *Answers* — Creating an Entry

The Bidding

- West opens 2♣.
- East bids 2♦, an artificial negative.
- West continues with 2NT.
- East now knows there is a golden fit in hearts. East rebids 4♥.
- Pass, pass, pass. The contract is 4♥. East is the declarer.

The Play

- The opening lead by South is the ♠J.
- Declarer has four losers and can afford only three. Declarer could take the spade finesse, discard a loser on the diamonds or lead toward the ♣K.
- This looks like an opportunity to take a spade finesse, but declarer must beware. If the finesse loses, North, the dangerous opponent, can lead the ♣Q to trap the ♣K, and declarer will lose four tricks. Declarer should win with the ♠A, draw trumps and discard a club loser on the extra diamond winner in dummy.

CHAPTER 7
Managing the Trump Suit

If you are playing in a suit contract, managing the trump suit is an important task. After all, the lowest trump card can have more value than an ace in another suit. You can also use the trump suit to help control the opponents' long suits and to establish your suits. Although the general guideline is to draw the opponents' trumps at the first opportunity, it is often best to delay drawing trumps altogether — or to draw some trumps, play another suit and then go back to drawing trumps.

Before deciding whether or not to draw trumps, you must consult your PLAN. Determine how many losers you can afford and how many you have. You need to know whether your losers are quick or slow. The trump suit is so important that managing it skillfully is a key to improving your game.

DRAWING TRUMPS

Generally, it's a good idea for declarer to draw trumps as soon as possible. Any outstanding trumps in the opponents' hands have the potential of defeating a contract if they can be used to ruff your winners. Let's start by looking at how to handle the trump suit itself.

Playing the Trump Suit

In many respects, the trump suit is like any other suit. Winners can be developed through promotion, length or the finesse. Since your side has named the trump suit, you probably have more cards in the suit than the opponents. You have a comfortable advantage when you hold eight or more trumps — the opponents have five or fewer. Depending on how the trump suit is distributed between your hand and dummy and which high cards are missing, drawing trumps can be handled in a variety of ways.

DUMMY: A J 8 3   When you have nine trumps, the opponents
DECLARER: K Q 7 4 2   have only four. With the four highest cards in the suit, you can draw trumps without losing a trick, even if the missing trumps divide 4–0.

Most of the time, you won't need to play four rounds of the suit to draw all of the missing trumps. If the missing trumps divide 3–1, you'll need to play only three rounds. If they divide 2–2, you'll need to play only two rounds.

DUMMY: Q 10 7 4

DECLARER: K J 8 5 3

You're missing the ace, but you can use one of your high cards to drive it out, promoting the rest of your trumps into winners. When you regain the lead, draw the remainder of the opponents' trumps.

When drawing trumps, you must often give up the lead. Generally, you should not be afraid to let the opponents have the lead when it is necessary to draw trumps. We'll see, however, that at times you can't afford to give up the lead too early. Your PLAN will tell you whether you must do other work first.

DUMMY: 7 6 4

DECLARER: A 8 5 3 2

Develop the trump suit through length. The opponents have five trumps. If they divide 3–2, you must give up two tricks to draw all of the trumps. If they divide 4–1, you will end up losing three tricks. If they are 5–0, you will have four losers. Fortunately, suits are rarely distributed 5–0.

DUMMY: 10 9 7 3

DECLARER: A Q J 8 5

You are missing the king. If you can afford a loser in the trump suit, you could play the ace and then drive out the king, losing only one trick (unless the king is singleton).

If you can't afford a loser, you must hope the king is on your right and can be trapped using a finesse. Cross to dummy with an entry in another suit and lead the 10. If a low card appears on your right, take a finesse by playing low from your hand. If the 10 wins the trick, you're still in dummy and can repeat the finesse.

When drawing trumps, you don't want to play more rounds of the suit than necessary. There are 13 trumps. If you have eight, the opponents have five. The easiest way to keep track of the missing trumps is to deduct the number of opponents' trumps that appear each time you play the suit so you will know how many are still outstanding. After a little practice, this will become second nature to you.

When to Draw Trumps

To decide whether or not to draw trumps, consult your PLAN. One of the times to draw trumps right away is when you don't have any more losers than you can afford — you don't have to ruff or discard any losers. Usually, the only thing that can go wrong is that the opponents may ruff one of your winners. This is why you want to draw trumps as soon as possible, even if you must give up the lead.

Look at this example:

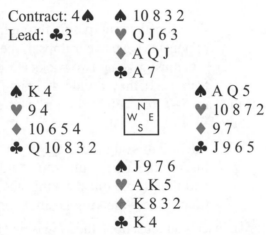

Contract: 4♠
Lead: ♣3

♠ 10 8 3 2
♥ Q J 6 3
♦ A Q J
♣ A 7

♠ K 4
♥ 9 4
♦ 10 6 5 4
♣ Q 10 8 3 2

♠ A Q 5
♥ 10 8 7 2
♦ 9 7
♣ J 9 6 5

♠ J 9 7 6
♥ A K 5
♦ K 8 3 2
♣ K 4

You can afford three losers. The only losers are in the trump suit where you are missing the ace, the king and the queen. In such a situation, start playing the trump suit right away. After winning the first trick, lead a trump to drive out one of the opponents' winners. As soon as you regain the lead, lead trumps again to drive out another high trump. In this fashion, you lose only three trump tricks, and it will be safe to take your winners in the other suits.

If you were afraid to draw trumps, either because of your anemic-looking trump suit or because you did not want to give up the lead, you would be defeated. When you tried to take your heart winners, West would ruff the third round with the ♠4. The opponents would still have three winners left in the trump suit. If you continued the policy of not drawing trumps, East would ruff the third round of diamonds with the ♠5, and you might be defeated two tricks.

It isn't the opponents' high trumps but their low trumps that could lead to defeat. In driving out the high trumps, you are also drawing out the low trumps, making it safe for you to take your winners.

Most of the time, when you compare the number of losers you can afford with the losers you have, you find that you need to eliminate a loser or two. For example, you may need to discard a loser on an extra winner in dummy. It's still a good idea to eliminate the opponents' trumps first, but you may not always be able to do this.

If you can draw trumps without giving up the lead, do so. You can't afford to give up the lead, however, if you have too many quick losers — tricks the opponents can take right away. It's safe to give up the lead only if some of your losers are slow — the opponents can't immediately take enough tricks to defeat you.

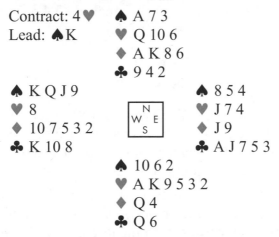

Contract: 4 ♥
Lead: ♠K

♠ A 7 3
♥ Q 10 6
♦ A K 8 6
♣ 9 4 2

♠ K Q J 9
♥ 8
♦ 10 7 5 3 2
♣ K 10 8

♠ 8 5 4
♥ J 7 4
♦ J 9
♣ A J 7 5 3

♠ 10 6 2
♥ A K 9 5 3 2
♦ Q 4
♣ Q 6

You can afford three losers. You have two in spades and two in clubs — one too many. Fortunately, dummy has an extra diamond winner on which you can discard one of your losers. After you win the ♠A, all of your losers are quick. If the opponents get the lead, they'll take all four of their tricks. Should you draw trumps or discard your loser first?

You can draw trumps without giving up the lead, so you should play trumps first. It takes three rounds to draw all of the trumps, but then you can safely play the ♦Q and lead the ♦4 to dummy's ♦A and ♦K to discard one of your losers.

What if you don't draw trumps first? When you try to take your diamond winners, East plays a trump on the third round. You can overruff to win the trick, but now you don't have an extra winner left in dummy on which to discard a loser. Down you go.

On the next deal, you must give up the lead to draw trumps. Should you do that before discarding your loser?

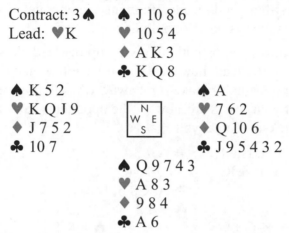

Contract: 3 ♠
Lead: ♥ K

```
              ♠ J 10 8 6
              ♥ 10 5 4
              ♦ A K 3
              ♣ K Q 8
♠ K 5 2                      ♠ A
♥ K Q J 9         N          ♥ 7 6 2
♦ J 7 5 2      W     E       ♦ Q 10 6
♣ 10 7            S          ♣ J 9 5 4 3 2
              ♠ Q 9 7 4 3
              ♥ A 8 3
              ♦ 9 8 4
              ♣ A 6
```

You can afford four losers. You have two spade losers, two heart losers and one diamond loser. One of the losers can be discarded on the extra club winner in dummy. Drawing trumps is a good idea but you will have to give up the lead twice. Should you play clubs first?

When considering giving up the lead, you need to look at your quick losers. The opponents have driven out your ♥ A, so you have two quick heart losers to go with the two sure trump losers. However, the opponents can't take a diamond trick right away if you give up the lead, since you still have the ♦ A and the ♦ K. (Your diamond loser is slow.) Therefore, it's safe to start drawing trumps.

When East wins the ♠ A, the opponents can take their two heart tricks. Whatever they lead next, you can win. Then you can lead spades again to drive out the ♠ K. Whatever they lead back, you can win and lead spades once more, drawing West's last trump. Now it's safe to play the club suit and discard your diamond loser.

If you don't draw trumps first, West ruffs the third round of clubs — you end up with five losers instead of four.

Now let's look at situations where you can't afford to draw trumps right away.

DELAYING DRAWING TRUMPS

On many deals, you can't afford to draw trumps right away. You can't give up the lead because you have too many quick losers, or you may need your trump suit for other purposes.

When You Have Too Many Quick Losers

If you have more quick losers than you can afford, you can't give up the lead without being defeated. You must eliminate some of your losers first. Look at this deal:

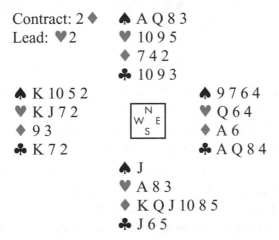

Contract: 2 ♦
Lead: ♥2

♠ A Q 8 3
♥ 10 9 5
♦ 7 4 2
♣ 10 9 3

♠ K 10 5 2
♥ K J 7 2
♦ 9 3
♣ K 7 2

♠ 9 7 6 4
♥ Q 6 4
♦ A 6
♣ A Q 8 4

♠ J
♥ A 8 3
♦ K Q J 10 8 5
♣ J 6 5

You can afford five losers but you have six — two hearts, one diamond and three clubs. After you win the ♥A, all of your losers are quick. If you start to draw trumps right away by driving out the ♦A, the opponents will take their winners. You must eliminate a loser first.

The only hope is dummy's ♠A and ♠Q. You can try a spade finesse for the king. If West has the ♠K, you can create an extra winner in dummy on which to discard one of your losers. Then you can afford to draw trumps. After winning the ♥A, lead the ♠J. If West doesn't cover, be careful to overtake the jack with dummy's queen; otherwise, you won't have an entry to dummy to play the ♠A and discard your loser.

If East had the ♠K, you would have ended up with an extra spade loser and gone down an extra trick. Nothing ventured . . .

Here is a deal where you must be careful to analyze whether your losers are quick or slow:

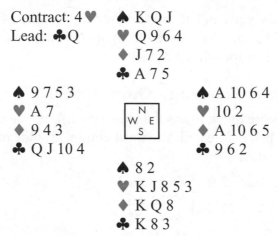

Contract: 4♥
Lead: ♣Q

♠ K Q J
♥ Q 9 6 4
♦ J 7 2
♣ A 7 5

♠ 9 7 5 3
♥ A 7
♦ 9 4 3
♣ Q J 10 4

♠ A 10 6 4
♥ 10 2
♦ A 10 6 5
♣ 9 6 2

♠ 8 2
♥ K J 8 5 3
♦ K Q 8
♣ K 8 3

You're missing the ♠A, the ♥A and the ♦A. You also have a club loser. When you *Analyze your alternatives,* you see the possibility of discarding your club loser on an extra spade winner in dummy once the ♠A has been driven out. Can you afford to draw trumps first?

On the surface, it looks as though you can. You must give up the lead to draw trumps but you have only three quick losers — the three aces. Your club loser is slow. Even after winning the first club trick, you'll have another club winner left to stop the opponents from taking a trick in that suit.

Looking ahead, however, you can see that you'll lose the race if you play the trump suit first. Upon winning the ♥A, the opponents will lead another club to drive out your remaining high card. Now you'll have a quick loser in clubs. When you establish your extra spade winner, you must let the opponents in the lead with their ♠A, and they can take a club trick to defeat your contract.

Instead, win the first trick with the ♣K, keeping the ♣A in dummy as a potential entry to your extra spade winner (if the opponents don't take their ♠A on the first round). Immediately lead a spade to drive out the opponents' ace. When a club is led back, you can win and play your extra spade winner to discard your club loser. Now it's safe to draw trumps and, when that is done, drive out the opponents' ♦A to make your contract. You, not the opponents, win the race.

When You Need to Ruff Losers

As we saw in Chapter 4, if you plan to ruff losers in dummy, be careful to keep a sufficient number of trumps in dummy for that purpose. This often affects your decision on whether or not to draw trumps.

Here is an example:

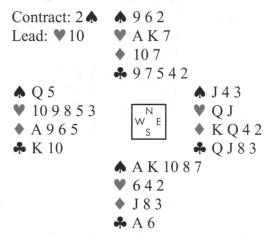

Contract: 2♠
Lead: ♥10

```
              ♠ 9 6 2
              ♥ A K 7
              ♦ 10 7
              ♣ 9 7 5 4 2
♠ Q 5                        ♠ J 4 3
♥ 10 9 8 5 3      N          ♥ Q J
♦ A 9 6 5      W   E         ♦ K Q 4 2
♣ K 10            S          ♣ Q J 8 3
              ♠ A K 10 8 7
              ♥ 6 4 2
              ♦ J 8 3
              ♣ A 6
```

The opponents lead the ♥10 against your 2♠ contract and the race is on. You can afford five losers. You have one trump loser if the missing trumps are 3–2, one heart loser, three diamond losers and one club loser. One of the losers will have to disappear. There is the possibility of ruffing one of your diamond losers in dummy. Should you start by drawing trumps?

You must preserve a trump in dummy to take care of your diamond loser, and you must give up the lead twice in diamonds before you are ready to ruff your loser. Each time you give up the lead, the opponents can lead trumps, trying to stop you from ruffing your loser in dummy. Therefore, you can't afford to play even one round of trumps.

Win the first trick and immediately lead a diamond. Suppose East wins and, seeing your plan, leads a spade. Win the trick and lead diamonds again. If East wins and leads another trump, win and lead your last diamond, ruffing it in dummy. You win the race and end up losing only one spade, two diamonds, one heart and one club.

When You Need the Trump Suit for Entries

Because the trump suit is usually the longest and most powerful suit in the combined hands, it's often needed as a source of entries to declarer's hand and dummy.

Here is an example:

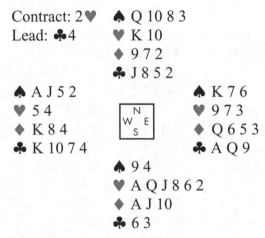

Contract: 2♥ ♠ Q 10 8 3
Lead: ♣4 ♥ K 10
  ♦ 9 7 2
  ♣ J 8 5 2

♠ A J 5 2 ♠ K 7 6
♥ 5 4 ♥ 9 7 3
♦ K 8 4 ♦ Q 6 5 3
♣ K 10 7 4 ♣ A Q 9

  ♠ 9 4
  ♥ A Q J 8 6 2
  ♦ A J 10
  ♣ 6 3

You can afford five losers if you are to make your contract of 2♥. You have two spade losers, two diamond losers and two club losers — one too many. You can't do much about the spade and club losers, but you have a chance to eliminate one of the diamond losers. Recalling the chapter on finesses, you want to lead a diamond from dummy and, when East plays low, insert the ♦ 10 (or the ♦ J). If the first finesse loses, you plan to lead another diamond from dummy and repeat the finesse. If East has either the ♦ K or the ♦ Q, you will lose only one diamond.

The problem with the plan is that it requires two entries to dummy so you can lead twice toward your hand. Where are the entries going to come from? Your strong heart suit provides the answer. The ♥ K and the ♥ 10 can be used as entries. This means you must delay drawing all of the trumps.

Suppose East wins the ♣A and the ♣Q and leads a third club, which you ruff. Lead a low heart to dummy's ♥ 10 and then temporarily stop drawing trumps. Lead a diamond from dummy and finesse the ♦ 10 when East plays small. West wins the ♦ K. Suppose West leads back the ♣ K, which you ruff. Lead a low heart to dummy's ♥ K and lead another diamond from dummy, finessing the jack when East plays low. This time, the finesse works since East has the ♦ Q. Now finish drawing trumps and take the ♦ A to make the contract.

Here is another example of using the trump suit to provide an entry.

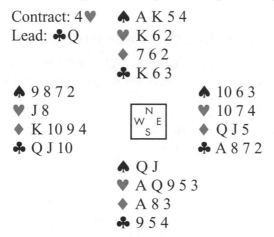

```
Contract: 4♥      ♠ A K 5 4
Lead: ♣ Q        ♥ K 6 2
                 ♦ 7 6 2
                 ♣ K 6 3

♠ 9 8 7 2              ♠ 10 6 3
♥ J 8         N        ♥ 10 7 4
♦ K 10 9 4  W   E      ♦ Q J 5
♣ Q J 10       S       ♣ A 8 7 2

                 ♠ Q J
                 ♥ A Q 9 5 3
                 ♦ A 8 3
                 ♣ 9 5 4
```

With the ♣ A placed unfavorably, your ♣ K is trapped and you lose the first three club tricks. Now the opponents lead a diamond and drive out your ♦ A. You can't afford any more losers in your contract of 4♥. Missing five trumps, you must hope they divide 3–2 to eliminate any losers in that suit. You still have two diamond losers but it may be possible to discard them on the extra spade winners in dummy. Since you need to take all four of your winners, you must be careful about entries. The only entry to dummy outside of the spade suit is the ♥ K.

You plan to play the ♠ Q and the ♠ J and then use the ♥ K to get to dummy. Next you can play the ♠ A and the ♠ K, discarding your diamond losers. But what about drawing trumps? If you don't draw all of them, the opponents may ruff one of your spade winners, and down you go. If you do draw all of the trumps, you'll have no entry left in dummy.

The key is to delay drawing the last trump until you are ready to use it as an entry to dummy. After winning the ♦ A, play the ♥ A and the ♥ Q. (This is not the time to start with the high card from the short side since you'll need the ♥ K later.) You watch with satisfaction as both opponents follow suit when you play the first two rounds of trumps. The missing trumps divide 3–2, but you can't draw the opponents' final trump yet. First, play the ♠ Q and the ♠ J, hoping the opponent with the trump follows suit. Now you're ready to play a low heart to dummy's ♥ K, drawing the last trump and putting you in dummy at the same time. Play the ♠ A and the ♠ K, discarding your diamond losers, and you are home. A well-played hand!

When You Need a Finesse in the Trump Suit

Sometimes you can't draw trumps right away because you need to take a finesse in the trump suit, and you're not in the appropriate hand.

Here is an example:

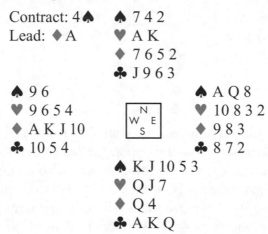

Contract: 4♠
Lead: ♦ A

```
            ♠ 7 4 2
            ♥ A K
            ♦ 7 6 5 2
            ♣ J 9 6 3
♠ 9 6                        ♠ A Q 8
♥ 9 6 5 4        N           ♥ 10 8 3 2
♦ A K J 10    W     E        ♦ 9 8 3
♣ 10 5 4         S           ♣ 8 7 2
            ♠ K J 10 5 3
            ♥ Q J 7
            ♦ Q 4
            ♣ A K Q
```

You can afford only three losers. West wins the first two diamond tricks and leads another high diamond which you ruff. You don't have any losers in hearts or clubs. You must avoid two trump losers to make your contract of 4♠. If East has the ♠ Q, you can take a successful finesse.

You need to lead from dummy toward your hand, so you must delay playing the trump suit. Play a low heart first to dummy's ♥ K. Now lead a spade from dummy and, if East plays a low spade, finesse with the ♠ 10 (or the ♠ J). When this play is successful, you can abandon playing trumps until you can get back to dummy with the ♥ A to lead another spade. With East having the ♠ Q, the opponents can't prevent you from making the contract.

MAINTAINING CONTROL

One advantage of having a trump suit is that it can be used to stop the opponents from taking their winners in a long side suit. Remember, however, if you run out of trumps, you will have lost control if the opponents get the lead and start taking their winners. Maintaining control involves keeping enough trumps to prevent this from happening.

When the Opponents Have the Outstanding High Trumps

One consideration in maintaining control of the trump suit is whether or not you can afford to draw trumps when an opponent has the highest remaining trump. Since your opponent will always take a trick with the high trump, it's usually unnecessary to drive it out. The reason for drawing trumps is to get rid of the opponents' low trumps so they can't do you any harm. If an opponent is entitled to a high trump, why not save your remaining trumps? Let your opponent use the high trump to ruff one of your winners. You'll get the trick back, since your remaining trump will now be promoted into a winner.

Knowing when not to draw an outstanding high trump is one of the keys to maintaining control in a suit contract.

Consider the following deal:

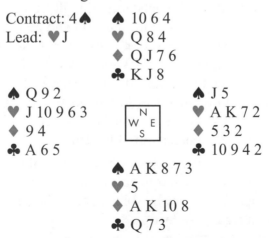

Contract: 4♠
Lead: ♥J

	♠ 10 6 4	
	♥ Q 8 4	
	♦ Q J 7 6	
	♣ K J 8	
♠ Q 9 2		♠ J 5
♥ J 10 9 6 3		♥ A K 7 2
♦ 9 4		♦ 5 3 2
♣ A 6 5		♣ 10 9 4 2
	♠ A K 8 7 3	
	♥ 5	
	♦ A K 10 8	
	♣ Q 7 3	

You can afford three losers. If the missing trumps divide 3–2, you have only one spade loser. In addition, there's one heart loser and one club loser. Since you have the number of losers you can afford, this appears to be a simple case of drawing trumps and taking your winners.

Let's look a little more closely. You'll have to give up the lead when you drive out the ♣A to promote your club tricks, so you must be careful to maintain control — keep enough trumps to stop the opponents from taking their heart winners. This will affect how you handle the trump suit.

The opponents win the first heart trick and lead another high heart which you ruff. Start drawing trumps by playing the ♠A and the ♠K. Both opponents follow suit, so the only outstanding trump is the ♠Q, a winner for the opponents. Should you play another round of spades to draw it out?

Let's see what happens if you do. You must play two of your trumps, one from each hand, to drive out the ♠Q. Since you ruffed the opponents' heart winner earlier, that leaves you with only one trump in your hand. Suppose West wins the ♠Q and plays another high heart. You can ruff this card with your last spade and take your diamond winners. But now you must lead a club to drive out the opponents' ace. When West wins the ♣A, West still has some hearts. Since you don't have any trumps left, West can take the remaining heart tricks to defeat the contract. You've lost control of the hand.

Suppose you don't draw the outstanding high trump. After playing the ♠A and the ♠K, leave West with the ♠Q and go about your business of driving out the ♣A. When West wins the ♣A, you still have two low trumps left in your hand. Even if West plays the ♠Q to draw your trumps, you still have one trump left. If West leads a heart next, you can ruff and play your remaining winners. You make the contract, losing just one spade, one heart and the ♣A. You have successfully maintained control by not drawing the outstanding high trump.

Incidentally, the above hand illustrates that it is often advantageous for the defenders to force declarer to ruff their winners. If declarer runs out of trumps, the opponents may be able to defeat the contract with their winners, if they can regain the lead.

Ducking to Maintain Control

We've seen in earlier chapters that ducking (not taking a trick when you can win it) is a useful technique to maintain entries in your suits or to remove entries from the opponents' hands (hold-up play). Playing the trump suit may offer another opportunity for taking your losses early through ducking. This time, the reason for ducking is to maintain control of the trump suit.

When your trump suit is weak but you have the ace, ducking a trick is a useful way of maintaining control while drawing trumps. You keep your ace to prevent the opponents from drawing too many of your trumps and then taking their winners. You'll still lose the same number of trump tricks, but you keep control.

Let's see how this helps on the following deal:

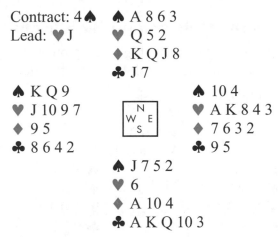

Contract: 4♠   ♠ A 8 6 3
Lead: ♥ J   ♥ Q 5 2
             ♦ K Q J 8
             ♣ J 7

♠ K Q 9   ♠ 10 4
♥ J 10 9 7   ♥ A K 8 4 3
♦ 9 5   ♦ 7 6 3 2
♣ 8 6 4 2   ♣ 9 5

             ♠ J 7 5 2
             ♥ 6
             ♦ A 10 4
             ♣ A K Q 10 3

You can afford three losers in 4♠. Provided the missing trumps divide 3–2, you have only two losers in spades and one in hearts. With such a weak trump suit, however, you must be careful not to lose control.

The opponents win the first heart trick and lead another heart which you ruff. Now you have only three spades left in your hand. You want to draw some of the opponents' trumps so they can't use their low trumps on your winners. You're willing to let them have two trump tricks but not three. Suppose you start by playing the ♠A and then another spade. West will win the ♠Q and play the ♠K to draw the last trump left in your hand. Now West can lead a heart, and you don't have any trumps left in your hand to stop the opponents from winning the trick. You lose two trump tricks and two heart tricks to go down in your contract.

Instead, after ruffing the second round of hearts, play a low spade from both hands, giving up a trick. If the opponents lead another spade, you can win the ♠ A and start taking your winners. Leave the remaining high trump outstanding — the opponent can have it anytime.

If the opponents win the first spade trick and play a high heart, you can ruff it. Now lead another round of trumps, winning the ♠ A. Again, leave the remaining high trump outstanding and go about the business of taking your winners. You end up losing only two spades and one heart.

By ducking the first round of trumps, you maintain control of the trump suit while drawing the opponents' low trumps.

When to Draw the Outstanding High Trump

Declarer doesn't always leave a high trump outstanding. Drawing it may be necessary to maintain control. Consider this deal:

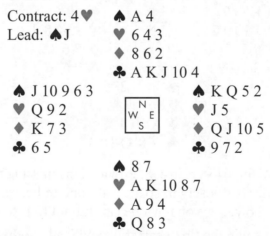

```
Contract: 4♥      ♠ A 4
Lead: ♠ J          ♥ 6 4 3
                   ♦ 8 6 2
                   ♣ A K J 10 4

♠ J 10 9 6 3                    ♠ K Q 5 2
♥ Q 9 2         N              ♥ J 5
♦ K 7 3       W   E            ♦ Q J 10 5
♣ 6 5           S              ♣ 9 7 2

                   ♠ 8 7
                   ♥ A K 10 8 7
                   ♦ A 9 4
                   ♣ Q 8 3
```

You have one spade loser, one heart loser if the suit breaks 3–2 and two diamond losers. That's one more than you can afford in 4♥. You plan to discard two of your losers on dummy's extra club winners.

After winning the ♠ A and playing the ♥ A and the ♥ K, should you draw the remaining high trump or start playing your club winners? Suppose you leave the high trump outstanding and start leading clubs. On the third round of clubs, West ruffs with the ♥Q. The opponents take their spade trick and then lead diamonds, driving out your ♦A. You have two club winners in dummy but you don't have an entry to them. You end up losing two diamond tricks and going down in the contract.

Instead, since you aren't in any danger of losing control, you should drive out the opponents' ♥Q. They can win this trick and take a spade trick, but now you're in control. Whatever the opponents lead next, you win and peacefully take your club tricks, discarding your two diamond losers. You make an overtrick, losing just one spade and one heart, rather than being defeated in your game.

DEVELOPING LONG SUITS

The trump suit can often be helpful when trying to develop tricks in a side suit.

Establishing Declarer's Side Suit

Consider the following deal:

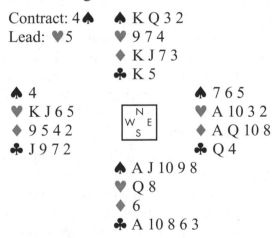

Contract: 4♠ ♠ K Q 3 2
Lead: ♥5   ♥ 9 7 4
              ♦ K J 7 3
              ♣ K 5

♠ 4   ♠ 7 6 5
♥ K J 6 5   ♥ A 10 3 2
♦ 9 5 4 2   ♦ A Q 10 8
♣ J 9 7 2   ♣ Q 4

              ♠ A J 10 9 8
              ♥ Q 8
              ♦ 6
              ♣ A 10 8 6 3

You can afford three losers. You must lose two heart tricks and the ♦A, so you can't afford to lose any club tricks. You have three possible club losers. With only two clubs in dummy, you can ruff your losers.

How many losers do you need to ruff? If the six missing clubs divide 3–3, you need to ruff only one of your losers in dummy (after playing the

♣K and the ♣A). Your remaining clubs will be established as winners. If, as is more likely, the missing clubs divide 4–2, you must ruff two of your losers to establish your remaining club. If the missing clubs break 5–1 or 6–0, you must ruff all three of your club losers. You'll be defeated since an opponent will ruff the first or second round of clubs. You can't draw trumps and still have three trumps left in dummy.

Suppose the opponents win the first two heart tricks and lead another heart, which you ruff. Since you don't know how the missing clubs will divide and you'll need trumps as entries back to your hand, delay drawing any trumps. Lead a low club to dummy's king (high card from the short side) and the ♣5 back to your ♣A. Now lead one of your club losers, planning to ruff it in dummy.

When West follows with a club, recall the advice in Chapter 5: when ruffing losers, use as high a trump as you can afford. Since you have enough high trumps in your hand to draw the opponents' trumps, you can afford to ruff with dummy's ♠Q (or ♠K). This prevents East from overruffing if East is also out of clubs.

If the missing clubs are divided 3–3, you don't need to ruff any more losers — you can draw the missing trumps and take your established club winners. On this deal, however, the clubs divide 4–2, so your remaining clubs are not established. Lead a spade to your hand and ruff another club high, using dummy's ♠K. Your last club is now a winner, so you can lead dummy's remaining spade to your hand and draw the outstanding trumps. Then you take your established club trick and make the contract, losing only two hearts and one diamond.

Notice how carefully you managed the trump suit on this deal. You delayed drawing trumps because you had to ruff some losers. You also used the trump suit for entries back to your hand, drawing some of the opponents' trumps in the process. Finally, once your side suit was established, you drew the remaining trumps so the opponents could not ruff your winner.

Establishing Dummy's Side Suit

Sometimes, you don't have enough winners in dummy on which to discard your losers. You often can create extra winners with the help of the trump suit.

Look at this deal:

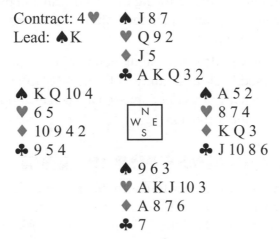

Contract: 4 ♥
Lead: ♠K

```
            ♠ J 8 7
            ♥ Q 9 2
            ♦ J 5
            ♣ A K Q 3 2
♠ K Q 10 4              ♠ A 5 2
♥ 6 5         N         ♥ 8 7 4
♦ 10 9 4 2  W   E       ♦ K Q 3
♣ 9 5 4       S         ♣ J 10 8 6
            ♠ 9 6 3
            ♥ A K J 10 3
            ♦ A 8 7 6
            ♣ 7
```

After losing the first three spade tricks, you must take the rest of the tricks in order to make your 4 ♥ contract. You have three diamond losers to worry about. Two of them can be discarded on dummy's extra club winners, but what can be done with the third loser?

The club suit does offer a further possibility. You have six clubs and the opponents have seven. If the missing clubs divide 4–3, you can establish a low club in dummy as a winner. You can't afford to give up a club trick, so you must establish the suit by ruffing one of dummy's low clubs.

Suppose the opponents win the first three spade tricks and then lead a diamond to drive out your ♦A. Once again, you must be careful in managing the trump suit. Can you afford to draw all of the missing trumps? You don't need dummy's trumps to ruff your losers, but you do need an entry to dummy once you have established the club suit. The ♥Q will serve that purpose.

After winning the ♦ A, play the ♥ A and the ♥ K to draw some of the opponents' trumps. Now you must delay drawing the final trump and go to work on the club suit. Lead a club to dummy's ♣Q. Take dummy's ♣A and ♣K and discard two of your diamond losers. Now lead a low club and ruff it high in your hand, to avoid an overruff. Next lead a trump to dummy's ♥ Q, drawing the last trump and putting you in dummy — you can take your established club winner and discard your remaining diamond loser.

You also could have ruffed a low club before playing the ♣A and the ♣K and then crossed back to dummy with the ♥ Q to take your three club winners. This usually is a safer approach to keep the opponents from ruffing one of your club winners.

GUIDELINES FOR DEFENSE

The defenders work together to try to defeat the contract. They are at a disadvantage since they can't see each other's hands. Each defender can see only one hand and the dummy. This makes it difficult for them to tell where their strengths and weaknesses lie as a partnership.

One way to overcome this is through the use of defensive signals. The defenders can give each other information through the cards that they play when a suit is led. We already have seen one way they can exchange information — by leading the top of touching honors. If your partner leads the queen, you know partner doesn't have the next-higher card, the king, but probably has the next-lower card, the jack. Here is another way the defenders can help each other.

Attitude Signals

The most common form of defensive signal is the *attitude signal.* This is the play of a card to tell partner whether or not you like (*i.e.,* have high cards in the suit and/or wish to have the suit led or continued) a particular suit. Traditionally, *a high card is encouraging* and *a low card is discouraging.* The terms high card and low card have no absolute meaning. Depending on what cards are available, an eight may be low, a four may be high. A high card is ideally a card higher than a six and a low card is something smaller. You may not always have a perfect card available, but when you do, you can help partner out.

Here is an example:

Contract: 3NT
Lead: ♥4

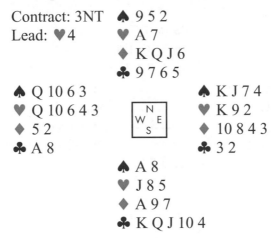

♠ 9 5 2
♥ A 7
♦ K Q J 6
♣ 9 7 6 5

♠ Q 10 6 3
♥ Q 10 6 4 3
♦ 5 2
♣ A 8

♠ K J 7 4
♥ K 9 2
♦ 10 8 4 3
♣ 3 2

♠ A 8
♥ J 8 5
♦ A 9 7
♣ K Q J 10 4

Your partner leads the ♥4 against 3NT. Declarer plays the ♥A from dummy at the first trick. Which card do you (East) play? Holding the ♥K, you like the suit that has been led and you want to encourage partner to lead it again at the next opportunity. Therefore, you play the ♥9, an encouraging card.

This makes the defense easy for your partner. Declarer needs to establish some club winners in order to make the contract, so declarer leads a club from dummy to the ♣K to drive out the ♣A. When your partner wins the ♣A, partner knows from your encouraging signal that you like hearts — and continues by leading another heart. You win the ♥K and lead the ♥2 back to partner, who takes three more heart winners to defeat the contract. Bridge is such an easy game!

Did it matter whether you played the ♥9 or the ♥2? After all, partner may have led another heart anyway and still have defeated the contract. Let's give your partner and dummy the same hands but exchange a couple of your cards and declarer's:

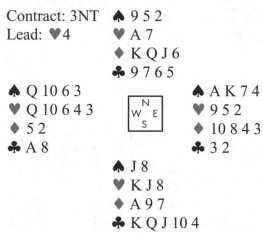

Contract: 3NT
Lead: ♥4

♠ 9 5 2
♥ A 7
♦ K Q J 6
♣ 9 7 6 5

♠ Q 10 6 3
♥ Q 10 6 4 3
♦ 5 2
♣ A 8

♠ A K 7 4
♥ 9 5 2
♦ 10 8 4 3
♣ 3 2

♠ J 8
♥ K J 8
♦ A 9 7
♣ K Q J 10 4

Your partner makes the same lead, and the same dummy comes down. Again, declarer wins the first trick with dummy's ♥A and leads a club to the ♣K. What does your partner do after winning the ♣A?

If partner leads another heart, declarer will end up with 11 tricks: three hearts, four diamonds and four clubs. On this deal, your partner must abandon the heart suit and lead a spade instead. Then the defenders can take four spade tricks along with the ♣A to defeat the contract.

How will partner know to shift to a spade? When declarer wins the first trick with dummy's ♥A, you want to discourage partner from continuing hearts since you don't have any interest in the suit. You can do this by playing a discouraging card, the ♥2. After winning the ♣A, partner knows you don't like hearts and can try another suit. Since declarer is establishing club tricks and dummy has diamond strength, it's quite likely that partner will lead a spade.

A Ruff for the Defense

The attitude signal can also be useful on a deal such as the following:

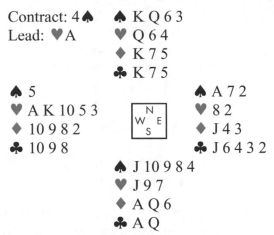

Contract: 4♠
Lead: ♥A

```
            ♠ K Q 6 3
            ♥ Q 6 4
            ♦ K 7 5
            ♣ K 7 5
♠ 5                        ♠ A 7 2
♥ A K 10 5 3      N        ♥ 8 2
♦ 10 9 8 2      W   E      ♦ J 4 3
♣ 10 9 8          S        ♣ J 6 4 3 2
            ♠ J 10 9 8 4
            ♥ J 9 7
            ♦ A Q 6
            ♣ A Q
```

Your partner leads the ♥A. You want to encourage partner to continue playing the suit, even though the ♥Q is in dummy. Why? If, as seems likely, partner also has the ♥K, partner can win it and then lead a third round of hearts for you to ruff. You'll still have the ♠A for the fourth defensive trick.

To encourage partner to continue leading hearts, play the ♥8 on the first trick. Partner may wonder why you like hearts, but trusting your attitude signal, should continue by leading the ♥K and another heart. Signaling requires partnership cooperation. One partner must make the appropriate signal, and the other partner must be watching for it.

Suppose we exchange several of your cards with declarer's:

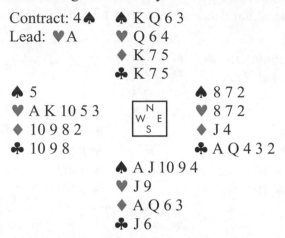

Contract: 4♠ ♠ K Q 6 3
Lead: ♥A   ♥ Q 6 4
             ♦ K 7 5
             ♣ K 7 5

♠ 5   ♠ 8 7 2
♥ A K 10 5 3   ♥ 8 7 2
♦ 10 9 8 2   ♦ J 4
♣ 10 9 8   ♣ A Q 4 3 2

             ♠ A J 10 9 4
             ♥ J 9
             ♦ A Q 6 3
             ♣ J 6

This time, you discourage partner from continuing hearts by playing the ♥2. This play tells partner you would prefer a switch to another suit. If partner chooses clubs, you'll win the ♣A and the ♣Q since you have dummy's king trapped. Partner's ♥K will be the fourth defensive trick. If partner chooses diamonds, again you can discourage by playing the ♦4. When partner later wins the ♥K, partner can try clubs — again, you'll defeat the contract.

What if your partner continued leading hearts? Then declarer would discard one of the club losers on the ♥Q and make the contract. By playing the ♥2 and having partner interpret this as a discouraging signal, you give the defense the opportunity to defeat the contract.

It's not always possible to give a clear-cut signal. On this hand, for example, you might have held the ♥9, the ♥8 and the ♥7. You want to discourage partner from continuing, but the lowest heart you have is the ♥7. You must play it and hope partner can see enough of the missing cards to realize that this is your lowest heart.

Similarly, on the previous deal, when you wanted to encourage partner to lead hearts, you might have been dealt the ♥3 and the ♥2. You would have to play the ♥3 and hope partner could figure it out. Of course, nothing will help if partner doesn't watch the cards you play — and you don't watch partner's cards.

BIDDING — SLAM BIDDING

There are large bonuses in the scoring for bidding and making a small slam (a contract to take 12 tricks) or a grand slam (a contract to take 13 tricks). Deciding whether to bid a slam adds a great deal of drama to the action.

Slam Bidding

The decision whether or not to bid a slam is similar to the decision to play in a partscore or game. The partnership must determine if they have enough combined strength to play at the slam level and which strain to play the contract in.

With 33 to 36 combined points, the partnership generally has enough strength to play in a small slam. With 37 or more points, the partnership should have enough strength for a grand slam.

At the game level, the partnership usually plays in 3NT, 4♥ or 4♠ since these contracts require fewer tricks than 5♣ or 5♦. At the slam level, the same number of tricks is required for every strain — 12 for a small slam and 13 for a grand slam. Since playing in a Golden Fit will often produce one more trick than playing in notrump, slams should generally be played in a Golden Fit if one can be found. Otherwise, the slam should be played in notrump.

Here are some examples of bidding a slam when your partner opens the bidding with 1NT.

♠ K Q J ♥ A Q 5 ♦ J 10 7 4 ♣ K Q 5	With 18 HCPs, you know there is enough combined strength for slam since partner has at least 15 HCP to open 1NT. With no known Golden Fit, bid slam in notrump by jumping directly to 6NT.
♠ A 10 8 ♥ A J 5 ♦ 10 ♣ A Q J 8 5 2	With 16 HCPs plus 2 points for the six-card club suit, you have enough combined strength for a small slam. Since opener has a balanced hand, opener must have at least two clubs — so there is a Golden Fit in clubs. Bid 6♣.

♠ A K 6   With 22 HCPs, you should have enough for a grand
♥ K J 10   slam. Jump directly to 7NT, since there is no known
♦ A 8 5   Golden Fit.
♣ A K 8 2

If you have enough combined strength for slam but you aren't sure
of the best strain, make a forcing bid. Reserve the right to make your
decision when you have more information. For example, suppose your
partner opens the bidding 1 ♥, and you hold the following hand:

♠ K Q 7 2   You have 20 HCP. Since partner has at least 13
♥ A J   points, the partnership should have enough com-
♦ A 9 5   bined strength for slam. What strain? At this point,
♣ A Q 10 5   you don't know if a Golden Fit exists, so you must
                    do some exploring. Respond 1 ♠, a forcing bid, and
                    wait to hear what partner does next. Maybe partner
will raise your suit and you can play in slam in spades. If partner rebids
hearts to show a six-card suit, you could bid slam in hearts. Partner may
show a second suit with a 2♣ rebid. Now you can bid a slam in clubs.
Partner may rebid 1NT to show a balanced hand — then the partnership
belongs in 6NT.

Inviting a Slam

Sometimes, you know the best strain but are not certain whether there
is enough combined strength for slam. In this case, you can invite partner
to bid a slam by bidding one level beyond game. With extra strength,
partner can accept the invitation and bid slam. If partner has the minimum
of the range promised, partner can pass, turning down the invitation.

Here are some examples of inviting slam when your partner opens
the bidding 1NT:

♠ Q J 6   Partner has 15 to 17 HCP. Combined with your 16
♥ K 10 8   points, you know the partnership has at least 31
♦ K Q 7   combined points. It could have as many as 33. Invite
♣ A J 9 3   partner to slam by bidding one level beyond game,
                    4NT. With a minimum hand of 15 HCP, partner will
pass. With some extra strength, partner will accept the invitation and bid
6NT.

♠ A Q J 10 8 3
♥ A 5
♦ 10 4
♣ K 6 5

With a total of 16 points — 14 HCPs plus 2 points for the six-card spade suit — you have enough once again to invite a slam contract. Since there must be a Golden Fit in spades, invite slam by bidding one level beyond game, 5 ♠.

Slam Conventions

Suppose partner opens the bidding 1 ♥ and you have the following hand:

♠ A 8 5 2
♥ Q J 9 4
♦ A K Q J
♣ 5

Since you have 17 HCPs plus 3 dummy points for the singleton club, the combined partnership strength is at least 33 points, enough for a small slam. Since there is a known Golden Fit in hearts, you could jump directly to 6 ♥.

This would work out unfortunately if partner had this hand:

♠ K Q J
♥ K 10 8 7 4
♦ 10 6
♣ K Q 10

The partnership does have enough combined strength for slam, but there are two quick losers, the ♥ A and the ♣ A. Given time, partner might discard the three club losers on your extra diamond and spade winners and make the slam. More likely, the opponents will be only too eager to take their two aces and defeat you.

It is obviously not a good idea to bid a slam missing two aces. The opponents can take their two tricks before you get an opportunity to develop your extra winners or discard your extra losers. Similarly, in a grand slam, you don't want to be missing an ace. How can you avoid such situations?

One way to avoid bidding a slam when too many aces are missing is to use the *Blackwood convention*. Once you have agreed upon a trump suit, a bid of 4NT is used as a conventional (artificial) bid to ask how many aces are in partner's hand. Partner responds as follows:

5♣	No aces or all four aces
5♦	One ace
5♥	Two aces
5♠	Three aces

Once you know how many aces your partner has, you'll know if the combined hands are missing too many aces. If they are, you can stop below slam. If not, you can bid slam.

Let's return to our earlier deal when partner opens the bidding 1♥ and you hold the following hand:

♠ A 8 5 2
♥ Q J 9 4
♦ A K Q J
♣ 5

Instead of jumping directly to 6♥, use the Blackwood convention (assuming partner is familiar with it) to find out if two aces are missing. Respond 4NT to ask how many aces partner has. Since you haven't bid another suit, partner will assume that hearts is the agreed upon trump suit.

If partner rebids 5♣, showing no aces, you can sign off in 5♥. If partner bids 5♦, showing one ace you know that the partnership is missing only one ace — you can bid 6♥. Note that the Blackwood convention doesn't tell you which aces partner has, only how many. If you need to know the specific aces partner has, you would have to use more sophisticated methods which are beyond the scope of this text.

If partner bids 5♥, showing two aces, you know that you have them all. Sometimes, after finding out that the partnership has all of the missing aces, you'll be interested in a grand slam. In a grand slam, you generally don't want to be missing any kings. You can use an extension of the Blackwood convention, a bid of 5NT, to ask how many kings partner holds. Partner responds in the same fashion as over 4NT, this time at the six level (6♣ with no kings, etc.).

One other frequently used slam convention is the *Gerber convention*. When your partner opens the bidding in notrump, you can't use the Blackwood convention since a trump suit hasn't been agreed upon. If you bid 4NT, one level beyond game in notrump, we saw earlier that partner would interpret it as an invitation to bid 6NT. Instead, jump to a conventional (artificial) 4♣, the Gerber convention, to ask for aces. Partner responds in a similar manner as when responding to the Blackwood convention:

4♦	No aces or all four aces
4♥	One ace
4♠	Two aces
4NT	Three aces

If your side doesn't have enough aces, you can sign off in a contract below the slam level. If you have enough aces, you can bid a slam. If you have all of the aces and are interested in a grand slam, you can use the conventional (artificial) bid of 5♣ to ask for kings. Opener will respond in a similar fashion (5♦ with no kings, etc.).

SUMMARY

Managing the trump suit is one of the key considerations when you come to the fourth step of the PLAN, *Now put it all together.* You must decide whether or not to draw trumps right away.

You should draw trumps right away when you don't need the trump suit for other purposes and:

- You have no more losers than you can afford.

- You have more losers than you can afford but can draw trumps without giving up the lead.

- You have more losers than you can afford but don't have too many quick losers.

You may have to delay drawing trumps when:

- You would have to give up the lead and have too many quick losers.

- You need the trumps for other purposes (ruffing losers, entries).

- You need to get to the other hand to take a finesse in the trump suit.

When drawing trumps, you must be careful to maintain control of the trump suit. If you run out of trumps, you can no longer stop the opponents from taking their winners and may lose control. One way to maintain control is to avoid spending a trump to draw an outstanding high trump unless you can afford to do so. If your trump suit is weak, you sometimes can **duck a trick to the opponents** to help maintain control.

The trump suit can also be used to help develop a long side suit, either in declarer's hand or in dummy.

When defending, you can use an **attitude signal** to tell partner whether or not you like a particular suit. **A high card is encouraging and a low card is discouraging.**

If the partnership holds 33 to 36 combined points, the contract should generally be a small slam. With 37 or more points, the partnership should be in a grand slam. Slam can be played in any Golden Fit.

You can invite your partner to bid a slam by bidding one level beyond game. With extra strength, partner will accept the invitation; otherwise, partner will pass.

If you have agreed on a trump suit and are interested in slam, you can find out the number of aces partner has by bidding 4NT, the **Blackwood convention.** If partner opens the bidding in notrump, you can find out how many aces partner has by bidding 4♣, the **Gerber convention.**

Exercise One — Playing the Trump Suit

If you decide the best plan is to draw all of the missing trumps, how would you draw the opponents' trumps with each of the following trump suits (high cards, promotion, length, finesse)? How many tricks would you have to lose if the missing high cards are favorably located and the suit is divided as you expect? How many times would you have to play the trump suit to draw all of the missing trumps?

DUMMY: 1) K Q 6   2) J 9 8 5   3) A 9 5   4) Q J 10   5) K 9 6 3
DECLARER: A J 9 5 4 2   Q 10 7 4   8 7 6 4 2   A 9 8 7 6   A 7 5 2

METHOD: _____   _____   _____   _____   _____

# of Losers: _____   _____   _____   _____   _____

# of Rounds: _____   _____   _____   _____   _____

Answers to Exercise

Exercise One *Answers* — Playing the Trump Suit

1) Use the high cards; there are no losers even if the suit breaks 4–0. Expect the trumps to divide 3–1 and take three rounds to draw all of them.

2) Use promotion, driving out the ace and the king. Play three rounds, losing the first two and winning the third. Expect the trumps to divide 3–2.

3) Use the length of the suit. Draw three rounds, losing the first two. Trumps should divide 3–2.

4) Start in dummy and finesse against the king. If the finesse works, you'll have no losers. Repeat the finesse and play a third round of trumps, expecting them to divide 3–2.

5) Using length, there will be only one loser if the missing trumps divide 3–2. Play three rounds to draw all of the trumps, losing the third round.

Exercise Two — Looking at Quick and Slow Losers

Against your 4♠ contract, the opening lead is the ♥Q. After winning the first trick with the ♥A, how many losers do you have in each of the following examples? Are they quick or slow?

1) DUMMY	2) DUMMY	3) DUMMY
♠ A Q 8 6	♠ Q 10 8 2	♠ J 9 6 4
♥ A 9 5	♥ A K 3	♥ A 8 4
♦ 7 4 2	♦ J 8	♦ A Q 3
♣ K 5 4	♣ K Q J 5	♣ Q 7 4
■	■	■
DECLARER	DECLARER	DECLARER
♠ K J 7 5 4	♠ K J 9 7 6	♠ Q 10 8 7 3
♥ 10 8 3	♥ 9 8 4	♥ 7 6 2
♦ Q	♦ Q 10	♦ K 5
♣ A Q J 2	♣ A 8 2	♣ A K 8

Quick Losers: _____	Quick Losers: _____	Quick Losers: _____
Slow Losers: _____	Slow Losers: _____	Slow Losers: _____
Total Losers: _____	Total Losers: _____	Total Losers: _____

Answers to Exercise

Exercise Two *Answers* — Looking at Quick and Slow Losers

1) There are three quick losers and no slow losers.
2) There are three quick losers and one slow loser.
3) There are four quick losers and no slow losers.

Exercise Three — Drawing Trumps

In each of the examples in Exercise Two, should declarer start by drawing trumps? Give a reason for your answer.

1) Draw   2) Draw   3) Draw
   Trumps?:_____   Trumps?:_____   Trumps?:_____

   Reason: _____   Reason: _____   Reason: _____

Exercise Four — Side Suit Establishment

How do you expect the missing cards to be divided in each of the following side suits? Assuming you have lots of entries to dummy, how many trumps will you need to establish the side suit if the missing cards are divided as you expect?

DUMMY:	1) A K 8 6 4	2) A K 9 6 4	3) A 9 7 6 3 2
DECLARER:	3 2	2	5
Expected Division:	_____	_____	_____
Trumps Revised:	_____	_____	_____

DUMMY:	4) A K 9 8 4 2	5) A Q 7 4 2
DECLARER:	5 3	K 5
Expected Division:	_____	_____
Trumps Revised:	_____	_____

Exercise Three *Answers* — Drawing Trumps

1) Draw trumps right away. You don't need the trumps for any other purpose and you have only three losers, which you can afford. If trumps divide 2–2 or 3–1, an extra trump will be available in dummy to ruff one of your heart losers after you cash the clubs and discard a heart from dummy.

2) Draw trumps. Although you have to give up the lead to do so, your heart loser is slow. Later you can discard your heart loser safely on the extra club winner.

3) You can't play trumps right away because you'd have to give up the lead — the opponents would take enough winners to defeat the contract. Eliminate one loser first by discarding it on the extra diamond winner and then give up the lead to draw trumps.

Exercise Four *Answers* — Side Suit Establishment

1) 4–2. You would need two trumps to establish the suit.

2) 4–3. You would need two trumps to establish the suit.

3) 4–2. You would need three trumps to establish the suit.

4) 3–2. You would need one trump to establish the suit.

5) 4–2. You would need one trump to establish the suit.

Exercise Five — Attitude Signals

You are defending a 3NT contract, and your partner leads the ♠5. Declarer plays the ♠A from dummy. Circle the spade you would play in each of the following examples?

1)   DUMMY
    ♠ A 6
    ♥ K Q 10 5
    ♦ 8 6 4
    ♣ Q 9 7 3
             YOU
♠ 5   [N W E S]   ♠ K 8 2
             ♥ J 4 3
             ♦ Q 9 7 3
             ♣ 10 4 2

2)   DUMMY
    ♠ A 6
    ♥ K Q 10 5
    ♦ 8 6 4
    ♣ Q 9 7 3
              YOU
♠ 5   [N W E S]   ♠ 8 4 2
             ♥ J 4 3
             ♦ A Q 9 7
             ♣ 10 4 2

Exercise Six — Bidding Slams

Your partner opens the bidding 1NT. What do you respond with each of the following hands?

1) ♠ K J 9
   ♥ A Q 3
   ♦ Q 9 4
   ♣ K Q J 2

2) ♠ A
   ♥ 10 8 2
   ♦ K Q J 8 6 3
   ♣ A Q 5

3) ♠ A K Q
   ♥ A 7 2
   ♦ Q J 10 7
   ♣ K Q J

Opener's
Range: 15 to 17
Responder's
Points: _____

Opener's
Range: 15 to 17
Responder's
Points: _____

Opener's
Range: 15 to 17
Responder's
Points: _____

Combined
Range: _____

Combined
Range: _____

Combined
Range: _____

Response: _____

Response: _____

Response: _____

Exercise Five *Answers* — Attitude Signals

1) Play the 8 to show that you like the suit.

2) Play the 2 to show that you don't like the suit.

Exercise Six *Answers* — Bidding Slams

1) Since you have 18 HCP, the combined total is 33 to 35. Bid 6NT.

2) You have 18 points, so the combined total is 33 to 35. Bid 6♦.

3) You have 22 points. The combined total is 37 to 39. Bid 7NT.

Exercise Seven — Inviting Slam

Your partner opens the bidding 1NT. What do you respond with each of the following hands?

1) ♠ J 7 3
   ♥ K Q
   ♦ A K 10 2
   ♣ K 10 9 5

2) ♠ K J 10 8 7 3
   ♥ Q 3
   ♦ A Q 8
   ♣ Q 5

Opener's
Range: 15 to 17

Responder's
Points: _____

Combined
Range: _____

Response: _____

Opener's
Range: 15 to 17

Responder's
Points: _____

Combined
Range: _____

Response: _____

Answers to Exercise

Exercise Seven *Answers* — Inviting Slam

1) You have 16 HCP. The combined total is 31 to 33. Bid 4NT to invite a slam.

2) You have 16 points. The combined total is 31 to 33. Bid 5♠ to invite a slam.

Exercise Eight — Responding to Blackwood

You open the bidding 1♠ and your partner responds 4NT, the Blackwood convention. What do you rebid with each of the following hands?

1) ♠ A K 9 7 3
   ♥ J 7 4
   ♦ 8 4
   ♣ A 5 4

2) ♠ K J 10 5 3
   ♥ K Q 10 9 3
   ♦ K J
   ♣ 5

3) ♠ Q 10 8 6 2
   ♥ A 2
   ♦ K Q 6 4
   ♣ J 2

# of aces: _____   # of aces: _____   # of aces:_____

Response: _____   Response:_____   Response: _____

4) ♠ A 10 8 7 4
   ♥ J 2
   ♦ A 6 3
   ♣ A 8 6

5) ♠ A J 10 7 3
   ♥ A 3
   ♦ A 9
   ♣ A 10 7 5

# of aces: _____   # of aces: _____

Response: _____   Response:_____

Answers to Exercise

Exercise Eight *Answers* — Responding to Blackwood

1) You have two aces; respond 5♥.
2) You have no aces; respond 5♣.
3) You have one ace; respond 5♦.
4) You have three aces; respond 5♠.
5) You have four aces; respond 5♣.

Exercise Nine — Delaying Drawing Trumps

(E–Z Deal Cards: #7, Deal 1 — Dealer, North)

Turn up all of the cards on the first pre-dealt deal. Put each hand dummy-style at the edge of the table in front of each player.

The Bidding

North passes. What is East's opening bid?

South passes. West has 12 total points and support for opener's suit. What does West respond?

North passes. How many points does East have? How many points is West showing? At what level does the partnership belong? Is there a Golden Fit? What does East rebid?

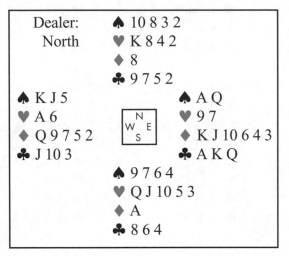

Dealer: North

♠ 10 8 3 2
♥ K 8 4 2
♦ 8
♣ 9 7 5 2

♠ K J 5   ♠ A Q
♥ A 6   ♥ 9 7
♦ Q 9 7 5 2   ♦ K J 10 6 4 3
♣ J 10 3   ♣ A K Q

♠ 9 7 6 4
♥ Q J 10 5 3
♦ A
♣ 8 6 4

How does the auction proceed? What will the contract be? Who will be the declarer?

The Play

Which player makes the opening lead? What will the opening lead be? Assuming dummy wins the first trick, which card will North play?

> ### Declarer starts by making a PLAN:
> 1. **P**ause to consider your objective
> 2. **L**ook at your winners and losers
> 3. **A**nalyze your alternatives
> 4. **N**ow put it all together

How can declarer eliminate a loser? Should declarer draw trumps first? If not, why not?

Exercise Nine *Answers* — Delaying Drawing Trumps

The Bidding

- East opens 1♦.

- West responds 3♦, the best bid available. (This is a tough decision because no bid we have discussed to date covers this situation.)

- East, with a maximum hand of 21 points, bids slam in the Golden Fit, 6♦.

- Pass, pass, pass. The contract is 6♦. East is the declarer.

The Play

- The opening lead is the ♥Q by South. Dummy wins the first trick, and North encourages with the ♥8.

- Declarer can't draw trumps first because there are too many quick losers and declarer would have to give up the lead. Instead, a heart loser is discarded on the extra spade winner in dummy by playing the ♠A and then overtaking the ♠Q with the ♠K to play the ♠J. Declarer then plays trumps.

Exercise Ten — Care in the Trump Suit

(E–Z Deal Cards: #7, Deal 2 — Dealer, East)

Turn up all of the cards on the second pre-dealt deal and arrange them as in the previous deal.

The Bidding

East passes. With a balanced hand too weak to open 1NT, what is South's opening bid?

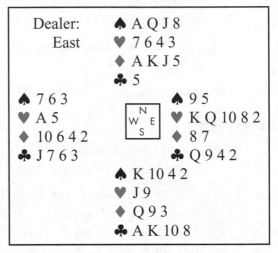

West passes. North has three suits which can be bid at the one level. Which suit does North bid first? Why? East passes. Without support for partner's suit, South still has room to bid a new suit at the one level. What does South rebid?

West passes. Counting dummy points, how many points does North have in support of opener's major? If opener has a minimum hand, is there enough combined strength for slam? What if opener has more than a minimum? What does North bid to invite partner to bid slam?

East passes. Does South accept partner's invitation? Why not? What will the contract be? Who will be the declarer?

The Play

Which player makes the opening lead? With the opponents having bid three suits, what might be a good suit to lead? If West leads the ♥ A, which card should East play?

Declarer starts by making a PLAN. How does declarer plan to eliminate the club losers? If the opponents start by playing three rounds of hearts, why must declarer be careful?

Exercise Ten *Answers* — Care in the Trump Suit

The Bidding

- South opens 1♣.

- North responds 1♦, bidding the suits up the line.

- South rebids 1♠.

- North has 18 dummy points and invites slam by bidding 5♠.

- With a minimum hand, South declines the invitation by passing. If South had more than a minimum hand, South would accept the invitation by bidding 6♠.

- The contract is 5♠. South is the declarer.

The Play

- West leads the ♥A and East plays high, the ♥10 or the ♥8, to encourage.

- Declarer can eliminate the two club losers by discarding one on the diamonds and ruffing one in dummy. Declarer must be careful if the opponents play three rounds of hearts — declarer must ruff with a high trump to avoid an overruff.

Exercise Eleven — Maintaining Control

(E–Z Deal Cards: #7, Deal 3 — Dealer, South)

Turn up all of the cards on the third pre-dealt deal and arrange them as in the previous deal.

The Bidding

South passes. What is West's opening bid?

North passes. With 6 points and support for partner's five-card suit, what does East respond?

South passes. Does West have a minimum, medium or maximum hand? What does West rebid?

```
Dealer:      ♠ Q 10 3
South        ♥ 10 8 6 4
             ♦ K Q 8 7
             ♣ 8 5
♠ A 9 7 6 2       N       ♠ K 8 5
♥ A K Q       W     E     ♥ J 9 3 2
♦ 4               S       ♦ J 10 3
♣ K Q 6 3                 ♣ J 10 7
             ♠ J 4
             ♥ 7 5
             ♦ A 9 6 5 2
             ♣ A 9 4 2
```

How does the auction proceed from there? What will the contract be? Who will be the declarer?

The Play

Which player makes the opening lead? What will the opening lead be? What is South's attitude toward the opening lead? Which card does South play?

Declarer starts by making a PLAN. How many losers can declarer afford? How many losers does declarer have? How must the missing trumps divide so that declarer has only one trump loser? Should declarer draw any trumps before playing winners? Why? Should declarer draw out the last outstanding trump? Why not?

Exercise Eleven *Answers* — Maintaining Control

The Bidding

- West opens 1♠.
- East responds 2♠.
- West has a maximum hand and bids 4♠.
- Pass, pass, pass. The contract is 4♠. West is the declarer.

The Play

- North leads the ♦ K. South encourages by playing the ♦ 9.
- Declarer can afford three losers. Declarer has only three losers as long as the missing trumps divide 3–2 and declarer doesn't lose control. Declarer should draw two rounds of trumps, leaving the last high trump outstanding, and then take the winners. If the last trump were drawn, the diamond suit would provide a source of winners for the defenders. Keeping a trump protects declarer from this.

Exercise Twelve — Establishing a Side Suit

(E–Z Deal Cards: #7, Deal 4 — Dealer, West)

Turn up all of the cards on the fourth pre-dealt deal and arrange them as in the previous deal.

The Bidding

West passes. What is North's opening bid?

East passes. How many dummy points does South have in support of partner's major suit? Is there enough combined strength for slam? What does South respond?

How does the auction proceed from there? What will the contract be? Who will be the declarer?

Dealer:	♠ A Q 10 8 6 4 2
West	♥ 9 3
	♦ J 5
	♣ A 6

♠ 3		♠ 7
♥ J 5	N W E S	♥ Q 10 7 6
♦ 8 6 4 3 2		♦ A 10 9 7
♣ K J 10 7 2		♣ 9 8 5 3

♠ K J 9 5
♥ A K 8 4 2
♦ K Q
♣ Q 4

The Play

Which player makes the opening lead? Assuming that the opening lead is the ♦ A (you should not lead away from an ace against a suit contract), which card will partner play? Why?

Declarer starts by making a PLAN. How many losers can declarer afford? How many losers does declarer have? How does declarer plan to get rid of the extra loser? If hearts break as expected, how many entries to dummy will declarer need to establish and take a heart trick? Can declarer afford to draw trumps first?

Exercise Twelve *Answers* — Establishing a Side Suit

The Bidding

- North opens 1 ♠.

- South has 20 points in support of partner's major suit, so there is enough combined strength for a slam. South responds 6 ♠.

- Pass, pass, pass. The contract is 6 ♠. North is the declarer.

The Play

- East leads the ♦ A and West discourages by playing the ♦ 2.

- Declarer has one loser too many and can discard a club on a heart winner after establishing an extra trick by ruffing the low hearts. Declarer needs three dummy entries to do this. Declarer can draw trumps first without giving up the lead.

CHAPTER 8
Putting It All Together

When there aren't enough tricks available to make the contract, use the third step of the PLAN — *Analyze your alternatives.* We have looked at several techniques for developing extra tricks or eliminating losers: promotion, length, finesses, discarding and ruffing losers. Within each suit, it's possible some of the time to combine two or more techniques. At other times, you must choose among the available techniques.

In the final step of the PLAN, *Now put it all together,* you must look at the deal as a whole rather than look at the individual suits. There may be a number of alternatives from which to choose. In some cases, you must combine the alternatives to give yourself the best chance. In other cases, you must choose the best alternative because you won't have the luxury of trying more than one.

Lets's see how to go about making these decisions.

COMBINING TECHNIQUES

When establishing tricks in a suit, it's often possible to combine the techniques of promoting high cards, developing long suits and finessing. In a suit contract, the trump suit provides additional possibilities. Some of these combinations have been discussed in earlier chapters, but there is an almost endless variety of suit combinations — this is part of the fascination of the game.

Promotion, Length and Finesses

Here are some examples of combining various techniques to get the maximum number of tricks from each suit. Assume you have sufficient entries and no more important considerations for the deal as a whole.

DUMMY: K Q 6 3 2   This suit can be developed with a combination
DECLARER: J 5 4   of promotion and length. The king can be used to drive out the ace, promoting the queen and the jack into winners.

There are eight cards in this suit. If the missing cards divide 3–2, dummy's low cards will also be tricks, giving you four tricks in all. If the missing cards divide 4–1, you can still develop one extra trick through length by giving up a second trick. You would end up with three tricks.

DUMMY: A Q J 2

DECLARER: 6 5 4 3

You can combine a finesse with length to try for all four tricks. Lead a low card toward dummy. If the opponent on your left has the king, your finesse will win. Then you need an entry back to your hand to repeat the finesse. Take the ace. If the missing cards divide 3–2, your remaining low card will be a winner.

DUMMY: A Q 4 3 2

DECLARER: 6 5

Lead toward dummy, taking a finesse. If the finesse is successful, play the ace and give up a trick. If the missing cards divide 3–3, your remaining two low cards are winners and you get four tricks. If the missing cards divide 4–2, you must give up a second trick and will end up with three tricks.

DUMMY: Q 3

DECLARER: A 7 6 5 2

Start by leading low toward dummy's queen. If your left-hand opponent has the king, you'll win a trick with the queen sooner or later. You also have a trick with the ace and, if the missing cards divide 3–3, will end up with four tricks. If they are 4–2, you must give up a second trick to establish a third winner.

DUMMY: Q 10 4 3 2

DECLARER: K 5

Start by using the king to drive out the opponents' ace, promoting the queen into a winner. Next, lead the 5 and finesse dummy's 10, hoping your left-hand opponent has the jack. If the finesse wins, play the queen. If the suit divides 3–3, your two low cards will be winners, giving you four tricks in all.

This last suit is developed through a combination of promotion, length and the finesse. In an actual deal, a number of things may go differently. The opponents may hold up their ace when you play the king. That doesn't stop you from leading toward dummy to try the finesse. The finesse may not work, but you may still get tricks through length. The suit will more likely break 4–2 than 3–3, but you can establish one additional trick through length. In the end, you may get anywhere from one to four tricks from this suit. Combining good technique with a little luck will do wonders in making tricks appear from thin air!

Knowing the best way to handle a particular suit combination still must be put into the context of a complete deal. Other considerations, such as entries, will also come into play. Let's look at a deal where you need lots of luck together with a knowledge of how to play a particular suit to bring home your contract.

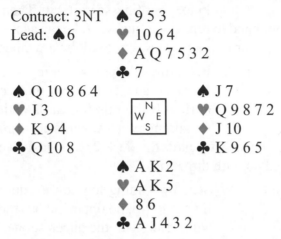

```
Contract: 3NT    ♠ 9 5 3
Lead: ♠6         ♥ 10 6 4
                 ♦ A Q 7 5 3 2
                 ♣ 7
♠ Q 10 8 6 4              ♠ J 7
♥ J 3            N        ♥ Q 9 8 7 2
♦ K 9 4        W   E      ♦ J 10
♣ Q 10 8         S        ♣ K 9 6 5
                 ♠ A K 2
                 ♥ A K 5
                 ♦ 8 6
                 ♣ A J 4 3 2
```

You need nine tricks in a 3NT contract. You start with six sure tricks: two spades, two hearts, one diamond and one club. It looks as if the diamond suit has some potential for producing extra tricks, but how should you handle this combination?

One extra trick can come from taking a finesse if West has the ♦ K. In addition, if the five missing cards divide 3–2, three extra tricks will come from length by giving up one trick. Is that good enough?

When putting it all together, don't forget to consider entries. The only entry to dummy is in the diamond suit itself. You can't take the finesse and then give up a trick, since you will have no entry to dummy's winners. Instead, since you must give up a trick even if the finesse works and the suit divides 3–2, incorporate a ducking play as well.

Win the first trick and play a low diamond from both hands, ducking a trick. Now the stage is set. When you win the next trick, lead your other low diamond and finesse with dummy's queen. You can breathe a sigh of relief when this works, since you would take no diamond tricks if it lost. Now you can play the ♦ A. When the suit divides 3–2, your remaining diamonds are all winners, and you are in dummy to take them.

You will end up with five diamond tricks and make an overtrick. You were lucky — East could have held the ♦ K. In that case, you would have taken no diamond tricks, and the contract would have been defeated by four tricks — quite a swing! Nonetheless, you needed to know how to play the diamond suit to give yourself a chance.

Using the Trump Suit

When you have a trump suit, there are further opportunities to develop tricks in side suits. Here are some examples:

DUMMY: 5 2

DECLARER: A Q 8 3

You have three potential losers. You can lead a low card from dummy, however, and finesse the queen. If this play wins, you can take the ace and ruff both of your remaining losers in dummy, ending up with no losers in the suit.

DUMMY: A Q 8 6 3

DECLARER: 5 4

You have only one loser in your hand. You can avoid losing a trick by taking a successful finesse. In addition, you can establish an extra winner by leading the suit again and ruffing it. If the suit breaks 3–3, dummy's remaining two cards will be winners, and you can use them to discard losers in other side suits. Even if the suit breaks 4–2, you can establish one extra winner by crossing back to dummy, leading the suit again and ruffing.

DUMMY: J 8 6 5 4 2

DECLARER: 7

This is a similar situation. If you need to develop an extra trick in this suit, start by giving up a trick. When you regain the lead, lead the suit from dummy and ruff. Cross to dummy, lead the suit again and ruff. If the missing cards divide 3–3, dummy's remaining cards are winners. If the missing cards divide 4–2, you cross to dummy, lead the suit again and ruff.

DUMMY: —

DECLARER: K Q J 10

You can promote three tricks by leading the king to drive out the ace. In a trump contract, you may be able to take three tricks without losing one. Lead the king. If your left-hand opponent plays the ace, ruff in dummy. Now the remaining cards are winners. If the ace isn't played, discard from dummy. If your right-hand opponent follows low, you can continue by leading the queen to see whether your left-hand opponent wants to play the ace. Whenever your opponent does play the ace, you can ruff and end up without any losers in the suit. This technique is called a ruffing finesse. You are finessing against the ace on your left, and you'll use dummy's trumps to ruff the ace when it appears.

CHOOSING AMONG TECHNIQUES

Sometimes you can't employ more than one technique to handle a suit. How you play the suit may depend on such factors as how many tricks you need or can afford to lose and whether there is a dangerous opponent.

Eight Ever, Nine Never

Consider the following layout where the only missing high card is the queen:

K J 10 6

— $\begin{array}{c} N \\ W \quad E \\ S \end{array}$ —

A 5 3 2

Declarer could take the ace and the king. If the queen doesn't appear, declarer could play the jack to drive it out, promoting the 10 into a winner. Alternatively, declarer could take the ace and lead low toward dummy. If West plays a low card, declarer could take a finesse against the queen by playing the 10 (or the jack). Which way should declarer play the suit?

If declarer needs just three tricks from the suit and can afford to lose a trick, then either way is fine. However, if declarer needs all four tricks and can't afford to give up the lead, a useful guideline for this situation is: eight ever, nine never.

Use this advice when you are missing a queen and must decide whether or not to take a finesse. With eight or fewer cards, take the finesse (ever). With nine or more cards, don't finesse (never) — play the ace and the king and hope one of the opponents has to play the queen. The ever and never are a bit extreme. When you look at the entire deal, you may see valid reasons for not finessing with eight cards or for taking a finesse with nine cards.

Here are some examples of suits where you would consider using the guideline *eight ever, nine never.*

DUMMY: A K J 6 5 2   With nine cards in the combined hands, play
DECLARER: 8 7 3   the ace and the king. This is the nine never case
                       — meaning, don't finesse for the queen.

DUMMY: A K J 6 3   With only eight cards, plan to finesse by lead-
DECLARER: 7 5 4   ing low to dummy's jack. If you have enough
                       entries, win the first trick with dummy's ace (or
                       king) and then come to your hand to finesse.
This gives you an extra chance in case your right-hand opponent started
with a singleton queen.

DUMMY: A J 3   Win the first trick with the king and lead low
DECLARER: K 6 2   toward dummy, finessing with the jack. If a
                       low card appears — eight ever applies when
                       you have fewer than eight cards.

DUMMY: K J 7 6 3 2   With nine cards, you normally play the ace
DECLARER: A 5 4   and the king first. If you could afford to lose a
                       trick in this suit, however, and dummy had no
                       other entries, it would be safer to take the ace
and then finesse with the jack if the queen did not appear. If the finesse
loses, you would still have a low card to lead to dummy's winners. If you
play the ace and the king instead, the queen may not appear if the suit
was originally divided 3–1. You can drive out the queen but you end up
without an entry to dummy. This is the type of consideration that makes
never too extreme.

Let's look at a complete deal and put the guideline to work:

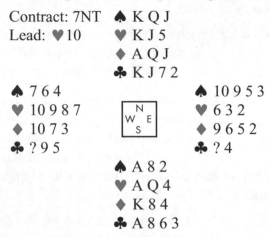

Contract: 7NT
Lead: ♥10

♠ K Q J
♥ K J 5
♦ A Q J
♣ K J 7 2

♠ 7 6 4
♥ 10 9 8 7
♦ 10 7 3
♣ ? 9 5

♠ 10 9 5 3
♥ 6 3 2
♦ 9 6 5 2
♣ ? 4

♠ A 8 2
♥ A Q 4
♦ K 8 4
♣ A 8 6 3

With nearly every high card in the deck, you have bid 7NT, as high as you can go. Unfortunately, the one high card you lack is the ♣Q. You have three tricks each in spades, hearts and diamonds. You must take all four tricks in clubs to make the grand slam.

You can delay things by taking your spade, heart and diamond winners, but eventually you must play the ♣A and lead a low club toward dummy. Naturally, West produces the ♣9 (if the ♣Q appeared, all the excitement would be over). Do you finesse dummy's ♣J or play the ♣K, hoping East has just the ♣Q left?

The guideline is there to help you out. *Eight ever* guides you to take the finesse. Does it work? If it does, you and your partner can score up your large bonus. If it doesn't, you can be content knowing you made the correct play.

Counting Tricks

Here's a suit combination we have looked at before:

7 4 2

— —

K Q 3

The best way to play this suit is to lead from dummy toward declarer's hand. If East has the ace and plays low, declarer wins the first trick with the queen (or the king). Then, after going back to the dummy, declarer leads another small card. Whether or not East plays the ace, declarer ends up with two tricks. If West started with the ace, declarer gets only one trick.

Alternatively, declarer can lead the king to drive out the ace and promote the queen. Declarer gets one trick no matter which opponent has the ace but gives up the chance to take two tricks.

Why would declarer ever settle for one trick? While the finesse may be the best play for a particular suit, declarer must take the whole deal into consideration. Declarer may need only one trick and not two. Dummy may not have two entries to allow declarer the luxury of leading twice toward declarer's hand. Dummy may have two entries, but declarer may need one for another purpose.

Here are some other examples where declarer must choose the best technique for developing a suit based on the number of tricks needed and declarer's ability to give up the lead:

DUMMY: A Q J

DECLARER: 8 7 2

If declarer needs only two tricks and can afford to give up the lead, declarer can play the ace, lead the queen to drive out the king, and promote the jack into a second winner. If declarer needs all three tricks or can't afford to lose a trick, declarer must try the finesse. Two entries will be needed in order for declarer to be able to finesse twice.

DUMMY: A Q 3

DECLARER: 10 9 6 5 4 2

If declarer needs all six tricks in this suit, a low card must be led to dummy's queen, hoping the left-hand opponent has the king. Then declarer plays the ace, hoping the suit divides 2–2. If declarer can afford to lose one or two tricks or is short of entries, declarer can play the ace and then lead the queen to drive out the king. If the suit breaks 2–2, declarer will take five tricks. If the suit breaks 3–1, declarer will take at least four tricks (five if the singleton is the king or the jack) provided there is an entry back to take the winners.

DUMMY: K 2

DECLARER: 5 4 3

Normally, declarer will lead toward dummy's king, hoping the left-hand opponent holds the ace. If this were a side suit in a suit contract, however, declarer might want to ruff a loser in dummy. When there are few entries to declarer's hand, declarer can lead the suit from dummy, giving up two tricks. In the end, declarer would be able to ruff a loser in dummy.

Here is a deal where a specific suit can't be played the way declarer would like to play it:

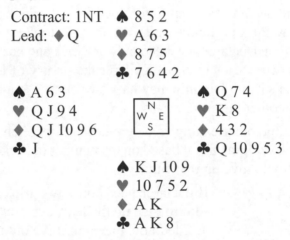

Contract: 1NT
Lead: ◆ Q

    ♠ 8 5 2
    ♥ A 6 3
    ◆ 8 7 5
    ♣ 7 6 4 2

♠ A 6 3   ♠ Q 7 4
♥ Q J 9 4   ♥ K 8
◆ Q J 10 9 6   ◆ 4 3 2
♣ J   ♣ Q 10 9 5 3

    ♠ K J 10 9
    ♥ 10 7 5 2
    ◆ A K
    ♣ A K 8

Declarer has one heart trick, two diamond tricks and two club tricks. Two more tricks are needed to make 1NT. Ideally, declarer would like to take a spade finesse, hoping East has the ♠Q. By repeating the finesse, declarer could take three tricks.

Dummy, however, has only one entry — even if East has the ♠Q, declarer can't repeat the finesse. Using the ♥A as an entry to dummy is also dangerous. Once the ♥A is gone, the opponents can take all of their heart winners along with any winners *they* establish.

Since declarer needs only two spade tricks, they can be developed simply by using promotion. After winning the first trick, declarer leads the ♠K to drive out the ace. The opponents drive out one of declarer's remaining high cards, but then declarer leads the ♠J to drive out the ♠Q. The defenders can take the winners they have established, but they don't have enough tricks to defeat the contract. When declarer regains the lead, the promoted ♠10 and ♠9 can be taken along with declarer's other winners to make the contract.

Safety Play

Another reason for playing a suit in a particular manner is safety. Sometimes you can afford one loser in the suit but you want to avoid two losers. Look at this layout:

```
            K J 4 2
               N
   —        W     E        —
               S
            A 7 5
```

If you need four tricks in this suit, you play the ace, lead a low card toward dummy and finesse the jack when West plays low, hoping West has the queen. If the finesse works, you play the king and hope the suit divides 3–3.

If you need only three tricks in the suit and can afford to lose one, the safest play is to take the ace and the king and then lead low toward dummy's jack. You still will take three tricks if the suit breaks 3–3, although one of the opponents will win a trick with the queen. You also will take three tricks when West has the queen, even if the suit breaks 4–2 or 5–1, since you end up leading toward dummy's jack.

Why is this called a safety play? Suppose the actual layout of the missing cards is:

```
            K J 4 2
                 N
   10 9 6 3    W     E    Q 8
                 S
            A 7 5
```

If you try for all four tricks, playing the ace and finessing dummy's jack, you lose to East's queen. Later when you play dummy's king, the suit divides 4–2 — you get only the two tricks you started with. By making the safety play of taking the king and the ace first, you find out about East's doubleton queen and no longer need to risk the finesse. By sacrificing the potential for a fourth trick, you increase your chances of safely winding up with three tricks.

The safety play is generally beyond the scope of this text. This example is included so you can see another reason why one method of playing a particular suit might be chosen over another method. Now let's move on to look at how you can select the best suit to develop when you have a choice.

COMBINING ALTERNATIVES

When putting it all together, you often have more than one suit from which you can get extra tricks or from which you must eliminate losers. In some cases, you have to develop two or more suits. At other times, you must combine your chances, so that you can turn to an alternative suit when you can't get the tricks you need in the first suit.

Which Suit First?

On many deals, you must be careful of the order in which you take your tricks, even if you don't have to develop them. Here is a simple example:

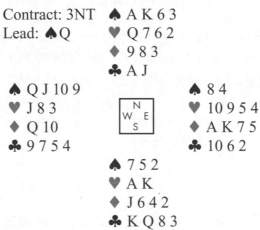

Contract: 3NT ♠ A K 6 3
Lead: ♠Q ♥ Q 7 6 2
            ♦ 9 8 3
            ♣ A J

♠ Q J 10 9   ♠ 8 4
♥ J 8 3   ♥ 10 9 5 4
♦ Q 10   ♦ A K 7 5
♣ 9 7 5 4   ♣ 10 6 2

            ♠ 7 5 2
            ♥ A K
            ♦ J 6 4 2
            ♣ K Q 8 3

You need nine tricks to make 3NT. At first glance, you seem to have everything you need. You have two sure tricks in spades, three in hearts and four in clubs. Suits in which you can't take all of your winners without using an entry in another suit are said to be *blocked*. In this deal, the heart and the club suits are blocked.

After winning the first trick with the ♠K, play the ♣A and the ♣J to unblock that suit. Now lead a heart to your king so you can take the ♣K and the ♣Q. Next take the ♥A to *unblock* that suit. Now lead a spade to dummy's ♠A and take the ♥Q as the ninth trick.

If you play the suits in a different order, you may find that you have trouble taking all nine of your winners. For example, if you play the ♥A and the ♥K, unblocking the heart suit, you won't have an entry to your club winners.

Here is a deal where you must not only develop two suits but also be careful to play them in the right order:

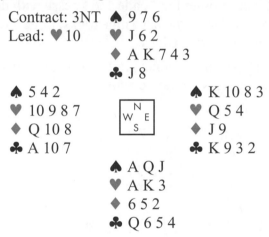

Contract: 3NT
Lead: ♥10

♠ 9 7 6
♥ J 6 2
♦ A K 7 4 3
♣ J 8

♠ 5 4 2
♥ 10 9 8 7
♦ Q 10 8
♣ A 10 7

♠ K 10 8 3
♥ Q 5 4
♦ J 9
♣ K 9 3 2

♠ A Q J
♥ A K 3
♦ 6 5 2
♣ Q 6 5 4

You have one sure trick in spades, two in hearts and two in diamonds. Four more are needed to make your contract of 3NT. One source of extra tricks is the spade suit. If East has the ♠K, you can win a finesse. You'll need two entries to dummy, so you can repeat the finesse and take two extra spade tricks. The diamond suit also can be developed. If the missing diamonds divide 3–2, you can establish two extra tricks by giving up one trick. By developing both suits, you can get four extra tricks.

You must be very careful to do everything in the right order. The only entries to dummy are the ♦A and the ♦K. These will be needed to take the spade finesses. One of them also will be needed as an entry to the diamond suit itself — that means you must duck an early diamond trick.

Neither of these techniques is new. We have looked already at the finesse and the ducking play when developing long suits.

After winning the first heart trick, duck a diamond. Assuming the missing diamonds are divided 3–2, this play establishes the suit while leaving the ♦ A and the ♦ K as entries. If the opponents play another heart, win the trick and lead a diamond to dummy's king. It isn't time yet to take the rest of your diamond winners, since you have work to do in the spade suit.

Lead a low spade from dummy. When East plays low, finesse with the ♠ J. When this trick wins, lead a diamond to dummy's ace. Since this is the last time you will be in dummy, take your other two diamond winners. Finally, lead another low spade and finesse with the ♠ Q. When this wins, take your ♠ A and you have nine tricks: three spade tricks, two heart tricks and four diamond tricks.

When you must promote winners in two suits, you generally should start by playing the longest combined suit first.

Look at this deal:

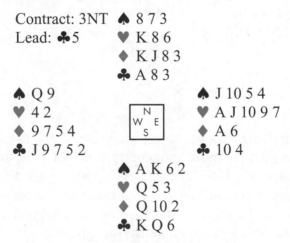

```
Contract: 3NT   ♠ 8 7 3
Lead: ♣5        ♥ K 8 6
                ♦ K J 8 3
                ♣ A 8 3
♠ Q 9                        ♠ J 10 5 4
♥ 4 2               N        ♥ A J 10 9 7
♦ 9 7 5 4        W     E     ♦ A 6
♣ J 9 7 5 2         S        ♣ 10 4
                ♠ A K 6 2
                ♥ Q 5 3
                ♦ Q 10 2
                ♣ K Q 6
```

You start with two spade tricks and three club tricks. Four more tricks are needed to make 3NT. Another spade trick is a possibility if the suit divides 3–3. The suit, however, most likely is divided 4–2. You can develop a heart trick by using one of your high cards to drive out the ♥ A. You also can promote three tricks in diamonds by driving out the ♦ A.

Which ace should you drive out first?

Since you have more diamonds than hearts, you should drive out the ♦ A first. Whatever the opponent leads back, you can win. Then you can drive out the ♥ A to establish your ninth trick.

What happens if you play the shorter suit first? Suppose you win the first trick in your hand and lead a heart to dummy's king. Because of East's holding, East will win the trick and establish some heart tricks by leading the ♥ J to drive out your ♥ Q. Now when you try to establish the diamond tricks you need, East will win the ♦ A and take the three established heart winners. Together with the ♥ A, these tricks will be enough to defeat your contract.

Combining Chances

When either of two suits will give you the extra tricks you need, you sometimes can combine your chances.

Look at the following deal:

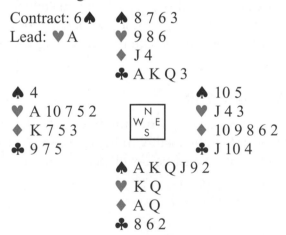

You can afford one loser in your small slam of 6♠. After taking the ♥ A, the opponent leads another heart, which you win with the ♥ K. You still have a potential diamond loser. When you *Analyze your alternatives,* you see two possibilities. You could lead a diamond from dummy, and if East produces a low diamond, finesse the queen. If East has the ♦ K, you make your contract; if West has it, you are defeated.

The second alternative is to discard your ♦ Q on an extra winner in dummy. If the missing clubs divide exactly 3–3, dummy's low club will become a winner. Unfortunately, the most likely division of the clubs is 4–2.

If you had to choose between the alternatives, the diamond finesse would look better. It's a 50–50 proposition while a 3–3 club break is much less than an even chance, but you don't have to choose. Why not try both? Two chances are better than one!

After drawing trumps (you don't want the opponents to ruff one of your club winners), which alternative should you try first? If you take a losing diamond finesse first, it will be too late to try the clubs. You must play the clubs first. If they divide 3–3, you can discard your ♦ Q, and you won't need to take the finesse. If the clubs don't break 3–3, your second option is to take the diamond finesse. On this hand, the clubs break 3–3. If you didn't give yourself this extra chance, you would be defeated, since the diamond finesse loses.

Many deals are similar to this one — first you can try one thing and then another if your first alternative doesn't work out. However, be careful to put your PLAN together so you can try everything in the appropriate order.

Help from Another Suit

When you can't see how to avoid losers in one suit, take a look at the whole deal to see if another suit will help you. We already have seen how a side suit can sometimes be developed to provide extra winners for discards.

Here is a different example:

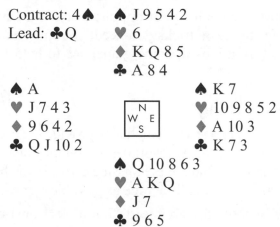

Contract: 4♠
Lead: ♣Q

♠ J 9 5 4 2
♥ 6
♦ K Q 8 5
♣ A 8 4

♠ A
♥ J 7 4 3
♦ 9 6 4 2
♣ Q J 10 2

♠ K 7
♥ 10 9 8 5 2
♦ A 10 3
♣ K 7 3

♠ Q 10 8 6 3
♥ A K Q
♦ J 7
♣ 9 6 5

You can afford three losers in your contract of 4♠. You have two trump losers, one diamond loser and two club losers. The opponents have driven out your ♣A at trick one, making all of your losers quick. Since you must give up the lead, you can't draw trumps until you have done something about eliminating your losers. You can't do anything about the ♠A, the ♠K and the ♦A, so you must eliminate the two club losers. This doesn't look easy. You can't discard them on extra winners in dummy, nor does it appear that you can ruff them in dummy.

If you look carefully, however, you will see a way to ruff your club losers! After winning the ♣A, play the ♥A, the ♥K and the ♥Q, and discard two clubs from dummy. Now dummy has no clubs left and you can ruff your two club losers. Once you have discarded dummy's clubs, it's safe to draw trumps since you no longer have too many quick losers. You'll lose only two spade tricks and the ♦A.

Make sure you take time to look at the entire deal, not just the individual suits. New possibilities will arise when you start combining the play of two or more suits.

CHOOSING AMONG ALTERNATIVES

You can't always combine your options when you have more than one alternative for the extra tricks you need; you must choose one and go with it. Let's take a look at some guidelines to help you make the right decision.

Go for the Sure Thing

Sometimes you have one suit which may provide the tricks you need, but only if the lie of the cards is favorable — you may need a successful finesse or a reasonable division of the missing cards. If you have a choice, select the suit that requires as little luck as possible.

For example, suppose declarer needs four tricks from one suit. Compare the following three layouts:

1) DUMMY	2) DUMMY	3) DUMMY
Q 5 3	Q 10 3	Q 5 3
■	■	■
DECLARER	DECLARER	DECLARER
A 7 6 4 2	K J 9 4 2	K J 6 4 2

In the first layout, declarer may be able to take four tricks. A finesse can be taken by leading toward dummy's queen, hoping the king is on declarer's left. In addition, the missing cards must divide 3–2. Since declarer needs a very favorable lie of the missing cards, this suit wouldn't be selected unless there were no alternative.

In the second layout, declarer has all of the missing high cards except the ace. By driving out the ace, declarer can promote four winners. It doesn't matter which opponent has the ace or how the missing cards are divided. Since this is a sure thing, declarer would definitely play this suit if there is a choice.

The third layout is closer to what declarer actually may get at the table. Declarer doesn't care which opponent has the missing ace, but since declarer doesn't have all of the high cards, the suit needs to divide 3–2. While this is not a sure thing, it is preferable to the suit in the first layout.

In a trump contract, you should also look for the sure thing when trying to eliminate losers.

Here is an example in a complete deal:

Contract: 4♠
Lead: ♣Q

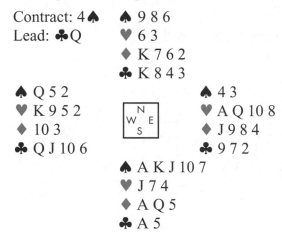

♠ 9 8 6
♥ 6 3
♦ K 7 6 2
♣ K 8 4 3

♠ Q 5 2
♥ K 9 5 2
♦ 10 3
♣ Q J 10 6

♠ 4 3
♥ A Q 10 8
♦ J 9 8 4
♣ 9 7 2

♠ A K J 10 7
♥ J 7 4
♦ A Q 5
♣ A 5

You're missing the ♠Q and you have three heart losers. You could lead a spade from dummy and take a finesse when East plays a low card. This will work when East has the ♠Q, a 50–50 proposition. You could also try discarding one of the heart losers on an extra winner in dummy. Dummy has no sure winner, but if the missing diamonds divide 3–3, dummy's remaining diamond will become a winner. The most likely divison of the diamonds, however, is 4–2.

The sure way to eliminate one of your losers is by ruffing a heart in dummy. This will work no matter who holds the ♠Q and how the diamonds break. After winning the first club trick, play a heart immediately. Suppose East wins and leads a spade. Don't be tempted to take the finesse. If it loses, West can lead another trump, and you may soon find yourself with no trump in dummy to take care of your loser. Win the spade and lead another heart. If East wins and leads another spade, again refuse to take the finesse. You have a sure thing going. Win the spade, lead your last heart and ruff it in dummy. You end up losing just two heart tricks and the ♠Q.

Go for the Right Number of Tricks

If you have a choice of suits to develop, be careful to pick the one which will provide enough tricks to make the contract. For example, take a look at the following deal:

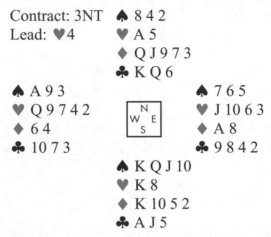

Contract: 3NT
Lead: ♥4

♠ 8 4 2
♥ A 5
♦ Q J 9 7 3
♣ K Q 6

♠ A 9 3
♥ Q 9 7 4 2
♦ 6 4
♣ 10 7 3

♠ 7 6 5
♥ J 10 6 3
♦ A 8
♣ 9 8 4 2

♠ K Q J 10
♥ K 8
♦ K 10 5 2
♣ A J 5

You need nine tricks in 3NT. You start with two heart tricks and three club tricks. In the spade suit, you can drive out the opponents' ace and promote three winners. In the diamond suit, you can also drive out the opponents' ace and develop four extra tricks.

Since you need four more tricks to make the contract, play the diamond suit after winning the first heart trick. That will guarantee the contract.

If you are tempted to play the spades first, look what happens. West wins the ♠A and leads another heart to drive out your remaining high card. Now you have eight sure tricks but still need to develop one more. Eventually, you must play a diamond to try to get your ninth trick. East wins the ace and leads another heart. The opponents get three heart tricks and their two aces to defeat the contract. Make sure you keep an eye on your objective when choosing which suit to play.

Go with Your Only Chance

Suppose you have a suit that could provide the tricks you need. Unfortunately, the opponents are hard at work trying to make things tough for you — they won't always give you time to develop the suit you like best. In such cases, you may have to choose another suit which, while not offering as good a chance for extra tricks, offers the only hope of making the contract. Here is an example:

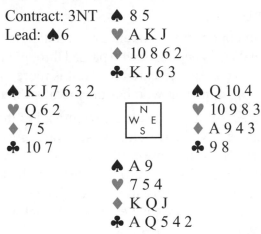

```
Contract: 3NT    ♠ 8 5
Lead: ♠6         ♥ A K J
                 ♦ 10 8 6 2
                 ♣ K J 6 3
♠ K J 7 6 3 2              ♠ Q 10 4
♥ Q 6 2          N        ♥ 10 9 8 3
♦ 7 5         W     E     ♦ A 9 4 3
♣ 10 7           S        ♣ 9 8
                 ♠ A 9
                 ♥ 7 5 4
                 ♦ K Q J
                 ♣ A Q 5 4 2
```

You start with eight sure tricks: one spade, two hearts and five clubs. You need only one more trick to make your contract of 3NT. The suit to develop appears to be diamonds. By driving out the opponents' ♦ A, you can promote more winners than you need. Unfortunately, you must watch out for the opponents. They have led a spade and are intent on driving out your ♠ A. If you let the opponents win a trick with the ♦ A, they'll take enough spade tricks to defeat the contract.

Do you have an alternative? You can lead a heart toward dummy and finesse the ♥ J when West plays low. If West has the ♥ Q, the finesse will succeed and you'll have your ninth trick. If East has the ♥ Q, down you go. The finesse is a 50–50 chance.

Even though the diamonds offer certain tricks, they don't give you a chance to make the contract. The opponents have already established their spade winners. Instead, go with the 50% chance of the heart finesse. The opponents haven't left you any other option.

Go with the Odds

If you must choose between two suits, either of which could provide the tricks you need, select the one which gives you the better chance.

Going with the odds is definitely a good idea, but how do you know what the odds are? Given the large number of possible suit combinations, the subject can become quite complex. Even a simple finesse, which looks like a 50% chance, can be affected by such things as the bidding or the division of the cards.

For example, an opponent who opened the bidding is more likely to hold a missing king than an opponent who passed throughout the auction; an opponent who has four or five cards in a suit is more likely to hold a missing queen than an opponent who has only two or three.

It is beyond the scope of this text to delve into all of the possibilities — for now, the concepts you have already seen will provide sufficient guidelines. A finesse for one missing card can be viewed as a 50–50 proposition. An odd number of missing cards will tend to divide as evenly as possible, and an even number of missing cards will tend to divide slightly unevenly. Based on this, here are the key concepts that will help you go with the odds in the most common situations:

- The odds for a successful finesse for one missing card are approximately 50%.*

- The odds of five missing cards dividing 3–2 are greater than 50% (68%).

- The odds of six missing cards dividing 3–3 are less than 50% (36%). The odds on a 4–2 division are 48%.

*See the appendix for more suit division probabilities.

Let's see how this information can be applied on the following deal:

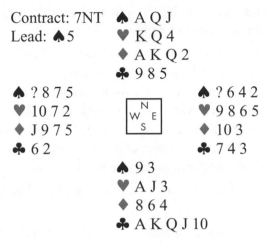

Contract: 7NT
Lead: ♠5

♠ A Q J
♥ K Q 4
♦ A K Q 2
♣ 9 8 5

♠ ?8 7 5
♥ 10 7 2
♦ J 9 7 5
♣ 6 2

♠ ?6 4 2
♥ 9 8 6 5
♦ 10 3
♣ 7 4 3

♠ 9 3
♥ A J 3
♦ 8 6 4
♣ A K Q J 10

You have to take all of the tricks in your grand slam, and the opponents have made you make a choice at trick one. You have 12 sure tricks: one spade, three hearts, three diamonds and five clubs. Do you take the spade finesse for your 13th trick, or do you win the ♠A — hoping the missing diamonds are divided 3–3, so that dummy has four diamond tricks? It's your play — the finesse is the percentage favorite.

GUIDELINES FOR DEFENSE

When you are defending, go through the same general thought process that declarer uses. Make your own plan. This is complicated by the fact that you can't see your partner's hand. You must use dummy, your hand and your imagination to see where the tricks for your side will come from.

The Defenders' Plan

The plan for a defender involves the same four steps that declarer goes through — but keep in mind that you are working with a partner. The first step is to determine the objective: *how many tricks do we need to defeat the contract?* Notice how "we" replaces the "you" from declarer's plan. Then you determine how far you are from the objective: *how many sure tricks do we have?* Determining the sure tricks is not as easy for a defender because you can't see your partner's cards. Instead, you must make use of any inferences you have — from the bidding, the cards your partner plays and the way declarer plays.

The third step is to determine how you can establish the additional tricks you need to defeat the contract: *where can we get extra tricks?* Again, you must imagine what the unseen hands look like, perhaps crediting partner with cards which are necessary to defeat the contract. Finally, put it into an overall plan: *how do we put it all together?* In what order will you take your tricks? How can you cooperate with partner to make sure you are both working along the same lines?

The defenders' plan will be discussed in more detail in the next book in this series, *Defense*.

For now, let's see how a defender would approach the following deal:

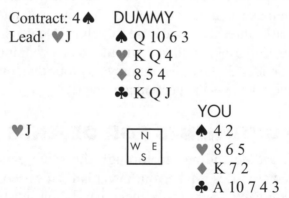

Contract: 4♠   DUMMY
Lead: ♥J   ♠ Q 10 6 3
                ♥ K Q 4
                ♦ 8 5 4
                ♣ K Q J

                        YOU
        ♥J   ♠ 4 2
                        ♥ 8 6 5
                        ♦ K 7 2
                        ♣ A 10 7 4 3

South opens the bidding 1♠. The contract becomes 4♠ — you and your partner pass throughout the auction. Your partner leads the ♥J. Declarer wins the first trick with the ♥A and draws trumps with the ♠A and the ♠K. Then declarer leads a club to dummy's ♣J. What is your plan?

To defeat 4♠, you need four tricks. The ♣A is a sure trick but you need to find three more. Since declarer has drawn trumps, you'll get no tricks from the spade suit. Declarer has all of the high hearts, so that suit offers no possibility. Once your ♣A is driven out, declarer will have all of the high clubs. That leaves diamonds as the only chance.

Although you have no tricks in diamonds yourself, remember that your partner is on the other side of the table to help you. You may not be able to visualize exactly what partner must hold, but you can see that your only hope of defeating the contract is to take three diamond tricks. If declarer has some of the missing high diamonds, don't worry. You can't defeat every contract, but you can give it your best try.

In putting it all together, you have the same considerations as declarer. For example, should you hold up the ♣A, refusing to win the first trick? That will do no good since declarer still has lots of entries to dummy. If declarer has only one club, this will be your last chance to win the ace.

Having gone through all of this, win the ♣A and lead a diamond, hoping the complete layout is something like this:

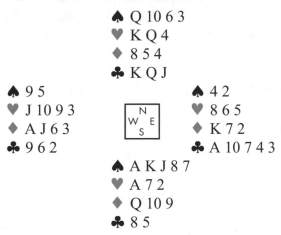

```
                  ♠ Q 10 6 3
                  ♥ K Q 4
                  ♦ 8 5 4
                  ♣ K Q J
   ♠ 9 5                         ♠ 4 2
   ♥ J 10 9 3         N          ♥ 8 6 5
   ♦ A J 6 3       W     E       ♦ K 7 2
   ♣ 9 6 2            S          ♣ A 10 7 4 3
                  ♠ A K J 8 7
                  ♥ A 7 2
                  ♦ Q 10 9
                  ♣ 8 5
```

When you lead a diamond, declarer's ♦Q is trapped. Whatever declarer plays, you and partner can take three diamond tricks to defeat the contract. One for the defense!

BIDDING — PREEMPTIVE BIDS

An opening suit bid of 2♦, 2♥, 2♠ or an opening bid at the three level or higher shows a hand with a long suit that is too weak to open the bidding at the one level (*i.e.,* fewer than 13 points). This is called a preemptive opening bid, or preempt.

The Theory behind Preemptive Bids

Why start the bidding at the two level or higher with a hand that is too weak to open at the one level? The advantage of a preempt is that it takes up a lot of room on the Bidding Scale and makes it difficult for the other partnership to exchange information.

For example, if you were planning to open 1♦ and the opponent in front of you opened 3♥, you would be faced with a difficult problem. How do you show partner that you have an opening bid with diamonds when the auction is already at the three level? A preempt may cause the opponents to reach the wrong strain, end up too high or too low or be unable to get into the auction at all.

Of course, a preempt may make if difficult for your partner to bid effectively, and there is also the danger that you may be doubled and defeated badly! You can minimize the risk and maximize the potential gain by preempting only with the appropriate type of hand.

Requirements for a Preemptive Opening Bid

- 2♦, 2♥, 2♠ openings promise a strong six-card suit and fewer than 13 total points.

♠ 5 2
♥ 8 2
♦ K Q J 7 3 2
♣ J 4 3

This hand contains a strong six-card diamond suit and 9 total points (7 HCP plus 2 points for the long diamonds). Nine points is not enough for a one-level opening bid, but qualifies as a perfect two-level preempt. The correct opening bid is 2♦. Preemptive bids at the two-level are called weak two bids.

- 3♣, 3♦, 3♥ and 3♠ openings promise a strong seven-card suit and fewer than 13 total points.

♠ 3 2
♥ A Q 10 7 4 3 2
♦ 4 3 2
♣ 8

This hand contains a strong seven-card heart suit and 9 total points (6 HCP Plus 3 points for the long hearts). Although this hand does not have enough points to open at the one-level, it is a perfect three-level opening. The correct opening bid is 3♥.

- 4♣, 4♦, 4♥ and 4♠ openings promise a strong eight-card suit and fewer than 13 total points.

♠ A K J 10 8 7 4 3   This hand contains a strong eight-card spade suit
♥ 7   and 12 total points (8 HCP and 4 points for the long
♦ 6 5 2   spades). Twelve total points is not quite enough for
♣ 8   a one-level opening bid, but this example is a great
                      four-level opening. The correct opening bid is 4♠.

In each of the above definitions, there are not enough total points for a one-level opening bid. The higher the level of the preempt, the more cards required in the long suit. A weak two bid requires a six-card suit, while three- and four-level opening preempts require seven-card and eight-card suits respectively. In addition, all of our preemptive openings must be based on a strong suit.

There are various definitions of what constitutes a strong suit, but the definition we will use is as follows:

A strong suit contains at least two of the top three cards (the ace, the king and the queen).

One advantage of a preempt is that it is very descriptive for partner. Knowing the type of hand you have, partner can respond accordingly.

The advantage of having a good long suit is that it is more difficult for the opponents to double the contract. Even if they do, the penalty is likely to be less than the value of a contract they could make.

Responding to a Preempt

The key to responding to a preempt is to think about what your partner's hand looks like. You should try to estimate the number of tricks you think you will win and how many losers you think there are with your partner's long suit as trump. ***Responding to a preempt is more about counting tricks than it is about counting points.***

Your partner opens with a weak two bid in spades, showing a strong six-card spade suit and fewer than 13 total points. This is your hand.

♠ Q 5 4   Once partner has shown long spades, this hand is
♥ 9   worth 13 points. It is unlikely that the partnership has
♦ 8 2   the 25 combined total points that 4♠ requires. But
♣ A K 9 5 4 3   take another look at this hand. Remember, respond-
                     ing to a preempt involves counting tricks, not points.
Think about what your partner's hand probably looks like.

There should probably be no losers in clubs. Your singleton heart will hold your partnership's heart losers to one. You have only two losers in diamonds. So, with only three probable losers, you should bid 4♠.

Preempts can make a mockery of point count as some good hands become bad and some bad hands become good. Visualizing partner's hand and counting tricks is the way to go!

Use the following guidelines in deciding how to proceed in the bidding when partner has opened the bidding with a preempt:

- Responding to a preempt is more about *counting tricks* than counting points. Visualize how your hand works with partner's hand and estimate the outcome of various contracts for both partnerships.

- Side suit aces and kings tend to be very valuable assets while queens and jacks are often worthless.

- The response of a game contract after a preempt is an absolute signoff.

- When you respond 3NT to a preempt, you either expect to run the opener's suit or you have a long solid suit of your own. In either case, stoppers in all suits are required.

Your partner bids 3♣ and you have the following hand.

♠ A 9   3NT is a contract certain to succeed. You have nine
♥ Q J 8   sure winners in notrump, eight diamond tricks and
♦ A K Q J 10 8 3 2   the ♠A. Your heart holding contains a stopper and
♣ —   may even win a trick. You also know your side has
                        a stopper in clubs. Again, 3NT is a great contract.

- After a preemptive opening bid, a new suit by responder that is not a game contract is a forcing bid. The opening bidder will raise with support and normally rebid the original suit without support.

Your partner bids 3♦ and this is your hand.

♠ A K J 9 8   Your bid is 3♠ which is forcing. With three-card
♥ A 7 5   support, partner should bid 4♠. Without support,
♦ A 10 3   partner would bid 4♦.
♣ 6 4

- Consider raising partner's preempt as a further preempt. If the contract you bid fails by two tricks or fewer and the opponents have a game contract, you will have stopped them from making their game contract.

REMEMBER, PREEMPTS ARE ALL ABOUT MAKING LIFE DIFFICULT FOR THE OPPONENTS!

Competing against a Preempt

If your opponent opens with a preempt, you still can make use of the overcall and the takeout double to compete. Since you are starting the auction at the three level or higher, you should have a hand stronger than an opening bid.

For example, suppose the opponent on your right opens 3♣.

♠ A 9 4   With a good six-card suit and 16 points, overcall
♥ A Q J 10 8 2   3♥.
♦ K 10 3
♣ 4

♠ K J 6 3   With support for the unbid suits and 15 HCPs plus
♥ A Q 8 2   3 dummy points for the singleton, make a takeout
♦ K Q 7 5   double.
♣ 4

♠ K 8 4   Although you have enough to open the bidding, you
♥ Q J 6   don't have enough to enter the auction at the three
♦ A J 4 3   level. Pass. The preempt has made your life difficult,
♣ Q 10 3   just as your opponent intended.

SUMMARY

When you try to establish extra tricks to make your contract, look for opportunities to combine the techniques of promoting high cards, developing long suits and finessing. In addition, the trump suit can be used in combination with the other techniques.

How you choose to handle a specific suit depends on circumstances such as how many tricks you need or can afford to lose and whether you can let the opponents get the lead.

A useful guideline when considering a finesse for a missing queen is **eight ever, nine never**. With eight or fewer cards, take the finesse; with nine or more, play the ace and the king.

When you put your PLAN together, sometimes you need to establish more than one suit. You must be careful to **play the suits in the appropriate order**, using your entries wisely. Usually you will establish your longest suit first in a notrump contract. Try to arrange your play so that you can try more than one alternative.

If you must choose among two or more alternatives, use the following guidelines:

- Go for the sure thing (select the alternative that requires the least amount of luck).
- Go for the right number of tricks (select the suit that will give you enough tricks to make the contract).
- Go with your only chance (select a suit that gives you some chance of making your contract).
- Go with the odds (select the suit that offers the best chance).

When you are defending, make a plan similar to the PLAN you make as declarer. You can't see your partner's cards, but with a little imagination, you may be able to see how your side can get enough tricks to defeat the contract.

A preemptive opening bid at the two level or higher shows:

- A six-card or longer suit.
- Less than the point count values for an opening bid at the one level.

If partner opens with a preempt, pass unless you believe that your hand fits well with partner's hand or unless your hand is good enough to proceed on your own. If the opponents open with a preempt, you can use the overcall and the takeout double to compete.

Exercise One — Combining Techniques

How would you play each of the following suits if you have plenty of entries between the two hands? How many tricks would you expect if the missing high cards lie favorably and the suit divides as you expect?

DUMMY: 1) Q J 10 5 2   2) 7 6 2   3) K Q 8 6 2
DECLARER: 8 4 3   A Q J 8 3   7 5

Method   _____   _____   _____

# of tricks: _____   _____   _____

DUMMY: 4) A Q 9 3 2   5) Q 10 3 2
DECLARER: 6   K 6 5 4

Method   _____   _____

# of tricks: _____   _____

Exercise Two — Choosing a Technique

How would you play each of the following suits to get the maximum number of tricks? What is the maximum number of tricks you could get?

DUMMY: 1) A J 6 3   2) A 8 4 2   3) A K J 3
DECLARER: K 9 4 2   K J 7 5 3   8 6 2

Method   _____   _____   _____

Maximum
# of tricks: _____   _____   _____

DUMMY: 4) 8 4 2   5) K 9 5 3 2
DECLARER: K Q 6   8 7 4

Method   _____   _____

Maximum
# of tricks: _____   _____

Exercise One *Answers* — Combining Techniques

1) Develop tricks by promotion and length. The missing cards should divide 3–2, allowing you to take three tricks after you drive out the ace and the king.

2) The combination of a successful finesse against the king and a 3–2 division of the missing cards will provide five tricks.

3) By using the finesse against the ace, you can get tricks with both the king and the queen. If the missing cards divide 4–2, you can set up a third trick by length. If they divide 3–3, you end up with four tricks.

4) A successful finesse followed by a 4–3 division of the missing cards will result in three tricks.

5) Leading the king to drive out the ace will promote one trick. A finesse against the missing jack will provide a second trick, and a 3–2 division of the missing cards will provide a third trick.

Exercise Two *Answers* — Choosing a Technique

1) Play the king and finesse the jack (eight ever). If the finesse works and the suit divides 3–2, you get all four tricks.

2) Play the ace and the king, hoping the queen will drop (nine never), giving you five tricks.

3) Try the finesse. If the suit divides very favorably, 3–3, you can take four tricks.

4) Lead toward the king and the queen to try for two tricks.

5) Try the finesse by leading toward the king and then hope for a 3–2 division to give you two more tricks.

Exercise Three — Combining Alternatives

You are in 3NT and your opponent leads the ♥J. Should you play the club suit or the diamond suit first when you gain the lead?

1) DUMMY	2) DUMMY	3) DUMMY
♠ 7 4 2	♠ K 4	♠ K Q 8
♥ 7 6 4 2	♥ 7 5 2	♥ 7 3
♦ K Q	♦ K Q 4	♦ 9 6 2
♣ K J 7 2	♣ J 10 8 3 2	♣ A Q 8 4 2

DECLARER	DECLARER	DECLARER
♠ A 8 6 3	♠ A 8 6 2	♠ A 4 2
♥ A 8 3	♥ A K 8	♥ A 2
♦ A 9 8 5	♦ 8 6 2	♦ A K Q 5
♣ A Q	♣ K Q 5	♣ 7 6 5 3

Exercise Four — Choosing an Alternative

You're in 3NT and the opponents lead the ♠Q. Should you play the club suit or the diamond suit first when you gain the lead?

1) DUMMY	2) DUMMY	3) DUMMY
♠ K 8 2	♠ 6 4 2	♠ 7 3
♥ 9 6 3	♥ Q J 3	♥ Q 10 3
♦ A Q J 7	♦ K Q J	♦ A K Q 3
♣ Q J 4	♣ Q 10 5 3	♣ J 10 4 3

DECLARER	DECLARER	DECLARER
♠ A 9 3	♠ A K 3	♠ A 2
♥ A K Q	♥ A K 8 2	♥ A K J 7
♦ 9 8 5	♦ 8 6 2	♦ 6 4 2
♣ K 10 9 5	♣ K J 8	♣ K Q 8 2

Exercise Three *Answers* — Combining Alternatives

      1) Clubs   2) Clubs   3) Diamonds

Exercise Four *Answers* — Choosing an Alternative

      1) Clubs   2) Clubs   3) Diamonds

Exercise Five — Defenders' Plan

You're defending a 4♥ contract and your partner leads the ♠Q. Declarer wins with the ♠A, draws trumps with the ♥A and the ♥K and finesses dummy's ♦Q. How many tricks do you need to defeat the contract? How many tricks do you have? Where will you get the extra tricks you need? What card must partner have to defeat the contract? What should you do after winning the ♦K?

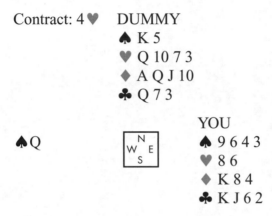

Contract: 4♥   DUMMY
♠ K 5
♥ Q 10 7 3
♦ A Q J 10
♣ Q 7 3

♠Q

YOU
♠ 9 6 4 3
♥ 8 6
♦ K 8 4
♣ K J 6 2

Exercise Six — Opening Preempts

Assuming your side is nonvulnerable, what is your opening bid with each of the following hands?

1) ♠ A K J 8 7 3 2   2) ♠ 8 4   3) ♠ K 4
   ♥ 6 3   ♥ 8 2   ♥ A K Q 8 4 3 2
   ♦ 8 5   ♦ 3   ♦ 6 4 2
   ♣ 10 9   ♣ A J 10 7 6 5 3 2   ♣ J

Bid:_____   Bid: _____   Bid: _____

Exercise Five *Answers* — Defenders' Plan

You need four tricks to defeat 4 ♥ and you have only one. The extra three tricks could come from the club suit if your partner has the ♣A. Lead the ♣2.

Exercise Six *Answers* — Opening Preempts

   1) 3 ♠   2) 4 ♣ (or 3 ♣)   3) 1 ♥

Exercise Seven — Responding to a Preempt

Your partner opens 3 ♥. What do you respond with each of the following hands?

1) ♠ K J 8
   ♥ 8 5
   ♦ K Q J 6
   ♣ Q 9 7 3

2) ♠ A 8 4
   ♥ K 2
   ♦ Q 7 6 3
   ♣ A K 7 5

3) ♠ A Q J 10 7 4 2
   ♥ 2
   ♦ A 4 2
   ♣ K 3

Response: _____   Response: _____   Response: _____

Exercise Eight — Competing against a Preempt

The opponent on your right opens 3 ♥. What do you do with each of the following hands?

1) ♠ A K Q 8 7 3
   ♥ 7 4
   ♦ A J 4
   ♣ 5 2

2) ♠ J 10 7 3
   ♥ 3
   ♦ A J 9 2
   ♣ A K J 4

3) ♠ Q 8
   ♥ K 9 2
   ♦ K Q 10 4
   ♣ K 8 4 2

Bid:_____   Bid: _____   Bid: _____

Exercise Seven *Answers* — Responding t a Preempt

    1) Pass   2) 4 ♥   3) 3 ♠

Exercise Eight *Answers* — Competing against a Preempt

    1) 3 ♠   2) Double   3) Pass

Exercise Nine — Combining Techniques

(E–Z Deal Cards: #8, Deal 1 — Dealer, North)

Turn up all of the cards on the first pre-dealt deal. Put each hand dummy-style at the edge of the table in front of each player.

The Bidding

North passes. With a good seven-card suit and not enough for a one-bid, what is East's opening bid?

What does South do?

What is East telling West about the hand? What does West do?

How many dummy points does North have in support of South's suit?

```
Dealer:      ♠ J 3 2
North        ♥ K 7
             ♦ A Q 8 7 2
             ♣ 9 7 5
♠ 6 5                      ♠ 8 4
♥ 4 3           N          ♥ A Q 10 9 8 6 2
♦ K J 6       W   E        ♦ 10 4 3
♣ K J 6 4 3 2    S         ♣ Q
             ♠ A K Q 10 9 7
             ♥ J 5
             ♦ 9 5
             ♣ A 10 8
```

Knowing that South must have more than a minimum hand to overcall at the three level, what does North bid?

How does the auction proceed? What is the contract? Who is the declarer?

The Play

Which player makes the opening lead? What will the opening lead be? What is East's plan for defeating the contract? After winning the first two tricks, what does East lead next?

Declarer starts by making a PLAN:

1. **P**ause to consider your objective
2. **L**ook at your winners and losers
3. **A**nalyze your alternatives
4. **N**ow put it all together

How many losers does declarer have? How can declarer eliminate a diamond loser? How can declarer eliminate a club loser?

What will declarer have to do with the diamond suit? Is there a potential entry to dummy's established winner? How must the missing diamonds divide? Why must declarer be careful with the trump suit?

Exercise Nine *Answers* — Combining Techniques

The Bidding

- East opens 3 ♥.

- South overcalls 3 ♠. West passes since East is showing a weak hand.

- North has 11 dummy points and raises to 4 ♠. The contract is 4 ♠. South is the declarer.

The Play

- West leads the ♥ 4, partner's suit. After winning two heart tricks, East returns the ♣ Q.

- Declarer has five losers. The diamond loser can be eliminated by a successful finesse for the ♦ K. The club loser can be discarded on the extra diamond that can be established in dummy by ruffing one diamond.

- The key to taking enough tricks to make the contract is the diamond suit. First, declarer can afford to play the ace and king of trumps to try to draw trumps. If the trumps are divided 3–1, declarer must postpone drawing the last trump. Then, declarer must try the diamond finesse and hope it works. After winning with the ♦ A, declarer ruffs the next round of diamonds to establish two winners. Declarer must end in dummy with the ♠ J to be able to discard the club losers on the established diamonds.

Exercise Ten — Eight Ever, Nine Never

(E–Z Deal Cards: #8, Deal 2 — Dealer, East)

Turn up all of the cards on the second pre-dealt deal and arrange them as in the previous deal.

The Bidding

East passes. With a hand not strong enough to open at the one level and a good seven-card suit, what does South bid?

How many dummy points does West have? How can West compete?

What should North do? Knowing that West must have a good hand to compete at the three level, how can East show strength?

```
Dealer:        ♠ 8 4 2
East           ♥ A Q 8 7
               ♦ 9 6 3
               ♣ Q 9 7
♠ K Q J 3              ♠ A 10 9 7 5
♥ K 6 5 3       N      ♥ 4 2
♦ 10         W     E   ♦ Q 4
♣ A 8 5 4       S      ♣ K J 6 3
               ♠ 6
               ♥ J 10 9
               ♦ A K J 8 7 5 2
               ♣ 10 2
```

What will the contract be? Who will be the declarer?

The Play

Which player makes the opening lead? What is the opening lead? After seeing the dummy, what will South do next?

Declarer starts by making a PLAN. How many losers does declarer have? How does declarer plan to eliminate a diamond loser? How does declarer plan to handle the club suit? What guideline is useful when considering how to play the club suit?

Exercise Ten *Answers* — Eight Ever, Nine Never

The Bidding

- South bids 3 ♦.

- With 16 dummy points, West doubles.

- North doesn't have to bid and probably should pass, fearing a penalty double. East has 11 points and shows strength by jumping to 4 ♠. The contract is 4 ♠. East is the declarer.

The Play

- South leads the ♦ A and shifts to the ♥ J, hoping partner has some tricks in the heart suit.

- Declarer has five losers (six if the clubs don't divide 3–2). Declarer plans to ruff a diamond loser in dummy and handle the club suit by taking a finesse for the queen (eight ever, nine never).

Exercise Eleven — Combining Alternative

(E–Z Deal Cards: #8, Deal 3 — Dealer, South)

Turn up all of the cards on the third pre-dealt deal and arrange them as in the previous deal.

The Bidding

What is South's opening bid?

Does West have enough to enter the bidding at the three level? Does North have anything to say?

How can East compete for the contract?

South passes. How many points does West have? What does West bid?

Dealer:	♠ 9 5 3
South	♥ 9 7 6 5
	♦ K J 8 7
	♣ 8 3

♠ K J 7 6 2		♠ A Q 10 8
♥ A Q 3	N W E S	♥ K 8 4 2
♦ 9 6 3		♦ A Q 4
♣ Q 6		♣ J 4

	♠ 4
	♥ J 10
	♦ 10 5 2
	♣ A K 10 9 7 5 2

How does the auction proceed from there? What will the contract be? Who will be the declarer?

The Play

Which player makes the opening lead? What will the opening lead be?

Declarer starts by making a PLAN. How many losers can declarer afford? How many losers does declarer have? What are declarer's alternatives? Must declarer choose one of the alternatives?

Exercise Eleven *Answers* — Combining Alternative

The Bidding

- South opens 3♣.

- West passes since an overcall at the three level would be dangerous with only 13 points. North passes.

- East doubles.

- West shows 13 points by jumping to 4♠.

- Pass, pass, pass. The contract is 4♠. West is the declarer.

The Play

- North leads the ♣8, partner's suit.

- Declarer can afford three losers and has two club and two diamond losers. One possibility of eliminating a loser is to take the diamond finesse. The other is to discard a diamond loser on dummy's last heart if the missing hearts divide 3–3. Declarer can combine both possibilities after drawing trumps. If the hearts don't break, declarer can try the finesse.

Exercise Twelve — The Best Alternative

(E–Z Deal Cards: #8, Deal 4 — Dealer, West)

Turn up all of the cards on the fourth pre-dealt deal and arrange them as in the previous deal.

The Bidding

West passes. What is North's opening bid?

East passes. How many points does South have? Is game possible? What does South bid?

How does the auction proceed from there? What will the contract be? Who will be the declarer?

```
Dealer:        ♠ K Q 10 8 7 5 3
  West         ♥ 8 6
               ♦ J 5
               ♣ 10 6
♠ A 6                      ♠ 9 4
♥ K 4 3         N          ♥ J 10 9 5
♦ K 10 6     W   E         ♦ A Q 8 7
♣ 9 8 4 3 2     S          ♣ J 7 5
               ♠ J 2
               ♥ A Q 7 2
               ♦ 9 4 3 2
               ♣ A K Q
```

The Play

Which player makes the opening lead? What will the opening lead be? If West gets to win the first trick, how would West plan to defeat the contract?

Declarer starts by making a PLAN. How many losers can declarer afford? How many losers does declarer have? What are declarer's alternatives for eliminating a loser? Can declarer try both alternatives? Does declarer take the heart finesse? If not, why not?

Exercise Twelve *Answers* — The Best Alternative

The Bidding

- North opens 3♠.

- With 16 points, a good fit and top cards, South has enough to try a game contract and bids 4♠.

- Pass, pass, pass. The contract is 4♠. North is the declarer.

The Play

- East leads the ♥ J. If West wins the first trick, West would plan to defeat the contract by hoping partner had the ♦ A — then the defense could take two diamond tricks along with the ♠ A and the ♥ K.

- Declarer has four losers and can afford three.

- Declarer can't afford to try the heart finesse. If it loses, the opponents will immediately take their two diamond tricks and spade trick and defeat the contract. Instead, declarer wins the ♦ A and discards one loser on the extra club winner in dummy.

CHAPTER 9
The Jacoby Transfer

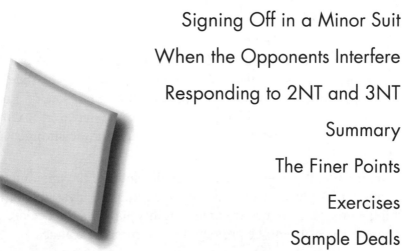

THE JACOBY TRANSFER

The Jacoby transfer is another very popular convention and works along with Stayman. It is one of the most widely used conventions in the bridge world. Jacoby transfers are used in response to 1NT, 2NT and 3NT opening bids. When you use the Jacoby transfer, the response of two of a suit has a different meaning than we were originally taught.

JACOBY TRANSFERS FOR THE MAJORS

> The 2 ♣ response to 1NT is still the Stayman convention.
>
> The 2 ♦ and 2 ♥ responses to 1NT are Jacoby transfer bids.

How do Jacoby transfers work? A Jacoby transfer bid promises at least five cards in the next higher-ranking suit. A 2 ♦ response to a 1NT opener promises at least five cards in hearts and requests the opener to bid 2 ♥. Likewise, a 2 ♥ response to 1NT promises at least five spades and requests the opener to bid 2 ♠. The opening bidder almost always completes the transfer by bidding two of the major suit that the responder promised by using a Jacoby transfer.

Jacoby transfer bids can be used with signoff hands, invitational hands, hands that are strong enough to force to game and hands that can even explore the possibilities of slam. They also can be used with balanced hands or unbalanced hands.

Why use Jacoby transfers? One of the best reasons to use Jacoby transfer bids is to assure that the 1NT opener will become the declarer if the responder's long major suit becomes the trump suit. If a partnership has a choice as to which player will be the declarer, it will be to their advantage on most deals to try to arrange for the stronger hand to be declarer.

Remember, the opening lead gives the defense the opening blow to the contract. A player with a 1NT opening bid will invariably have a lot of high cards. If it can be arranged that this player is the declarer, some of those high cards will be protected from immediate attack.

Look at this hand and suppose spades are trump:

♠ Q J 4
♥ A Q J 3
♦ K J
♣ K 8 4 3

Each of the three side suits contains high cards that are vulnerable to attack. It will be more difficult for the defenders to attack these suits effectively with this hand as the declarer than it would be if this hand is the dummy.

So, the word *transfer* is part of the name of Jacoby *transfer* bids because it transfers the declaration from the (weak) responder hand to the (strong) opener hand.

After the 1NT opener completes the transfer, the responder is well-placed to continue describing the hand with the next bid. The responder can take advantage of this opportunity to give partner some more information about the strength and/or distribution of the hand.

Signing Off in Partscore in a Major Suit

To sign off in two of a major after a 1NT opening bid, transfer to your five-card (or longer) major suit and pass when your partner completes the transfer.

Opener	Responder	
1NT	2♦	♠ 6
2♥	Pass	♥ A 8 7 6 2
		♦ 9 6 3 2
		♣ 10 5 4

This hand contains 5 total points. That is not enough to explore for game, so you should opt to play in partscore with hearts as trump.

Inviting Game in a Major Suit

To invite game after a 1NT opener, responder needs 8 or 9 points. When playing Jacoby transfers, responder can show an invitational hand with a five-card or longer major suit by first transferring to the major suit. With the rebid, responder clarifies the hand.

A Jacoby transfer followed by a 2NT rebid describes an invitational hand with exactly five cards in responder's major.

Opener	Responder	♠ K Q 3 4 2
1NT	2♥	♥ K 8 2
2♠	2NT	♦ 10 5
		♣ 7 5 4

This hand has 9 total points, enough to invite a game contract opposite a 1NT opener.

With an invitational hand containing a six-card (or longer) major suit, transfer to your major. After the transfer is completed, rebid three of your major.

Opener	Responder	♠ 4 3 2
1NT	2♦	♥ A Q J 8 4 2
2♥	3♥	♦ 10 4 3
		♣ 8

With two distribution points added to the 7 HCPs, this hand has enough to invite game in hearts. There is a Golden Fit in hearts, since the 1NT opener promises at least two cards in the suit.

Bidding Game in a Major

With 10 or more points, responder knows there is game and makes sure that it is bid. The final contract may be a major suit but may also be notrump.

A Jacoby transfer followed by a 3NT rebid shows exactly five cards in the major and asks the 1NT opener to choose between 3NT and four of the major as the final contract.

Opener	Responder	♠ A Q 8 5 4
1NT	2♥	♥ Q J 7
2♠	3NT	♦ K 5
		♣ 7 5 3

Responder has more than enough points to make sure the partnership reaches game. The only question is which is the best game. If the opener has only two spades, the contract will be 3NT; otherwise, the contract will be 4♠.

Opener's Rebid after the Transfer

When responder transfers, opener is expected to accept the transfer by bidding the requested suit at the cheapest level.

	Opener	Responder
♠ K Q 8 5		
♥ J 9	1NT	2♦
♦ A K 4 3	2♥	
♣ K 9 8		

Accept partner's transfer by bidding 2♥. Partner will clarify the hand after you make the transfer. Don't forget that partner may "pass" holding a hand with few points and just a five-card suit.

♠ A 8 5   With a minimum strength hand for your 1NT open-
♥ J 10 5 4   ing, even with four-card support for partner's suit,
♦ A Q 7 2   you have no reason to believe the final contract be-
♣ K J   longs higher than 2♥. Simply accept the transfer.
However, there is one exception. With a maximum hand including four-card support for partner's major, the 1NT opener should jump to the three level in responder's suit. This is called *super-acceptance*.

♠ A 5   With 17 HCP, this is a maximum 1NT opening bid.
♥ A Q 9 5   In addition, once the responder is known to have
♦ K 10 5 4   at least a five-card heart suit, a short-suit point for
♣ K J 4   the doubleton spade should be counted. The strong
four-card heart support in this hand definitely makes
it worth a jump to 3♥.

There are two reasons why it is a good idea for the 1NT opening bidder to super-accept a Jacoby transfer bid when holding four-card support for partner's major and a maximum hand.

1. If responder's hand was not quite strong enough to issue an invitation to game, responder might reconsider after opener super-accepts the transfer.

2. If responder has interest in a possible slam, the bidding will proceed more easily if responder learns right away that partner has a great hand in support of responder's long major suit.

THE SUBSEQUENT AUCTION

After the initial transfer and opener's acceptance of the transfer, the auction can proceed in several ways.

- Responder can pass to play in partscore in the major suit.
- Responder can invite game by bidding 2NT or raising the major suit.
- Responder can jump to game in notrump or in the major suit.
- Responder can bid a new suit.

A Jacoby transfer followed by the bid of a new suit is forcing to game and describes a hand with at least a five-card major and at least four cards in the suit that was just introduced. This type of sequence does not imply necessarily that the responder might have interest in playing in a slam contract.

When responder has both majors

Bridge players use the term *two-suiter* to describe a hand that has one suit with at least five cards in it and another suit with at least four cards in it. A major two-suiter is a two-suited hand in which spades and hearts are the two long suits. There are a few special bidding sequences to help responder bid these types of hands.

With less than invitational strength and five-five in the majors, responder should transfer to the longest and strongest major suit and then pass when partner completes the transfer.

Opener	Responder	
		♠ 10 8 7 5 4
1NT	2♦	♥ Q 10 7 5 4
2♥	Pass	♦ 4
		♣ J 9

There is no guarantee that hearts will make a better trump suit, but the odds are that at least as many tricks will be available if hearts are trump.

With less than invitational strength and five-four in the majors, responder should transfer to the five-card major and pass when partner completes the transfer.

Opener	Responder	
1NT	2♥	♠ J 9 8 5 3
2♠		♥ K J 8 6
		♦ 8 5 3
		♣ 4

Length is more important than strength when it comes to selecting a trump suit. It is entirely possible that a heart contract will play better than a spade contract, but the odds are that the partnership will have more spades between the two hands.

With invitational strength and five-five in the majors, responder should bid 2♦ to transfer to hearts and rebid 2♠ when partner completes the transfer.

Opener	Responder	
1NT	2♦	♠ Q 8 5 4 3
2♥	2♠	♥ A J 7 4 3
		♦ 4
		♣ 8 7

This special sequence describes an invitational hand with five-five in the majors. Opener might pass 2♠, but opener might also bid 3♥, 4♥ or 4♠ at the next turn to bid depending on the hand's strength and distribution in the majors. *This is the one sequence where a Jacoby transfer followed by the bid of a new suit is not forcing to game.*

With invitational strength and five-four in the majors, responder should use Stayman, planning to raise 2♥ or 2♠ a level or to rebid two of the five-card major when opener responds 2♦.

Opener	Responder	
1NT	2♣	♠ Q 8 4 3
2♦	2♥	♥ A Q 10 5 3
		♦ 4
		♣ 7 5

When opener denies a four-card major by responding 2♦, responder should rebid the five-card major. This sequence describes an invitational hand with five hearts and four spades. If opener names a major, this hand becomes strong enough to raise opener's major to game.

With a game-forcing hand and five-five in the majors, responder bids 2 ♥ after partner's 1NT opening to transfer to spades and rebids 3 ♥ when partner completes the transfer.

Opener	Responder	
1NT	2 ♥	♠ Q J 8 5 4
2 ♠	3 ♥	♥ A Q J 9 6
		♦ 4
		♣ A 7

This is the proper sequence to show a game-forcing hand. Remember, in order to show an invitational hand, responder would have transferred first to hearts and then bid spades.

With a game-forcing hand and five-four in the majors, responder should use Stayman, planning to raise 2 ♥ or 2 ♠ and to rebid three of the five-card major over 2 ♦.

Opener	Responder	
1NT	2 ♣	♠ K J 8 5 4
2 ♦	3 ♠	♥ A Q 9 4
		♦ 8 4
		♣ 5 3

This sequence describes a game-forcing hand with five spades and four hearts. Opener will bid 3NT when holding only two spades and will raise to 4 ♠ with three-card spade support.

Signing Off in a Minor Suit

After a 1NT opening, there is no way to sign off in 2 ♣ or 2 ♦ (since 2 ♣ is Stayman and 2 ♦ is a transfer), but it is possible to sign off in 3 ♣ or 3 ♦. When Jacoby transfers are being used, the 2 ♠ response to 1NT is *freed up* since it is no longer needed as a natural bid. You may use the 2 ♠ response to sign off in 3 ♣ or 3 ♦. Here's how this works:

Opener	Responder	
1NT	2 ♠	♠ 4
3 ♣	3 ♦	♥ 8 4 3
		♦ Q J 9 7 5 4
		♣ 4 3 2

The 2 ♠ response asks opener to bid 3 ♣. Responder will pass 3 ♣ if the long minor suit is clubs and will bid diamonds when the long minor suit is diamonds, as in this case. Unlike Jacoby transfers where the opener may super-accept with an appropriate hand, opener has no such option over partner's 2♠ response to the opening 1NT bid.

Other Responses to 1NT

1. Responder can bid 3♣ or 3♦ directly over partner's 1NT opening bid to describe a hand with invitational strength and a strong six-card minor suit. When responder makes such a bid, opener places the contract in 3NT when opener thinks 9 tricks can be taken in notrump opposite such a hand. Otherwise, opener should pass. The opener's decision as to whether or not to bid 3NT after a 3♣ or 3♦ response is more about judgment than it is about whether opener is holding a minimum or maximum hand.

	Opener	Responder
♠ J 10 7 6	Opener	Responder
♥ A K 4 3	1NT	3♣
♦ A 6	?	
♣ K 6 5		

Even though this hand has only 15 HCP, making it a minimum notrump opening bid, opener should bid 3NT with this great fit. With this next hand, a maximum notrump opening bid, opener should pass because there is no fit.

	Opener	Responder
♠ A K Q 5	Opener	Responder
♥ J 4 3	1NT	3♣
♦ A Q J 7	?	
♣ 10 5		

2. The direct 3♥ and 3♠ responses to a 1NT opening bid suggest at least six cards in the suit that was bid and a hand that is strong enough to be interested in slam.

	Opener	Responder
♠ Q J 10 5 4 3	Opener	Responder
♥ A 7 5	1NT	3♠
♦ 5	?	
♣ A K 7		

The 3♠ response describes a hand with six cards in the suit bid and a hand strong enough to try at least for a small slam. Your 16 point hand along with partner's 15-17 HCP suggests the possibility of a small slam. If partner has a maximum hand or even a minimum with some good cards in spades and a lot of aces and kings, partner will cooperate in your slam investigation. Otherwise, partner will bid 4♠ and leave any further exploration to you.

Check *The Finer Points* for a summary of all of the defined responses to a 1NT opening bid.

WHEN THE OPPONENTS INTERFERE

When using Jacoby transfers, you and your partner need to have agreements about what to do when the opponents interfere in the auction. What do you do if an opponent overcalls 2♥ over your partner's 1NT opening bid and you want to show a spade suit? Does a 2♠ bid now show spades or is it a transfer to clubs. Without firm agreements, the partnership can run into difficulty.

The standard agreement when the opponents interfere is to continue to use transfer responses to 1NT if an opponent doubles, since no bidding room has been used. If an opponent overcalls, however, the partnership has to abandon transfer bids.

WEST	NORTH (Opener)	EAST	SOUTH (Responder)
	1NT	2♥	?

Responder

♠ K J 10 8 4
♥ Q 3
♦ 10 7 4 3
♣ J 7

Bid 2♠. This is natural and non-forcing. Opener will treat this bid as mildly invitational, since you could have passed with a very weak hand.

The situation is different if an opponent interferes following a conventional response. Bids carry the same meaning that they would if there were no interference. However, the opponent's bid may present other options.

WEST	NORTH (Opener)	EAST	SOUTH (Responder)
	INT	Pass	2♥
Double	?		

Opener

♠ A Q 8
♥ 8 6 2
♦ Q J 5
♣ A K 4 3

Bid 2♠. Accept the transfer bid with three-card support for partner's suit.

Opener

♠ 8 3
♥ A 10 6
♦ A Q 4
♣ K Q 8 6 3

Pass. If West had passed, you would accept the transfer and bid 2♠. West's double gives you the option of passing. Your side may still stop in 2♠, but partner may decide to do something else knowing that you do not have spade support.

Opener

♠ 10 4
♥ A J 10 8 4
♦ A K 4
♣ A 9 2

Redouble. This suggests to partner that your side's best contract could be 2♥ redoubled. If you can take 8 tricks, you'll get a game bonus. Of course, partner could have another opinion and bid again.

RESPONDING TO 2NT AND 3NT
AFTER A 2NT OPENING BID

Now that you know the mechanics of the Jacoby transfer after a 1NT opening bid, you should be happy to learn that most of what you know also can be applied to Jacoby transfers after a 2NT opening bid.

- 3♦ is a transfer to 3♥.

- 3♥ is a transfer to 3♠.

- To sign off in three of a major, the responder will pass when the opener completes the transfer.

- After a 2NT opening bid and a Jacoby transfer, the responder's 3NT rebid asks opener to choose between 3NT and four of the responder's major.

One important difference between bidding over a 1NT opening and bidding over a 2NT opening is that there are no bidding sequences that are defined as being invitational to game when the opening bid is 2NT. All sequences are either forcing to game or sign- offs.

Check *The Finer Points* for a summary of all the defined responses to a 2NT opening bid.

After a 3NT Opening Bid

The partnership also can use the Jacoby transfer after an opening bid of 3NT showing a strong balanced hand of 25 to 27 HCP.

- 4♦ is a transfer to 4♥.

- 4♥ is a transfer to 4♠.

Opener	Responder	♠ 3
3NT	4♦	♥ J 9 8 6 4 3 2
4♥		♦ 8 4
		♣ 7 5 4 3

There is no guarantee that 4♥ will be a successful contract, but it is likely to be better than 3NT.

SUMMARY

If the partnership is using both Stayman and the Jacoby transfer as discussed in this chapter, responder's bids send the following messages:

Responses to 1NT

- 2♣ is the Stayman convention.
- 2♦ is a Jacoby transfer and asks opener to bid 2♥.
- 2♥ is a Jacoby transfer and asks opener to bid 2♠.
- 2♠ is used to sign off in 3♣ or 3♦. Opener must rebid 3♣ over 2♠.
- 2NT is invitational to 3NT.
- 3♣ and 3♦ are invitational to 3NT and show a strong six-card suit.
- 3♥ and 3♠ are invitational to slam and show at least six cards in the suit bid.
- 3NT is a signoff bid.

Opener's Rebid

In response to a transfer bid of 2♦ or 2♥:

- Opener simply bids the requested suit at the two level.
- Opener can super-accept by jumping to the three level in the requested suit when holding a maximum-strength hand and four-card support for the responder's suit.

In response to a transfer bid of 2♠:

- Opener bids 3♣. Responder may then pass to play a partscore in clubs. If responder bids 3♦, opener passes to play a partscore in diamonds.

Responder's Rebid after a Jacoby Transfer Bid

- Responder passes with minimum values to play a partscore in the major suit.

- A rebid of 2NT is invitational, showing five cards in the major suit.

- A raise to 3♥ or 3♠ is invitational, showing a six-card or longer suit.

- A raise to 4♥ or 4♠ is a signoff bid.

- A jump to 3NT shows five cards in the major suit and asks opener to choose between 3NT and four of the major suit.

- The bid of a new suit is natural and forcing.

Handling Interference

If the opening notrump bid is doubled:

- Responder's bids retain their conventional meanings.

If there is an overcall directly over the notrump bid:

- The Jacoby transfer no longer applies. All of responder's bids are natural, except a cuebid of the opponent's suit, which replaces Stayman.

If there is interference after the transfer bid:

- Opener can pass with a minimum hand and a doubleton in the requested suit.

- Otherwise, opener can bid if there is room available.

2NT and 3NT openings

- Jacoby transfer bids also can be used after opening bids of 2NT or 3NT.

The Finer Points

INT Responses

Although you know most of the responses to 1NT now, here is the complete list of defined responses to an opening 1NT bid when playing Stayman and Jacoby transfers. Any other direct responses not listed here are currently not defined and thus presumed to be natural.

2♣ Stayman –
: Opener rebids a four-card major when holding one and 2♦ otherwise.

2♦ and 2♥ –
: Jacoby transfer bids. The opener usually completes the transfer.

2♠ –
: Used to sign off in 3♣ or 3♦. Opener must rebid 3♣ over 2♠.

2NT –
: Invitational to 3NT. Opener passes with a minimum hand and bids 3NT with a maximum.

3♣ and 3♦ –
: Invitational to 3NT. These bids promise a strong six-card suit.

3♥ and 3♠ –
: Shows interest in playing in at least a small slam and at least six cards in the suit bid.

3NT –
: A signoff bid. Opener should always pass.

4♣ –
: The Gerber convention (asking how many aces opener was dealt.)

4NT –
: Invitational to 6NT. Opener passes with a minimum hand and bids 6NT with a maximum.

5NT –
: Invitational to 7NT. Opener bids 6NT with a minimum hand and bids 7NT with a maximum.

6NT –
: A signoff bid. The opener should always pass.

7NT –
: An obvious signoff bid.

2NT Responses

Here is a complete summary of all the defined responses to a 2NT opening bid. All direct responses that are not listed here are currently not defined and thus presumed to be natural.

　　　　3♣ Stayman - The opener rebids a four-card major when holding one and 3♦ otherwise.

　　　　3♦ and 3♥ - Jacoby transfer bids. Opener usually completes the transfer.

　　　　3NT – A signoff bid. Opener always should pass.

　　　　4♣ - The Gerber convention (asks how many aces opener was dealt.)

　　　　4NT – Invitational to 6NT. Opener passes with a minimum hand and bids 6NT with a maximum.

　　　　5NT – Invitational to 7NT. Opener bids 6NT with a minimum hand and bids 7NT with a maximum.

　　　　6NT – A signoff bid. Opener always should pass.

　　　　7NT – An obvious signoff bid.

Transfer Announcement

When you are playing "duplicate" bridge, you need to let your opponents know that you are playing Jacoby transfers when the bid comes up. Here's how you do that. You use what is called an "announcement" to alert your opponents. The 1NT opening bidder should say "transfer" when responder makes a transfer bid. If you are just playing in a friendly game at home, you and your partner may want to practice Jacoby transfer bids – just tell your opponents that you are playing that convention ahead of time. They may want to learn Jacoby transfers, too.

Exercise One – Using Jacoby Transfer Bids

Partner opens 1NT. What do you respond with each of the following hands? What do you plan to do next?

1) ♠ J 10 8 6 5 4
   ♥ 5
   ♦ 8 4
   ♣ J 8 6 4

2) ♠ 8 3
   ♥ K J 9 5 4 3
   ♦ 6 4 2
   ♣ K 6

3) ♠ 10 9 8 7 6 5
   ♥ A K
   ♦ 5 4
   ♣ K 4 3

4) ♠ 9 8 7
   ♥ Q J 7 5 4
   ♦ Q 5 4
   ♣ K 4

5) ♠ —
   ♥ K Q J 4 3
   ♦ 5 4 2
   ♣ A Q 9 7 4

6) ♠ A 10 5 4 3
   ♥ 10 5
   ♦ K Q 6
   ♣ Q 4 3

7) ♠ 10 9 5 4 3
   ♥ Q J 9 4 3
   ♦ 5 4
   ♣ 7

8) ♠ A 9 7 5 4
   ♥ 10 9 5 4 3
   ♦ Q 8
   ♣ 6

9) ♠ A K 5 4 3
   ♥ Q J 6 5 3
   ♦ 9 4
   ♣ 9

Answers to Exercise

Exercise One *Answers* – Using Jacoby Transfer Bids

1) 2 ♥ transfer. Pass partner's 2 ♠ rebid.

2) 2 ♦ transfer. Raise to 3 ♥, invitational.

3) 2 ♥ transfer. Raise to 4 ♠.

4) 2 ♦ transfer. Bid 2NT, invitational.

5) 2 ♦ transfer. Bid 3 ♣, forcing, to show second suit.

6) 2 ♥ transfer. Jump to 3NT.

7) 2 ♦ transfer. Pass partner's 2 ♥ rebid.

8) 2 ♦ transfer. Rebid 2 ♠, invitational, over partner's 2 ♥ response.

9) 2 ♥ transfer. Rebid 3 ♥, forcing, over partner's 2 ♠ response.

Exercise Two – Opener's Response to a Jacoby Transfer

You are North and open 1NT with the following hand:

♠ K Q 4 3
♥ A 8
♦ A J 7 3
♣ Q J 5

What is your rebid in each of the following auctions:

1)
WEST	NORTH	EAST	SOUTH
	1NT	Pass	2♦
Pass	?		

2)
WEST	NORTH	EAST	SOUTH
	1NT	Pass	2♥
Pass	?		

3)
WEST	NORTH	EAST	SOUTH
	1NT	Pass	2♦
Pass	2♥	Pass	3NT
Pass	?		

4)
WEST	NORTH	EAST	SOUTH
	1NT	Pass	2♦
Pass	2♥	Pass	2NT
Pass	?		

Exercise Three – Responding with Minor Suits

Partner opens 1NT. What do you respond with each of the following hands? What do you plan to do next?

1) ♠ 4
♥ 8 5 3
♦ 7 4 3
♣ Q 8 7 6 5 4

2) ♠ J 8 4
♥ 3
♦ Q 8 6 5 4 3 2
♣ 7 6

3) ♠ J 10 4 3
♥ 4
♦ Q J 5 4 3
♣ 8 6 4

4) ♠ K Q
♥ 4 3 2
♦ 7 3
♣ A Q J 9 4 3

5) ♠ K 8
♥ 5 4 2
♦ 10 5
♣ K J 10 5 4 2

6) ♠ 3
♥ 8 6 5
♦ K Q J 5 4 3
♣ 6 5 4

Exercise Two *Answers* – Opener's Response to a Jacoby
                                                            Transfer

1) 2 ♥. Accept the transfer.

2) 3 ♠. With a maximum and four-card support, super-accept the transfer.

3) Pass. Partner is showing a game-going hand with a five-card heart suit, asking you to choose between 3NT and 4 ♥.

4) 3NT. Partner has shown an invitational hand with five hearts. Accept the invitation with a maximum but no heart fit.

Exercise Three *Answers* – Responding with Minor Suits

1) 2 ♠ transfer. Pass partner's 3 ♣ bid.

2) 2 ♠ transfer. Bid 3 ♦, signoff, over partner's 3 ♣ bid.

3) Pass. Since you cannot signoff at 2 ♦, you hope partner will be able to make 1NT. This hand shows one of the few disadvantages of Jacoby transfers.

4) 3NT. Since you do not have enough combined points for slam, bid game in notrump.

5) 3 ♣ invitational. Partner can pass or accept to play in a notrump game or 5 ♣.

6) 3 ♦ invitational. Partner can pass or accept to play in a notrump game or 5 ♦.

Exercise Four – The Subsequent Auction

As North, you open 1NT with the following hand:

♠ K Q J 4
♥ A 8 5 4
♦ A 9 5
♣ J 3

What is your next bid with each of the following auctions?

1)	WEST	NORTH	EAST	SOUTH
		1NT	Pass	2♠
	Pass	?		

2)	WEST	NORTH	EAST	SOUTH
		1NT	Pass	2♠
	Pass	3♣	Pass	3♦
	Pass	?		

3)	WEST	NORTH	EAST	SOUTH
		1NT	Pass	3♣
	Pass	?		

4)	WEST	NORTH	EAST	SOUTH
		1NT	Pass	2♣
	Pass	2♥	Pass	3NT
	Pass	?		

Exercise Five – Handling Interference

Partner opens 1NT and the opponent on your right overcalls 2♦. What call do you make with each of these hands?

1) ♠ 7 4 3
   ♥ Q 8 4 3
   ♦ 10 9 4 3
   ♣ J 9

2) ♠ K J 5 4 3
   ♥ 4 3
   ♦ J 8
   ♣ Q 8 4 3

3) ♠ A 8
   ♥ K J 8 7 6
   ♦ K 7
   ♣ 9 6 5 2

4) ♠ 10 4
   ♥ Q J 8 4 3 2
   ♦ 5 3
   ♣ A K 5

5) ♠ A K 5 4
   ♥ J 10 5 4
   ♦ A 8
   ♣ 9 6 2

6) ♠ J 3
   ♥ 9 5 2
   ♦ K Q 5
   ♣ Q 8 4 3 2

Exercise Four *Answers* – The Subsequent Auction

1) 3♣. Accept the transfer.

2) Pass. Partner is showing a weak hand with a long diamond suit.

3) Pass. Partner is showing an invitational hand with long clubs. Decline the invitation with your minimum hand since you do not have a great club fit.

4) 4♠. Partner must have four spades to have started with Stayman, so play in your known four-four spade fit.

Exercise Five *Answers* – Handling Interference

1) Pass. With a weak hand its best to defend and hope to defeat the contract.

2) 2♠, natural and mildly invitational. Jacoby transfers no longer apply.

3) 3♥, forcing, asking opener to choose between 3NT and 4♥.

4) 4♥. You want to be in game in hearts and can no longer use a Jacoby transfer.

5) 3♦. A cuebid of the opponent's suit replaces Stayman when there is interference.

6) 2NT. Make an invitational raise, which is the same thing you would have done without the interference.

Exercise Six – Responding to 2NT

Partner opens the bidding 2NT (20-21 HCP). What do you respond with each of these hands? What's your plan?

1) ♠ 10 6 5 4 3 2
   ♥ 5 4
   ♦ 9 5 4
   ♣ 3 2

2) ♠ 9 4
   ♥ Q J 8 4 3
   ♦ K 8 4
   ♣ 8 2

3) ♠ Q 10 9 8 7 5
   ♥ K 4
   ♦ J 10 6
   ♣ 8 4

4) ♠ K 9 8 6 5
   ♥ Q 8 5 4
   ♦ 7 3
   ♣ J 5

5) ♠ 4 3
   ♥ J 8 4
   ♦ Q 8 4 3
   ♣ K 8 7 5

6) ♠ Q 9 5
   ♥ K Q 8
   ♦ K 9 6 2
   ♣ A 8 4

Exercise Six *Answers* – Responding to 2NT

1) 3♥ transfer then pass. Partner will play in 3♠.

2) 3♦ transfer then bid 3NT. Partner will choose either 3NT or 4♥.

3) 3♥ transfer then bid 4♠.

4) 3♣ Stayman. If opener shows a four-card major, raise to game; if opener bids 3♦, bid 3♠, showing the five-card spade suit and asking opener to choose between 3NT and 4♠.

5) 3NT. Settle for game in notrump.

6) 6NT. Partnership has at least 34 HCP, enough for slam.

Exercise Seven – The Proper Declarer

(Deal 1)

Turn up all of the cards on the first pre-dealt deal. Put each hand dummy-style at the edge of the table in front of each player

The Bidding

North is the dealer and opens 1NT. Does South have enough points to go to game? What should South bid? What will North answer? What will South now bid? What does this bid show? What should North do? What will happen if North passes and plays 3NT?

What is the final contact? Who is the declarer?

```
Dealer, North    ♠ A K 5
                 ♥ 10 9 8
                 ♦ A Q J 2
                 ♣ K 4 3
      ♠ J 6 4 3              ♠ 10 9 8 7
      ♥ K 6 2      N         ♥ 7 5
      ♦ 10 8     W   E       ♦ 7 6 4 3
      ♣ Q J 10 9   S         ♣ A 8 6
                 ♠ Q 2
                 ♥ A Q J 4 3
                 ♦ K 9 5
                 ♣ 7 5 2
```

The Play

Who makes the opening lead? What is the opening lead?

How many tricks can the declarer afford to lose? How many losers does he have? How can he get rid of a loser? Can the declarer afford to draw trumps first?

Exercise Seven *Answers* – The Proper Declarer

The Bidding

- Yes.
- 2♦, a Jacoby transfer to hearts.
- 2♥
- 3NT.
- A game-going hand with 5 hearts.
- Bid 4♥.
- North will not make his contract. The opponents will take 4 clubs tricks and the K♥.
- 4♥.
- North.

The Play

- East.
- 10♠.
- Three.
- Four possible losers – 1 heart and 3 clubs.
- Pitch a club on a long spade.
- No, in order to draw trumps declarer must take the heart finesse. If it loses, it will lose to the danger hand, West, who will lead the Q♣ trapping North's K♣.

Exercise Eight – Handling Major Suits

(Deal 2)

Turn up all of the cards on the second pre-dealt deal and arrange them as in the previous deal.

The Bidding

East is the dealer. What should East open? Does West have enough points to go to game? How should West describe to East this two-suited hand for the majors? What should the final contract be? Who should be the declarer?

```
Dealer, East    ♠ 5
                ♥ 9 8
                ♦ J 8 5 4 2
                ♣ K Q 8 7 3
♠ K 9 7 6 4           ♠ A Q 8 3
♥ A Q J 10 2    N     ♥ K 7 6
♦ 7 6        W   E    ♦ Q 3
♣ 5             S     ♣ A 10 6 4
                ♠ J 10 2
                ♥ 5 4 3
                ♦ A K 10 9
                ♣ J 9 2
```

The Play

Who is on lead? What should South lead? East should be extremely happy to be in a major suit since the combined hands do not contain a diamond stopper. How should East approach playing the hand? Why? What may happen if the final contract is 3NT?

Exercise Eight *Answers* – Handling Major Suits

The Bidding

- 1NT.
- Yes.
- Transfer to spades by bidding 2♥ and then rebid hearts.
- 4♠.
- East.

The Play

- South.
- A♦.
- With spades as trump, East should look at the hand from West's perspective.
- East will then see that West's hand works very well with his own. It is easy to see that West's hand when working with East's only has 2 diamond losers.
- There is the possibility that the defense can take 5 diamond tricks and defeat the contract.

Exercise Nine – Super-Acceptance

(Deal 3)

Turn up all the cards on the third pre-dealt hand and arrange them as in the previous deal.

The Bidding

South is the dealer. What does South do? What does West bid? What should East do? What will West rebid? What will East do? What is the final contract Who is the declarer?

```
Dealer, South   ♠ 8
                ♥ 9 5 4 3
                ♦ A 8 3 2
                ♣ 10 9 8 6
♠ K Q J 2              ♠ A 10 7 4 3
♥ A 10       N        ♥ Q 6 2
♦ K Q 10 9  W   E     ♦ J 7 6
♣ Q 4 2        S      ♣ J 5
                ♠ 9 6 5
                ♥ K J 8 7
                ♦ 5 4
                ♣ A K 7 3
```

The Play

North is on lead. What will North lead?

How many losers can West afford to have? How many does he have? How can West get rid of a loser? What happens if South returns a low heart?

When West gets in the lead should he pull trump?

Exercise Nine *Answers* – Super-Acceptance

The Bidding

- Pass.
- 1NT.
- Bid 2♥ to transfer to spades.
- West has a maximum 17 HCP notrump with four spades so West should super-accept by bidding 3♠.
- Bid 4♠.
- 4♠.
- West.

The Play

- 10♣.
- Three.
- With the club lead, hopefully, 2 club losers, 1 diamond loser, 1 heart loser.
- There is nothing that can be done about the 2 club losers and the 1 diamond loser. Declarer has to think of trying to get rid of a heart loser. When South wins the trick with the K♣ he can cash the A♣ or try another suit. If he cashes the A♣ West's club is now good for a heart pitch in East's hand. When West knocks out the A♦ the diamond suit provides another heart pitch from the dummy eliminating the hearts except for one which will be played on the Ace.
- This is a scary return for declarer. It is a return that puts the declarer to an immediate test. However, West should recognize that if he plays the A♥, he will have one too many losers. Therefore, he would have to play low from his hand and hope that the Q♥ will win the trick. Luckily for declarer the hearts are in a favorable position.
- Yes, there are enough trumps in both hands to pull the trump since both defenders play to the first trump trick.

Exercise Ten – Finding the Queen

(Deal 4)

Turn up all of the cards on the fourth pre-dealt hand and arrange them as in the previous deal.

The Bidding

West is the dealer. What does West do? Who should open the bidding? What should the opening bid be? West passes. How should North proceed? What should South do? What is the final contract? Who is the declarer?

```
Dealer, West   ♠ 4
               ♥ 10 9 7 6 4 2
               ♦ K 9 5
               ♣ A 7 3
  ♠ 10 9 7 3              ♠ Q J 8 5 2
  ♥ A J 3        N        ♥ 8 5
  ♦ 6 3        W   E      ♦ Q 7 4 2
  ♣ K Q J 10     S        ♣ 5 2
               ♠ A K 6
               ♥ K Q
               ♦ A J 10 8
               ♣ 9 8 6 4
```

The Play

Who makes the opening lead? What should the opening lead be?

How many losers does South have? How can some of the losers be eliminated? What do you do eliminate a diamond loser? How do you know who to finesse against?

Exercise Ten *Answers* – Finding the Queen

The Bidding

- Pass.
- South.
- 1NT.
- North should transfer to hearts and rebid 3♥ to show an invitational hand with a six-card suit.
- South should accept the transfer by bidding 2♥ and then should go to game recognizing that the partnership has a Golden Fit in hearts.
- 4♥.
- South

The Play

- West.
- K♣.
- No losers in spades since the small spade can be ruffed in dummy. Two possible losers in hearts. One possible loser in diamonds since the queen is missing. Two losers in clubs since one is covered by the ace and one can be ruffed in the dummy.
- After the K♣ lead, win the trick and play the A♠ and K♠ pitching away a club from the dummy. The play eliminates a loser in clubs. Only then can you pull the trump. When you see you do, in fact, have 2 heart losers, you need to find a way to eliminate a diamond loser.
- Finesse against East.
- West has showed up with the ♣K Q J and the ♥A J. If he also had the Q♦, he would have opened the bidding. Therefore, East has that card.

APPENDIX

Glossary of Terms

Probabilities of
Suit Divisions

Attitude — The play of a card to tell your partner whether you like a particular suit. Traditionally, a high card is encouraging and a low card is discouraging.

Blackwood Convention — Once you have agreed on a trump suit, a bid of 4NT is conventional (artificial) and asks partner how many aces are in partner's hand.

Broken Sequence — Two touching high cards followed by a gap and then the next highest card. For example ♥K Q 10 or ♠Q J 9.

Contract — The final bid in the auction that commits declarer's side to take the specified number of tricks in the strain named.

Convention — A call that conveys a meaning other than the one that would normally be attributed to it. For example, the use of 2♣ to ask opener for a four-card major (Stayman) in response to an opening bid of 1NT.

Cover — Playing a higher card than the one led. For example, playing the king when an opponent leads the queen or the jack.

Crossruff — Ruffing losers in both declarer's hand and dummy and thus using the trump cards separately.

Dangerous Opponent — The opponent that declarer wants to prevent from gaining the lead, either because that opponent has established winners or can lead a card that would trap one of declarer's or dummy's high cards.

Declarer — The player for the side that won the contract who first bid the strain named in the contract.

Defense, Defenders — The side that did not win the contract.

Discard — The play of a card, other than a trump, of a different suit than the suit led.

Discarding a Loser — Playing a losing card on a potential winning card in another suit.

Distribution — The number of cards held in each suit by a particular player; the number of cards held in a particular suit by a partnership.

Draw Trumps — To lead trumps until the opponents have none left.

Drive Out (a high card) — To lead a suit and force an opponent to play a high card to win the trick.

Duck — To play a low card from both hands and surrender a trick that could have been won, usually with the object of preserving an entry.

Entry — A card that provides a means of winning a trick in a particular hand.

Equals — Cards with the same trick-taking potential. For example, the ace and the king in a suit held by the same player.

Establish — To make one or more cards in a suit into winners by forcing out the opponents' higher cards.

Favorably Divided — Having the outstanding cards in a suit divided the way the declarer would like them to be — as evenly as possible.

Finesse — An attempt to win a trick with a card that is not as high as one held by an opponent by playing the card after that opponent has played.

Fourth Highest — The fourth highest card of a long suit (counting down from the top). Also referred to as fourth best.

Grand Slam — A contract to take 13 tricks.

Holding — The cards one is dealt in a particular suit or in the entire hand.

Hold-up Play — Refusal to win a trick you could win in order to make it difficult for the opponents to take tricks. You break their communication and strand their winners in one hand.

Honor Sequence —Two or more honor cards in consecutive order of rank. For example, the ♥K and the ♥Q.

Jacoby Transfer Bid – A conventional response to an opening bid of 1NT where 2♦ shows hearts and 2♥ shows spades. Similar responses can be used over other notrump opening bids.

Lead — The first card played to a trick.

Length — The number of cards held in a particular suit, often implying five or more.

Like a Suit — To have high cards in the suit and/or to want the suit led or continued.

LHO — Left-hand opponent, the player on your left.

Lose Control — Have no trumps left when the opponents get the lead and start taking their winners.

Loser — A card in declarer's hand (or dummy) that could lose a trick to the opponents.

Maintain Control — Have a sufficient number of trumps to prevent the opponents from taking enough tricks in their suits to defeat your contract when they get the lead.

Overruff — To play a higher trump than one played by an opponent when you are void in the suit led.

Overtake — Play a higher card than the one already played by your side, usually for the purpose of creating an entry.

PLAN — The four basic steps that declarer goes through before starting to play a hand.

Promotion — The increase in the trick-taking potential of a card as the higher-ranking cards in the suit are played.

Quick Loser — A trick the opponents can take as soon as they gain the lead.

Repeated Finesse — A finesse that can be taken more than once.

RHO — Right-hand opponent, the player on your right.

Ruff(ing) — To play a trump on a trick when you're void in the suit led.

Sacrifice — To give up a trick with the hope of getting one or more in return; to bid too high to prevent the opponents from playing in the contract of their choice.

Safe Suit — A suit that can be led without giving an opponent a trick that the opponents are entitled to.

Second Hand — The player who plays the second card to a trick.

Sequence — Two or more cards in the same suit in consecutive order or rank. For example, the king, the queen and the jack.

Side Suit — A suit other than the trump suit.

Slow Loser — A trick the opponents can take eventually but not immediately, since declarer has one or more winners left in the suit.

Small Slam — A contract to take 12 tricks.

Stayman Convention — A conventional (artificial) response of 2♣ to an opening bid of 1NT, asking opener to bid a four-card major suit.

Strong Two-bid — An opening suit bid at the two level which shows at least 22 points and is forcing to game.

Sure Trick — A trick which can be taken without giving up the lead.

Third Hand — The player who contributes the third card to a trick; the partner of the player leading to a trick.

Trap (a high card) — A position where a high card can't win a trick because the opponent next to play has a higher card.

Trump — The suit named in the contract.

Two-way Finesse — The choice within a suit of which way to finesse for a missing card. For example, A–J–4 opposite K–10–3.

Unfavorably Divided — Having the outstanding cards in a suit divided the way the declarer would not like them to be — as unevenly as possible.

Winners — Sure tricks declarer can take without giving up the lead.

Probabilities of Suit Divisions

Two cards are missing		Three cards are missing	
1-1	52%	2-1	78%
2-0	48%	3-0	22%

Four cards are missing		Five cards are missing	
2-2	40%	3-2	68%
3-1	50%	4-1	28%
4-0	10%	5-0	4%

Six cards are missing		Seven cards are missing	
3-3	36%	4-3	62%
4-2	48%	5-2	31%
5-1	15%	6-1	7%
6-0	1%	7-0	1%

An even number of cards rates to divide unevenly (except with two cards missing).

An odd number of cards rates to divide as evenly as possible in all cases.

ARE YOU A MEMBER?

The American Contract Bridge League (ACBL) is dedicated to the playing, teaching and promotion of contract bridge.

The membership of 160,000+ includes a wide range of players — from the thousands who are just learning the joy of bridge to the most proficient players in North America. The ACBL has long been the center of North American bridge activity. The organization is looking forward to celebrating its 75th Anniversary in 2012. ACBL invites you to join in the excitement of organized bridge play.

ACBL offers sanctioned games at local clubs, tournaments, on cruise ships and on the Internet! The ACBL is a service-oriented membership organization offering considerable benefits to its members, including reduced playing fees at tournaments!

If you are not a member of the ACBL, join today to take advantage of the reduced rates for first-time members and to receive our outstanding bridge magazine — *The Bridge Bulletin*! You will receive an ACBL player number, and any masterpoints (the measure of achievement for all bridge players) you win at ACBL clubs and tournaments will be automatically recorded to your account!

You can enjoy the fun, friendship and competition of bridge with an ACBL membership. Join today by visiting our web site **www.acbl.org**. ACBL is a Great Deal!

American Contract Bridge League
6575 Windchase Drive
Horn Lake, MS 38637-1523
www.acbl.org